A New Era
of Nonviolence

To the memory of Muhammad Bouazizi and to my millions of mentors from around the world who are showing humankind how to wage conflict creatively and constructively without violence. Some are so poor they cannot buy books. Some cannot read. Most do not speak English. Most suffered under harsh rule and thought they needed guns to be free. They used to believe they were the followers. Slowly, they and all of us are beginning to understand: They are the leaders. War will be ended by those who pay the costs in lives, civil society more than the soldiers, and the soldiers more than the elites who both profit from war and command that it begin.

Acknowledgments

Every scholar is indebted to all the rest. I am grateful to those who started peace education, peace research, and a new way to view our duties to the generations. Elise Boulding, Johan Galtung and the grandparents of us all. Some, like Galtung, like Marc Pilisuk, are still with us, and the mark of all of them is upon our work.

Astonishingly, Dr. Robert J. Gould has managed to keep me employed at Portland State University since 2001, no easy feat. Others have allowed me to teach courses, beginning with Dr. Kent Shifferd and including Dr. Michael Sonnleitner, Terri Barnes, and Dr. Rebecca Glasscock, keeping my focus on bringing the increasing volume of peace and conflict studies research and neoteric state of the professional arts to students. And yes, Johan, paying the mortgage.

Al Jubitz and the Jubitz Family Fund have supported my work with PeaceVoice, trying to help peace intellectuals become *public* peace intellectuals, and for that I remain grateful. Indeed, Al announced that his goal is to end war on Earth in his lifetime, and this book is part of our struggle to achieve that modest goal.

Exceedingly helpful comments and constructive criticism from Dr. Kent Shifferd and Dr. Patrick Hiller dramatically improved early drafts and are greatly appreciated. Naturally, remaining errors are mine.

I am most grateful to Laura Finley, one of our most prolific and brilliant young peace scholars, for her most excellent Foreword. You will hear much more from Laura for many more years.

All nonviolent activists are paying it forward, and they, along with the children who did nothing to deserve the violence and who in fact deserve all that is good, are the ones in my heart. Whitefeather, the Anishinabe man for whom my peace house is named, lights the spirit path, along with Lynn Fitz-Hugh, to whom I owe a great debt of gratitude for 29 years of friendship and more.

Table of Contents

Foreword
by Laura Finley

In *War Talk*, Arundhati Roy wrote: "Our strategy should be not only to confront empire, but to lay siege to it. To deprive it of oxygen. To shame it. To mock it. With our art, our music, our literature, our stubbornness, our joy, our brilliance, our sheer relentlessness—and our ability to tell our own stories. Stories that are different from the ones we're being brainwashed to believe. The corporate revolution will collapse if we refuse to buy what they are selling—their ideas, their version of history, their wars, their weapons, their notion of inevitability."

In the thoughtful and important book you are now holding, Tom Hastings provides a critical and thorough assessment of civil wars and violent engagements and shows how we can all benefit from "refusing what they are selling." Hastings identifies root causes and provides a blueprint for what is needed to transform a culture of violence into a culture of peace. This book offers global and domestic, current and historical examples to emphasize that there is always a nonviolent alternative.

Far from preaching to the choir, Hastings' book is intended to inspire politicians, corporate leaders, journalists, educators and others to pursue the more socially, economically, and psychologically beneficial option: peace.

Importantly, Hastings explains that, while we all suffer when violent conflict occurs, the effects are disproportionately felt by civilians and especially the poor and marginalized of the world. Much of these struggles involves resource scarcity that can be alleviated with careful attention to power dynamics and a critical assessment of who benefits from the status quo. We need to question who frames our history and in what ways. We need to assess how the Just War doctrine is used as an excuse

1

to intervene, and how the concept that war benefits the economy is deeply flawed. Indeed, nonviolence is always better for the economy. Importantly, Hastings points out that sustainability is conflict reduction. Violence, and the threat of it, has a huge carbon footprint, with the military consistently ranking as the most prolific user of oil and destroyer of natural resources. The "conflict industry"—all those who benefit (financially, politically, and socially) from conflict—must be made public, critiqued, and dismantled.

As Hastings notes, what is needed is creative, strategic, nonviolent leadership to transform our social institutions. Nonviolence, as he describes it, is a commitment to strive for fairness, justice and respect in human relationships. This will address not just direct violence but also the structural violence of poverty, which is the biggest predictor of civil war. This work is a call on both governments and civil society to draw on historical examples of successful nonviolent action and to utilize local data to transform communities. After violent conflict, peace-building must include truth and reconciliation processes, rebuilding of critical infrastructures, and treatment of both victims and combatants, including child soldiers. To do so will require envisioning what that better world can and should look like, and extensive training in conflict analysis, resolution, restoration and transformation.

Hastings draws on his lengthy experience as a journalist to highlight the many ways media contributes to the problem of violent conflict but how peace journalism can be a part of the solution. The United States and other militaristic cultures deify the warrior and warrior image, reifying the alleged rightness of violence as a solution and those who do it as patriotic and brave. Media is a major contributor to the "othering" that both has, and still does, set the stage for and justifies colonialism, resource and cultural destruction, and violent conflicts. Yet media can also be a tool to resist such othering, providing citizens with alternate stories, options, and imagery. In addition, peace education and research hold the power to show the failure of war. Peace research, education and media can help us pay attention to and reject militarism, not just during crises but also between them.

While law can be helpful in creating more peaceful and just societies, it can also be used to justify and expand violent cultures. Some of the laws themselves are violent, and in many cases, it is the enforcement of those laws that is violent.

Importantly, Hastings calls on civil society to utilize all its assets to develop a peaceful world. He notes how women are not always considered in peace-building initiatives, and documents some of the many historical examples of female-initiated and/or female-led peace-building efforts.

In sum, this book is an important contribution, one that should be read not just by those in the field of peace and conflict studies but rather by all those interested in creating a world in which violence is a thing of the past and peace is viewed as the normal, only realistic way to live. I am confident that his book will play an important role in inspiring our refusal to accept the inevitability of militarism and violence.

Laura Finley, Ph.D., Barry University, is a criminologist and sociologist. She serves on the Board of Directors of the Peace and Justice Studies Association and is the author of several books, academic journal articles, and many op-eds.

Preface: War Is Over

What do I mean, "War is over?" I mean that most interstate war is over. Yes, the U.S.-led invasions of Afghanistan and Iraq are the exceptions, and there are cross-border incursions in central Africa with great concern about Syria, but essentially the old nation versus nation wars are growing extinct since the end of the Cold War. So what I mean is that our traditional notion of war is over and, most importantly, we are now able to substitute nonviolent methods for every war that can be categorized as just. The idea of this book is that there is now no more viable Just War doctrine, because many nonviolent options preclude violence as a last resort. I hope to unpack this notion adequately for you.

To borrow and massage Winston Churchill's dictum that democracy is the worst form of government except all others, we have entered an era where the research is revealing that nonviolence is the worst form of conflict management, except for all other methods (Chenoweth & Stephan, 2011; Karatnyky & Ackerman, 2005; Stephan & Chenoweth, 2008). Wars between nation-states are Just So Twentieth Century—they are now rare-to-nonexistent on our fair planet. The wars we see now are almost all civil wars, with a small handful of invasions.

There are those atavistic defenders of war as the only real arbiter of conflict and the only real alternative to passive victimhood. Some are so devoted to the tradition of war that they even creatively reframe the invasion of Iraq in 2003 as a success—e.g., some of the analysts represented in some of the submissions in the Bacevich et alia, 2013 compilation of analyses. Nonetheless, those are the wars for which the mighty militaries of the world continue to prepare. The generals are always best prepared to fight the last war. They get ready, even over the past generation, since the end of the Cold War, and those are the wars still analyzed by many scholars and other analysts (e.g., McDonald, 2011; Woolsey, 2003). The academics, it seems, are always prepared to predict the previous outcomes, and intelligence chiefs are always framing all contests as war. Thus we still have huge armadas of aircraft carrier battle groups, thousands of nuclear missiles in the ground, on board submarines, and on bomber aircraft, and divisions of tanks—all designed to wage the large wars nations waged on each other for the past few thousand years, culminating with the attacks on Hiroshima and Nagasaki.

In all, an estimated 191 million humans were slaughtered in wars in the 20th century (Howard, Shegog, Grussendorf, Benjamins, Stelzig, & McAlister, 2007). The lull in interstate wars may be the calm before the storm, or we may have in fact evolved past them, but nothing should be taken for granted, and in fact it is time to step up our efforts to end all types of wars anywhere. The focus of this book, then, is toward that goal, focusing on the sorts of wars we see nowadays.

Is this the tilt of this book? It is—both bias and basis—and it is a bias—the primary bias—of my field of Peace and Conflict Studies, just as good health is a bias for those who study medicine. We see the possibility of more interstate war as low. Still, so many old conflicts continue to reassert themselves in so many cases, such as the Turkey-Greece conflict that has resulted in several wars and again threatens (Kouskouvelis, 2013), and there are novel sources of interstate conflict brewing—e.g., as the ice melts in the circumpolar region and as the ocean floor oil looks more possible in light of high demand (Klare, 2012; Shabaev, 2009), the low surficial levels of ethnic and interstate conflict with hidden collective memory reservoirs of antipathy may phase change into sudden hot conflict. It remains at the moment, however, that the facts on the ground are that civil wars of various sorts are killing more civilians than they kill soldiers (Bannon & Collier, 2003) and are our primary planetary conflict management challenge at this time—and in fact preventing civil wars is very likely the strongest factor in preventing what may be their frequent sequelae, interstate wars, as we see, for example, at the time of this writing, happening again in the countries surrounding the African central nation-state, the Democratic Republic of Congo, and the Middle Eastern central nation-state of Syria. Increasingly, from the grassroots and from the head of the UN, militarization is not the answer (Ban on ... 2012).

The problem of direct violence at the point of impact is in poor countries, which experience 90 percent of those fatalities, and the low-income countries in Asia, Latin America and Africa experience even higher percentages of deaths from indirect causes, otherwise known as structural violence (Pinto, Crespin, John, Mtonga, Valenti, & Zavala, 2010). In whatever new ways this set of old problems is emerging, we need to address them effectively and immediately.

This is not to discount the idea that violent intervention can also stop wars in progress. The "surge," which sent 130,000 additional United States troops to Iraq in the aftermath of the civil war begun by the 22 February 2006 anonymous bombing of the Golden Mosque in Samarra, Iraq, did help to temporarily quell the violence that the United States itself initiated in March 2003. The United States invaded and removed a strongman who actually was forcibly presiding over a country experiencing much less civil war than after the United States intervened. Saddam Hussein had already "surged" and clamped down on most conflict in his own brutal but equally effective fashion. Military analysts predicted as early as one month after the bombing that a U.S. military intervention would be necessary (O'Hanlon, 2006), but they considered no real alternatives. Studies, including one by war researchers Aysegul Aydin and Patrick M. Regan (2012), show that in some select instances—in particular the intervening nation-states who are not competing with combatants for influence in the nation suffering a civil war—violent intervention can shorten some wars (though it may also shorten the time period before the next outbreak). If we own a tank, the fastest path from point A to point B might be over some family homes; sometimes the fastest achievement of a goal carries long-term costs. The presumption is that nonviolence will generally have lower costs and therefore is the sole conflict management method under consideration in preventing civil wars, invasions, and occupations. Other works can address the advisability of violence.

Of course, it seems logical to many nations to continue to prepare for wars with other nations. The United States has made enemies around the world and has national interests from the ocean floors to the mountain tops literally around the planet. U.S. planners tend to view the conflict environment much as one Pentagon official framed it, that we are either at war or in "a period of pre-hostilities." Indeed, former CIA director James Woolsey (2003) framed the coming period of struggle between democracy and transnational Islamism as "World War IV" (and the Cold War as "World War III"). This framing of human history and our future as war-to-war war is not the sole province of the United States. Israel routinely notes out loud and with great defensiveness that it is surrounded by 22 Muslim nations that all regard Israel as more or less illegitimate, illegal, and without a right to exist. So it has universal conscription, no gender exceptions, which feeds into the same sort of mandate for those surrounding countries that may feel threatened by Israel's vastly superior military and its most open "secret" arsenal of hundreds of nuclear weapons—an arsenal that naturally demands reciprocity from those surrounding Muslim-majority states, in the never-ending rounds of tit-for-tat escalatory nuclear proliferation. Some of those nations are so brutal to their own citizens—Syria is a salient example—that expatriate males frequently identify compulsory military service as one compelling reason to emigrate[1] (Beitin, 2012). These positive feedback loops of residual interstate threat and militarism have enormous trailing effects.

Sadly, all too many of those engaging in the various insurrections since World War II have used the anachronistic violent strategies, tactics, philosophies and conflict methods that served humanity with such bloody mediocrity in past generations, centuries and millennia. From the endless popgun wars emanating from some Islamic islands in the Philippines to the reversion to 1920s-style "flying columns" tactics in Northern Ireland (Prince, 2007), civilians are ill-served by these antique means. Waging nonviolent insurrection should have completely supplanted violence by now if strategists had been keeping up with the current millennium, but that is a struggle that is sadly far from over.

The ultimate war—only experienced once so far—is nuclear war, the sort of mass annihilation that makes all other weapons of mass destruction look comparatively insipid. Since the 1945 attacks on Hiroshima and Nagasaki, further use is "unthinkable." Wars since those fateful and tragic explosions on Japanese cities have generally either been insurrections or invasions and occupations, with only scattered episodes of nation-state versus nation-state attack—indeed, Kofi Annan noted as long ago as 1999 that 90 percent of all war is civil war (Stoll, 2010). War as humanity has known it, it seems, is mostly either ended or is on a long vacation. We hope for the former and yet wars still rage.

Much of the work of peace activists, peace societies, peace organizations, peace educators, peace academics and peace researchers has also focused greatly on the path dependency caused by the 20th century experience of massive multi-state wars or multi-state interventions, invasions, and occupations. Indeed, even in 1969 Berenice A. Carroll, a leading peace researcher, noted in the *Journal of Peace Research* that most theories of how wars start and stop only examined interstate wars, "concerned almost exclusively with wars between 'States,' or international wars" (p. 297). In our intellectual and real world environment of some decades later, that notation is finally becoming quaint, a long overdue development.

And so the wars nowadays are uprisings, for the most part, or the predations of the War on Terror, which has set back the various attempts to construct a global peace system. Indeed, the human rights, democracy capacity, and peace-building work of the EU was greatly attenuated and somewhat transmogrified into more traditional security investments following the September 11, 2001, terror attacks, and the lobbying in favor of the most peace-oriented aspects of the EU was made far less effective (Kárníková, 2012).

Terrorism is, for the most part, just a desperate attempt at insurrection by those who cannot earn the respect and devotion of enough people to wage a real uprising. It is the weakest of the wars and yet has garnered the greatest devotion of attention from the military superpower, the United States. Peace and conflict scholars would, if asked, advise governments to treat terrorism as a law enforcement issue, not as a war and peace question, but those scholars are not consulted and the governments are making policy with as much success as if they were driving with their eyes shut. The War on Terror led to two invasions and occupations and now is going viral by unmanned killer aircraft, widening the war to several more nations. In recognition of the changing nature of war, the shift has begun in the U.S. military to deploy counterterrorism and counterinsurgency forces all over the world, to more than 160 of the 193 nation-states that belong to the UN, according to U.S. Army chief of staff, General Ray Odierno (Pincus, 2012).[2] Power projection from the United States is partially geopolitical hegemony and partially a conflict industry perpetual marketing infrastructure. The idea that there is any other approach to the desires of people to be free has barely penetrated the consideration of defense intellectuals. Felter (2012, p. 183) is representative.

> In this era of diminishing resources, determining effective and efficient approaches to combating insurgent threats—whether by host nation governments themselves or by third party interventions—remains an important requirement for defense planners and policy makers.

Similarly, other mainstream analysts write of "balancing" the ideals of America—democracy, freedom, fair play, liberation from oppression—with the national interests, otherwise regarded as "realism" (see, for example, Atlas, 2012). These interests are presumably consensual, but in actuality handed down as unspoken received wisdom from murky sources, probably military exigency coupled with cheap human and natural resources. In stark terms, it is less about a Cold War or a War on Terror than it is about maintaining the flow of inexpensive goods and high profits to the center nations, where the periphery population (the average citizen) has a much higher standard of living than does an average citizen in a periphery nation. This disparity can only be gained and maintained by raw military force, inevitably resulting in wars. That is realism according to the conventional wisdom, however papered over in outstanding rhetoric lauding democracy and excoriating threats to it. This is, of course, easier to achieve in a society that has not experienced war on its soil, and U.S. civil society is generally more approving of war than others, especially when those other countries, e.g., Iran, have had war waged in their country in recent memory (Torabian & Abalakina, 2012).

Our thinking as conducted by institutions and by replaceable employees of institutions creates path dependency that works to override our basic impulses. Neuroscientists note that, while there is adaptive aggression amongst many animal species, very little of that goes beyond ritualized posing into actual violence. Humans, too, are essentially hard-wired against actual intraspecies violence, and, paradoxically, need to employ our unique cognitive powers to overcome the good sense that is part of the area of the human brain that reasons we should not kill our own. "Under normal circumstances, the human frontal cortex provides significant inhibitory input to the hypothalamus and amygdala, major aggression promoting regions, to check unnecessary or abnormal aggression," note Bedrosian and Nelson (2012, p. 26). In other words, what is simple in other species becomes quite complex for humans. We can not only rationalize in order to circumvent our natural barriers to killing our own, we are clever enough to promote that sort of rationalization in others, taking advantage of other hard-wired needs, such as identity, and thus can do what no other animal (except perhaps some species of ants) can do, commit organized, collective violence, against members of our own species, no less. War. Rare disorders, such as psychopathy, can thus become structural, institutional, and foreign policies can come to virtually mimic behavior normally proscribed by nature and seen only in genetic anomalous or seriously traumatized individuals. Our work involves transforming that process.

Just as violent crime incidence is profoundly affected for and against by environmental factors such as trauma, abuse or neglect in childhood and adolescence (Bedrosian & Nelson, 2012), we can logically extrapolate and presume that social institutions that tend toward psychopathic behavior (arguably, killing in the name of a government) need to be transformed culturally and legally by a determined civil society. Transformation does not mean extermination; it means achieving the goal by positive, constructive means. Wanting my shoe off, I can unholster my Tech 9 and shoot off my foot or I can transform that process by bending over and untying my shoe and removing the shoe. The handgun is faster, unless you count all the time costs consequential to blowing off my foot after the achievement of the stated goal of taking off my shoe. Stopping societally reproved behavior has similar, if much more subtle, analogs. That will be our exploration in this book. Violence is always shooting ourselves in the foot, but there are times when we need to make many calculations indeed about alternatives. Civil society power is a trickle-up, inside-out, wicking-up, bottom-up, roots-shoots-fruits, bubble-up sort of power that only becomes intuitive for most of us sometime after proceeding through the long double helix of unlearning the old assumptions and methods and learning the new ones. We are barely beginning to see the academic research learning how to even discuss this, and the power elites—from U.S. presidents to Iranian prime ministers—still granularize almost every discussion and decision at the nation-state level in terms of interventions and solutions (Beyerle, 2008; Chenoweth & Cunningham, 2013). They are then shocked when the solution rises to meet them, overtakes them, and enfolds them in some fashion. Intelligence services are barely beginning to understand, and armed forces continue to generally fail. Fortunately, on the nonviolent civil society side of the planning and action, there is no waiting for the state actors. When John Lennon and Yoko Ono did their "War Is Over If You Want It" campaign, they were presciently acknowledging and announcing exactly the truth of many campaigns that followed, and they were stating the flat truth about war and peace that we simply need to learn to effect. Did they mean the individual *You* or the collective, civil society *You* or the member-of-the-armed-forces *You*? Yes. They meant them all, and all were in fact beginning to jell.

While the CIA and war-oriented political scientists (the vast majority of all political scientists, though that is beginning to crumble more around the edges as new research gains prominence) did no better at predicting Arab Spring than they did at predicting the fall of the Berlin Wall, scholars of nonviolence were noting the places where things could shift suddenly (e.g., DuVall, 2007). Arab Spring erupted first in Tunisia, and then almost simultaneously in Egypt, Syria, Yemen, Jordan, Oman, Libya, Morocco, and Bahrain (Sougato Baroi, 2012). That is a wide movement to miss in the instability prognostication business, a failure described by one expert as spectacular (Klug, 2012). Seeming to steal rhetoric from the Occupy movement in the United States, one former CIA Middle East-North Africa (MENA) expert called the Arab Spring uprisings in Tunisia and Egypt "leaderless" (Cannistraro, 2011, p. 37), which is another misread of a coalition of campaigns and organizations that civil society produced over time, each organization with its own leaders. Examining predictions from the CIA and the scholars who inform them, the maps they drew of the MENA region *in the very year of Arab Spring* showed complete stability in Egypt and Tunisia, unmasking the fundamental failure of that approach to intelligence. But from Jack DuVall, a public intellectual specializing in nonviolent civil society power analysis in 2007:

> When millions of Lebanese took to the streets to demonstrate against Syrian occupation in 2005, many said they were inspired by the Orange Revolution. Suddenly autocrats all over the Middle East realized that they weren't exempt from people power. Today, there is vigorous nonviolent action underway against authoritarian rulers or military occupiers in Zimbabwe, West Papua, Western Sahara, Egypt, Iran, Tunisia, Tibet, and a score of other countries in Africa, Asia and the Middle East.

Examining war from a historical periodicity point of view, we can note that the Correlates of War (COW) research project reveals that civil wars have always been more common than interstate wars (though when interstate wars break out involving more than two nations, as they have tended to do, this skews the results, because a war involving 20 nations still only "counts" as one war). Still, for example, between the end of the Cold War and 1997, just one interstate war was waged, compared to 24 civil wars.

Is civil war merely a terror campaign, as most targeted rulers assert? One might consider the dynamics of terrorism and insurrection to be alike in that both tend to rise up against some "legitimate" power, terrorism against any targeted government and insurrection against one's own. Where they overlap and intersect is when insurrectionists fail to only target military targets and instead resort to attacking civil society, especially certain identity groups (e.g., Sunnis attacking a Shi'a marketplace, or Hindus attacking a train full of Muslims).

So, if indeed terrorism and insurrection spring from a similar impulse to attack the government in power, nearly the same solutions might help to attenuate or transform these sorts of wars.

Those solutions will fall into two major strands. One, insofar as possible, remove the grievances that drive the conflict. Two, assuming serious grievances remain, convince as many of the conflict parties as possible that nonviolent conflict management methods are best. This book will thus be divided into two sections, "Ending civil wars" and "Ending invasions and occupations." The first section is broken into two parts, "Reduce grievances" and "Promote nonviolent conflict management." In real life, and in the explorations that follow, it is all connected. This book could be one long, complex, impenetrable, indigestible paragraph of connected material. Even a dedicated editor would not read it. The organization is an attempt at conflict forensics and suggestions for possible fixes for bits of the overall problem, which of course is violent social conflict writ large, i.e., war. War has been used by humans but that time is over; now humans are being used by war, a meme with a nasty life of its own, as Barbara Ehrenreich (1997) warned. This meme is completely maladaptive and needs to wither and perish so that humankind can flourish. Instead of finding hope in new military alliances (e.g., Ryan, 2006), we can find a stronger hope in new peace alliances.

Throughout this book I will try to examine what we've learned from what we've tried and to hypothesize how we can synthesize those lessons into new, adaptive approaches. Taking a lesson from obscure and distantly related efforts and attempting to extract a universal, or at least widely applicable, principle is a potentially helpful strategy.

Definitions

All the following are distilled from various sources and are for the purposes of this volume. There is debate about several of these terms in the literature.

Civil Society: Nongovernmental, nonmilitary society. This can happen at the local, provincial, national, nation-state, international and transnational levels. Formal **civil society organizations** are also known as nongovernmental organizations.

International: Connections to, between, and among nation-states (cf. **transnational**)

Nonviolence: Nonviolence traditionally is action that doesn't use violence or the threat of violence. **Strategic nonviolence** is a commitment to only use nonviolence for the duration of a campaign or a movement. **Pacifism** is a lifelong commitment to nonviolence but does not necessarily include any campaign or movement work.

Peace: Positive peace is peace and justice by peaceable means. Negative peace is imposed peace by violence or the threat of violence.

Terrorism: Violence that targets civilians in order to achieve some political purpose, even if that political purpose doesn't seem to involve politics. State terrorism is conducted by nation-states. Knowing that civilians will die in an attack makes that attack terrorism by intent, the standard of criminality.

Transnational: Civil society connections across national boundaries (cf. **international**)

Abbreviations, Acronyms, Initialisms

ADR	Alternative Dispute Resolution
ALEC	American Legislative Exchange Council
AVRP	Armed Violence Reduction and Prevention
BATNA	best alternative to a negotiated agreement
BDS	boycott, divestment, and sanctions
CCD	Center for Citizen Diplomacy
COIN	counterinsurgency
CPT	Christian Peacemaker Teams
CRE	conflict resolution education
CSO	civil society organization
DDR	demobilization, disarmament, and reintegration
EU	European Union
HSIO	highly structured intergovernmental organization
ISI	Inter-Service Intelligence [Pakistan]
MENA	Middle East-North Africa

MPT	Muslim Peacemaker Teams
NCI	nonviolent conflict intervention
PBI	Peace Brigades International
R2P	Responsibility to Protect
TBI	traumatic brain injury
UDHR	Universal Declaration of Human Rights
WMD	weapons of mass destruction
WTI	World Tribunal on Iraq

Section I:
Ending Civil Wars

The traditional means of controlling rulers—constitutional limitations, elections, self-restraint in the rulers themselves, and violent revolution—have been demonstrated to have significant limitations and disadvantages.

—Gene Sharp (1980, p. 21)[1]

From the end of World War II until the close of the millennium, wars between nations cost humankind 3 million of its own, enormous sums of money, and resulted in a great deal of resource consumption and pollution (Hastings, 2000). During that same period—1945–1999—civil wars imposed a far harsher, indeed staggering, cost on humanity in every respect, including more than five times the number of people whose lives themselves were robbed of them, more than 16 million—and that is only the immediate carnage, not counting those who die later as a direct result (Letendre, Fincher, & Thornhill, 2010). The time to shift focus from worrying more about wars between nation-states to wars within nation-states is long overdue. All war is a crime against humanity, and there have been attempts to outlaw it and enforce that (Tsagourias, 2012); civil wars are the biggest crime of all. They not only kill us, they routinely take all the money, and much of the best brainpower, leaving us behind in the race to solve all the other problems—hunger, disease, poverty and pollution—and war exacerbates every one of those problems. Any evolutionary advantage that war ever may have held for participants has vanished. Arguably, in a sea of wilderness dotted by islands of human disturbance it was as maladaptive as it is now, but for different reasons. There may have been a period—a time of drastically inferior morals and ethics, before humankind questioned imperialism and the "right" to enslave and acquire new lands and subjects by violent conquest—when war was less toxic, less capital-intensive, and bore profits for victors that enhanced their society's success. That is passé—though that seems like news to some who want to fix the problems of militarism and human mismanagement of nature by the application of more militarism and more intense management of nature (Orr, 2008). This is pure, dangerous folly. And, as we shall see, there are superior alternatives.

What is the sequence of events required to end civil wars? Naïve peace students and hawkishly naïve citizens alike often assert no one can work for peace before learning to be at peace within. Similarly, scholars from other fields who have little understanding of peace history and civil society antiwar movements and organizations labor under the false assumption that most peace groups are pacifist (e.g., Hrynkow, 2012). In truth, waiting for inner peace or for most peace groups to declare some pacifist orientation will be a wait in vain. People want what works, strategic nonviolence gives them that better than violence does, and this will be how wars are ended; civil society will decide that peaceful means are best, that civil society has shown it has the power to change policies or even regimes if necessary, and then civil society will assume responsibility for ending or preventing war after war. The number of people who find inner peace and the number of peace groups who declare a philosophical orientation toward pacifism will be essentially irrelevant (I assert this as a committed pacifist). Finding inner peace is a laudable goal, and a few leaders or members of movements may achieve that. If great numbers of people find inner peace that makes it far less likely that wars will break out. Similarly, the numbers of civil society organizations that declare themselves pacifist and thus unable to support war of any sort will contribute to the sustainability of any peace. But ending civil war cannot and will not wait for these hoped-for developments. With whatever amount of pacifism and emotional centeredness exists, we will proceed to stop civil wars by any nonviolent means at our command. Indeed, what we will see is that nonviolence is the new normal, the new realism, the new realpolitik (Boaz, 2013; Dudouet, 2013; Zunes, 2011).

From the other end of the spectrum, those who favor violence and domination often justify their brutality by claiming to be acting to prevent war. The Germans told the Danes in 1940 that they had taken control in order to protect Denmark against a British invasion (Ackerman & DuVall, 2000). Israel claimed, also illegally, on 31 May 2010 that it needed to board the *Mavi Marmara* in international waters in order to prevent war matériel from reaching Hamas, despite the finding of no war matériel on that ship (Buchan, 2011). Mainstream U.S.-received wisdom is that the surge in Iraq was the only way to end the civil war started by the U.S. invasion.[2] Indeed, the relentless misappropriation of the language of peace in the name of committing violence has a long, dark history that at least demonstrates that humankind would prefer to have peace and only with elaborate excuses are we going to permit violence, which is exactly backward from the usual *pons asinorum* Hobbesian notion that peace is the unnatural state only achieved negatively, by threat or commission of violence.

Rationalizing conflict transformation from destructive to constructive— from violence and the threat of and preparation for violence to nonviolence— means examining, evaluating, and assessing the costs and benefits of both general approaches. Table 1 compares these, and this book is an attempt to evaluate the assertions in this table and explore the paths toward nonviolence—the what, why, and how of methods of preventing and ending civil war. Some say that this needs to be done by eliminating greed, opportunity, and political instability; some claim that sanctions and the threat of sanctions are most effective (Karreth & Tir, 2013); some assert that this is only possible by an array of what we now discuss, reduction of grievances (Kubo, 2010).

Table 1: Cost/Benefit and Conflict Management Methods

	Violence	*Nonviolence*
Human life	High cost/low benefit	Low cost/low benefit
Environment	High cost/low benefit	Low cost/low benefit
Economy	High cost/some benefit	Low cost/low benefit
Technology	High cost/high benefit	Low cost/low benefit
Resource capture	High cost/high benefit	No cost/low benefit
Cooperative relationships	Some cost/some benefit	Some cost/high benefit
Hegemonic power	High cost/high benefit	No cost/no benefit

Political scientist Kathleen Gallagher Cunningham (2013) found that certain characteristics in an insurgent group tended to be associated with their choice of violence, that is, civil war, or nonviolent methods of insurgency. While no characteristic is a certain determinant, groups within a nation who are large, have kin in neighboring nations, are internally fragmented, and are part of an economically poor state, tend toward violence. Groups with grievances who operate in non-democracies, who are from smaller minorities and who may be geographically dispersed tend to choose nonviolent insurgency. Both groups in her study are excluded from meaningful political participation, are discriminated against economically, and want independence. Exceptions indicate possibilities more than probabilities, of course, but as the success rates of nonviolence become more known and understood, those possibilities increase. Carrington (2013) offered similar findings.

PART 1

Reduce Grievances

The self-immolation of a young Tunisian graduate named Muhammad Bouazizi in December 2010 set the whole region aflame.
— Arshad M. Abbasi (2012, p. 7)

The past is never dead. It's not even past.
— William Faulkner[1]

Identifying grievances that help prompt or justify or trigger civil war is important, and the short sections that follow attempt to do some of that. But there are other problems that may not trigger a civil war, but which, once transformed, can help stop or end a civil war. Gender issues are an example, as are certain structural conditions, such as availability of potable water or health care. Therefore, these sorts of weaknesses that can be transformed into strengths will simply be mentioned where helpful, salient, or germane.

With all grievances, it is critical to bear in mind the long collective memory, the nurturance of old wounds, old defeats, and the sense of duty to rectify those wrongs, however distant in the past. The benefits and pleasures and sense of belonging that our ancestors bequeathed upon us all also come with obligations that, in some cases, directly conflict with the responsibilities we have to our children, our heirs, and the generations to come. Nonviolence is about choosing a future, not past debt. A Kurd in Armenia, Syria, Iran, Iraq or Turkey may feel the pain of her people all the way back to the Arab invasion and then-new rule of Mesopotamia beginning in 637. Jews and Arabs trace their conflict even further back. Clinging to ideas of revenge means endless violence, something civil societies everywhere face. That decision framework will doom a people to long suffering and, if ever again victorious, a future of paranoia toward others who will then harbor their own collective memories of fresh insults and new pain. Facing the past means accepting all of our pieces of responsibility; facing the future means creating no new reasons for war. Seeking justice using nonviolence is about ending present and future discriminatory practices, not exacting vengeance (however emotionally desired and justified by old doctrines) for past grievances. While the longing for revenge may never be excised from the human spirit, we can create stronger normative barriers that keep the retributive measures in the realm of ideation, not operationalizing.

Causes of war vary over time. At this writing, there are 10 wars[2] raging across the world: four wars in Africa, four in the Middle East/Central Asia, one in South Asia, and one in North America. The casus belli for these wars (as represented in the Uppsala Conflict Data Program, which is recognized as the valid data by the UN) is myriad and shifting. The longest running war on Earth that is still producing more than 1,000 battlefield deaths annually is the civil war in Burma, which began in 1948, and the newest war, which broke out in 2012, is nominally over the imposition of Shari'a law. One country— Sudan, but also South Sudan—has two separate wars slaughtering its citizens, one over pastoral (nomadic) rights and lands and one over the oil-rich borderland region between Sudan and South Sudan (the world's newest nation), complicated by the ongoing war in Darfur. The war in North America—in Mexico—is classified as a drug war and is radically complicated by the U.S. supply of weaponry and money to both sides; the funds and arms to the Mexican government are from the U.S. government, while the funds and arms to the drug cartels are from the black markets in the United States. As with all wars, the combatants and their elite sponsors fare better than do the innocent civilians caught in the crossfire.

> *Every nation or group that initiates violence believes that war is forced on it by the other side and so turn to just-war doctrine to explain the atrocities they are about to inflict on their fellow humans.*
> —Kent Shifferd (2011, p. 82)

Shifferd is correct about the people of a nation or tribe or breakaway group—they are brought to the belief that not only is war justified, it is compelled by the corner into which another, unjust and violent, power has driven one's own peace-loving people. The most clearly aggressive wars are framed that way and people do not have the conscience, discipline and simple investigative motivation to challenge that frame.

What are the elements of this doctrine? From *Wikipedia*:

Criteria of Just War theory
Just War Theory has two sets of criteria. The first establishing jus ad bellum, the right to go to war; the second establishing jus in bello, right conduct within war.

Jus ad bellum: Just cause
• The reason for going to war needs to be just and cannot therefore be solely for recapturing things taken or punishing people who have done wrong; inno-

cent life must be in imminent danger and intervention must be to protect life. A contemporary view of just cause was expressed in 1993 when the U.S. Catholic Conference said: "Force may be used only to correct a grave, public evil, i.e., aggression or massive violation of the basic human rights of whole populations."

Comparative justice

- While there may be rights and wrongs on all sides of a conflict, to overcome the presumption against the use of force, the injustice suffered by one party must significantly outweigh that suffered by the other. Some theorists such as Brian Orend omit this term, seeing it as fertile ground for exploitation by bellicose regimes.

Competent authority

- Only duly constituted public authorities may wage war. "A just war must be initiated by a political authority within a political system that allows distinctions of justice. Dictatorships (e.g., Hitler's Regime) or deceptive military actions (e.g., the 1968 U.S. bombing of Cambodia) are typically considered as violations of this criterion. The importance of this condition is key. Plainly, we cannot have a genuine process of judging a just war within a system that represses the process of genuine justice. A just war must be initiated by a political authority within a political system that allows distinctions of justice."

Right intention

- Force may be used only in a truly just cause and solely for that purpose—correcting a suffered wrong is considered a right intention, while material gain or maintaining economies is not.

Probability of success

- Arms may not be used in a futile cause or in a case where disproportionate measures are required to achieve success.

Last resort

- Force may be used only after all peaceful and viable alternatives have been seriously tried and exhausted or are clearly not practical. It may be clear that the other side is using negotiations as a delaying tactic and will not make meaningful concessions.

Proportionality

- The anticipated benefits of waging a war must be proportionate to its expected evils or harms. This principle is also known as the principle of macro-proportionality, so as to distinguish it from the jus in bello principle of proportionality.

In modern terms, just war is waged in terms of self-defense, or in defense of another (with sufficient evidence).

Jus in bello

Once war has begun, just war theory (Jus in bello) also directs how combatants are to act or should act:

Distinction

- Just war conduct should be governed by the principle of distinction. The acts of war should be directed towards enemy combatants, and not towards non-combatants caught in circumstances they did not create. The prohibited acts include bombing civilian residential areas that include no military targets and committing acts of terrorism or reprisal against civilians. Moreover, combatants are not permitted to target with violence enemy combatants who have surrendered or who have been captured or who are injured and not presenting an immediate lethal threat.

Proportionality

- Just war conduct should be governed by the principle of proportionality. An attack cannot be launched on a military objective in the knowledge that the incidental civilian injuries would be clearly excessive in relation to the anticipated military advantage (principle of proportionality).

Military necessity

- Just war conduct should be governed by the principle of minimum force. An attack or action must be intended to help in the military defeat of the enemy, it must be an attack on a military objective, and the harm caused to civilians or civilian property must be proportional and not excessive in relation to the concrete and direct military advantage anticipated. This principle is meant to limit excessive and unnecessary death and destruction.

Fair treatment of prisoners of war

- Enemy soldiers who surrendered or who are captured no longer pose a threat. It is therefore wrong to torture them or otherwise mistreat them.

No means malum in se

- Soldiers may not use weapons or other methods of warfare which are considered evil, such as mass rape, forcing soldiers to fight against their own side or using weapons whose effects cannot be controlled (e.g., nuclear weapons).

The paradox, of course, is that no proposed war can ever again meet the criteria because there is always a nonviolent alternative and last resort is never reached. Gene Sharp's list of 198 ways is old and out-of-date, but they should all be tried earnestly before waging war. Nonviolent actionists have invented many more since his 1973 list. It is virtually impossible to achieve last resort.

In truth, it is the leadership who generally has another agenda but slowly convinces the masses to go along with the war. The Just War doctrine is just a framing tool to provide plausible deniability, but the research into nonviolence is making that deniability less and less plausible every day.

Stop the Violence

How democracy germinates is a good predictor of its success. Because democracy is bottom-up politics, a government installed from the top—especially if it needs a military escort to function—is unlikely to be stable.

—Cynthia Boaz and Jack DuVall, *Sojourners*
(September/October 2006)[3]

*The project of armed humanitarian intervention—the use of force to stop
mass killings within countries—has achieved a new prominence since the
end of the cold war.*

—Rajan Menon (2012, p. 310)

No one likes violence against their people, against themselves, against
their society, or their way of life. People want sovereignty, individually and
collectively. They don't want imposition; domination is simply very hard to
achieve without violence or the threat of violence. That produces the first and
most basic grievance: Stop the violence. The essential disagreement is whether
the violence is stopped by adding to the level of violence (e.g., armed "humanitarian intervention," no fly zones, arms transfers, or "mediation with muscle")
or by lowering it directly by using other means to force change. In the early
days of Arab Spring the struggles in Tunisia, Egypt, and then Yemen, Bahrain
and Syria were all essentially nonviolent (Abbasi, 2012; Boesak, 2011). They
were also characterized as such by mainstream media worldwide and by observing academic specialists. Indeed, Dr. Chibli Mallat, visiting professor in Islamic
Legal Studies, Harvard Law School, wrote then, in early 2011, in the journal
Middle Eastern Law and Governance, "In Bahrain, Yemen and Syria, the refusal
to resort to violence is a conscious choice of hundreds of thousands of people"
(p. 136). The world watched as first Tunisians, then Egyptians, and Yemenis
used nonviolence to depose leaders who had imprisoned and tortured dis-
senters—and then the world self-importantly injected itself into the same
struggle in Libya, "helping" by providing arms to the rebels and air attacks on
Qaddafi's forces, and thus "outside intervention may even have hardened the
attitude of some pro-regime loyalists" (Dalacoura, 2012, p. 65). That hardening
had horrific, bloody results. The Libyan Arab Spring, begun nonviolently in
Benghazi in March 2011, received military aid and support that same month
and descended into war that cost tens of thousands of lives, with the nearly
instant blowback in the form of the assassination of the U.S. ambassador on
11 September 2012, also in Benghazi. At this writing, the same outside "help"
is stiffening the resolve of Bashar al-Assad in Syria and arguably prolonging
that civil war even as it prevents it from returning to its nonviolent roots, the
only roots that might stop the violence. From Alvarez-Ossorio (2012):

> The roots of Syrian Arab Spring were almost all nonviolent, even several
> months into the Arab Spring. Most of these groups (with the exception of the
> Salafi elements) agreed about the need to avoid violence, reject sectarianism,
> and prevent foreign intervention. On August 29, 2011, the LCC stated, "While
> we understand the motivation to take up arms or call for military intervention,
> we specifically reject this position as we find it unacceptable politically, nation-
> ally, and ethically. Militarizing the revolution would minimize popular support
> and participation in the revolution. Moreover, militarization would undermine

the gravity of the humanitarian catastrophe involved in a confrontation with the regime. Militarization would put the revolution in an arena where the regime has a distinct advantage and would erode the moral superiority that has characterized the revolution since its beginning."

Indeed, the quick UN and United States and NATO aid to the Libyan rebels constituted what might be called the Libya Effect on the uprising in Syria, where anti-regime activists, considering the inimical nature of the relationship of Bashar al-Assad to the United States, watched the other Arab leader who had such a hostile relationship to the United States get militarily attacked. While the U.S. policy is nominally tilted toward preventing a civil war in Syria (Council on Foreign Relations, 2012), the policies on the ground are making it progress faster and with more lethality. The violent insurgents there almost certainly expected commensurate help and indeed continue, as of this writing, to demand it. In street terms, they were sucker-punched, left fighting with violence against a regime with more access to violence and no compunctions about using it. Thus the nonviolent uprising in Syria, begun the same month as Libya's, was eclipsed some 11 months into it by a violent rebellion tragically sure of its status as a rebellion sure to get protection from the world, even though all the elements of a nonviolent uprising remain in Syria (Kahf, 2013).

Even if the world is bristling with weaponry and the people prepared to use violence, the violence won't break out if grievances do not rise to the point that the violence seems advisable. This is a function of the scheme that looks at necessary, contributory, and sufficient categories of causation. There are certain factors that must exist in order for mass violence to occur. One is the capacity to react to conflict with the willingness to use violence. This capacity might include some malleable factors, such as belief systems that permit or do not permit violence, but also include individual and collective neurological functions that may revert to the use of violence in response to certain exigencies. Indeed, that neurological research is exiting its infancy and is becoming compellingly interesting, offering ideas on countering natural and induced impulses to violence—not meant as a stand-alone approach, but as a potential complementary approach to violence mitigation (Bedrosian & Nelson, 2012). Sufficiency means that, at the least, all necessary conditions have been met, but usually include other, contributory causes as well. Contributory causes— e.g., poverty, land theft, injustice, human rights violations, oppression, resource capture, despoliation, child abduction, religious sectarian repression—are innumerable. Some combination of necessary and contributory causes combine to produce sufficiency, a combination unique in every conflict but which may be examined for potential lessons in grievance reduction in other societies or at other times. By definition, conflict does not launch into violence until sufficiency has been achieved. Reducing or eliminating conflict factors is thus working to lower the aggregate levels of causal factors below that of sufficiency; working on each factor becomes valuable, and working on all will assist in lengthening the time spans between outbreaks of hot conflict. Conflict is inevitable and eternal, but mitigating the causes enough to keep the conflict below the level of sufficiency can at least prevent war (Boulding, 2002).

Working to develop sustainable systems that keep the conflict far below the level required to produce shooting war is the path to sustainable peace. Despite the convenience of seeing uprisings as a package of regional trends—Velvet Revolution, Colored Revolution—the etiologies are more distinct than that, and the trajectories are often quite particularistic (Dalacoura, 2012). Most of that work falls on the shoulders of the citizens of the country in question. For instance, the citizens of Syria could have kept their Arab Spring uprising nonviolent and avoided scores of thousands of deaths as the nonviolent uprising transitioned into violence, into civil war. After all, at this writing, three of the four leaders who were deposed by Arab Spring were defeated by nonviolence, and only when violence occurs does a dictator act with "justification" to crush the uprising. Bashar al-Assad saw what happened in Tunisia, Egypt, and Yemen—all of which were victories for nonviolent people power. Earlier in this struggle, the editorial board of the *Christian Science Monitor* noted, "His ruthless crackdown on cities like Homs and Hama is designed to force people to take up arms, which in turn allows him to warn Syrian minorities to stick with him and endorse his iron fist. He seeks to turn the protests into a sectarian, violent cause" (Editorial, 2012). As unfair as it is, this is how asymmetrical nonviolent struggle works. Civil society can stop civil war. Each act of violence by the rebels feeds the momentum toward more violence, higher costs, and less positive progress (Whelan, 2012). Although this is the new realism, analysts are stuck in old frames, calling armed revolution "realism."[4]

But what happens when external parties want war? Jihadis from all over came to Syria to join battle. The United States and others started to provide material support for the violent uprising, and we see Turkey, Israel, Iran, Russia, Saudi Arabia and even tiny Qatar embroiled in this conflict (Egin, 2013; Lesch, 2012; Whelan, 2012). This meddling may or may not have good intentions, but adding to the level of violence accomplishes just that; it adds to the level and duration of violence, and blame for the deaths is internationally attributed to the Assad regime, while on the ground in Syria the people suffer from rebel attacks that kill civilians too, making the rebellion almost as unpopular as the regime, creating a very different reality than the external world understands (al-Gharbi, 2013). The bad old days of proxy wars between hegemons via their surrogates continue, with Russia arming Assad and the United States arming the Free Syrian Army (FSA), mostly through other nations such as Saudi Arabia and Qatar (Alpher, 2012). Voices from the Middle East caution against the notion that armed intervention will help Syria. Mehdi Hasan (18 June 2012, p. 21) writes in *New Statesman,*

> What does it actually mean to "intervene" in Syria? Supplying arms to unknown and unaccountable rebel groups with dodgy human rights records? Carving out chunks of sovereign Syrian territory for "safe havens" that may not be very safe (think Srebrenica)? Dropping bombs from 15,000 feet on crowded cities (think Fallujah)?

Responsibility to Protect is a value, a mandate, and all suggestions for methods to achieve that protection should be considered as a function of a cost/benefit analysis in as holistic a sense as possible. Does R2P mean that when human rights violations are detected one nation has the R2P? Does it fall to the nation with the most fearsome military, to the nation with the best diplomatic abilities and track record, to the nation that has proven itself capable of nonviolently tossing out brutal human rights violators in their own countries, or is it the responsibility of some supranational body, either regional or global? Humankind has not resolved this question, and it is urgent to do so (Douzinas, 2013; Eckert, 2012; Zifcak, 2012). Otherwise, war rhetoric from the militarily powerful nations—who just happen to be the largest arms exporters—demands that weaponry flow to the violent rebels or, every once in a long while, that the armed forces of an alliance or even one nation-state intervene—something that may incentivize the armed rebels to cause or prompt the regime to cause more civilian casualties in order to trigger this sense of responsibility to offer military assistance, strategies that seemed successful in the 1990s in the Balkans—in Bosnia and then Kosovo (al-Gharbi, 2013). The phenomenon of more dead bodies seems to create the rationale for producing more dead bodies. It is always done in the name of humanitarian protection. The Nazis invaded in order to protect other nations from the British, they claimed. The United States invaded Iraq to protect Israel, the Kurds, Americans, Shi'a Iraqis—all were propped up as potential or historical victims of Saddam Hussein, all were used as props to justify an invasion. Both the United States and the Soviets intervened with massive numbers of ground troops and bombing campaigns to save Afghans from themselves, to protect women forced to live under the worst Shari'a law, and of course to protect others from the predations of Afghanistan. The death toll of these rationalized armed interventions, like so many others, skyrockets once the "help" arrives, usually in the form of bombing first to soften the targets. In regional conflict, R2P is even used to justify the flow of arms into a civil war, as we see being done by the government of Turkey, which has chosen to flip its historic high watermark of good relations with Syria as seen in 2009 to its new function as the primary transshipment point for arms entering Syria to rebel forces and concomitant denunciation of Bashar al-Assad by Turkish officials (Demirtaş, 2013; Egin, 2013). Costas Douzinas (2013, p. 51) notes that "rights have mutated from a relative defense against power to a modality of its operations." Who could argue against standing up for human rights? No one, unless one could show that human rights were violated by those claiming to be acting in their defense.

Thus, even though the R2P was first affirmed officially at a UN Global Summit in 2005, the rhetoric is old and remains vulnerable to dissembling and insincerity, as we see in the circumstances in Libya cf. Syria. The world was seemingly united in allowing a military intervention into the Arab Spring uprising in Libya; the UN Security Council moved with rare rapidity to announce an investigation (25 February 2011) into possible genocide or crimes against humanity violations by the Qaddafi regime and then permit military action (26 February 2011) (Zifcak, 2012). This nearly instantaneous progression from "investigation" to intervention approval never happened regarding Syria, despite apparently very similar behaviors on the parts of Bashar al-Assad and Moammar Qaddafi. As has been the case so often in the history of the Security Council, two cases with identical merits are treated entirely differently, often likely due to ideological affinities or other partnerships between the accused government and a member of the Security Council. In this stark case, the Russian client connection to Syria seems to have polluted that process. At other times, political fears will introduce contamination into the deliberations, as we saw with the Clinton administration and UN failure to do anything meaningful as the Rwandan genocide occurred in 1994. Violence is simply not reliable; can the world organize a more reliable and effective response to such violations using only nonviolent methods? Is that something to hope the UN does or will civil society need to take the lead? And can violence produce anything besides more violence or the passive-aggressive longing for more of it on the part of the losing party?

Hamburg (2010, p. 10) lists and describes the advances in these efforts, and cites "restraints on weaponry as well as promotion of democracy, fostering equitable socioeconomic development," and other means by which the UN and EU have been developing preventive countermeasures to possible outbreaks of mass violence. Do either the UN or EU have the resources to prevent all such outbreaks? Probably not, but with a shift in funds from the militaries of the world to such preventive efforts, more assurance of success could be achieved.

Other new conflicts continue to threaten, and the violence is causing great pain. The civil war in Syria is building at this time, not waning, with 6,000 killed in the civil war in March 2013 alone, at least 298 of them children, some due to the al-Assad military attacks and the rest as a result of the FSA rebel attacks (Owen, 2013). The image of the Syrian civil war as a brutal regime versus a people's uprising that is careful to avoid killing civilians is not borne out by the facts,[5] nor is it unlikely that a violent uprising will result in an extremist Islamist government bent on destruction of Israel by any means, even worse than the nefarious methods of Bashar al-Assad (Carpenter, 2013).

Other initiatives are under way to replace the armed interventions with nonviolent alternatives, though some also advocate multilateral or regional or UN armed intervention.[6]

Reuters journalist Crispian Balmer (2012), writing of the 2012 tensions in Palestine and the possibility of another intifada, quotes an Israeli who monitored the potential causal factors professionally.

> Yuval Diskin, the recently retired head of the Shin Bet internal security agency, was sounding the alarm. "When the concentration of gas fumes in the air is so high, the question is only when the spark will come to light it."

This is not an easy science to master. Some have made the attempt based on low-n lifetime observation and made bad bets resulting at times in disaster. Che Guevara was known for many things, including for his "triggering event" theory of revolution, and then in favor of using violence to trip that trigger. Of course, that is the least effective way to produce escalation that will redound well on the militarily weaker side, since civil society in the affected countries and the world hold far more sympathy with the victims of violence than they do with the perpetrators. The First Intifada, indeed, was triggered by the deaths of four Palestinians who were in the path of an Israeli army tank transporter. The high tension leading to this Reuters article was produced by the shooting of a Palestinian youth of 17 by Israeli troops. Unacceptable "normal" oppression and senseless deaths of innocents, coupled with generations of occupation, all contribute to this explosive atmosphere.

What follows is a partial list of contributory causes. Reduction or elimination of these causes removes or reduces the total weight of causes of war, and it is often the total weight of all necessary and contributory causes that finally crosses that tipping point from expressed grievance to hot conflict. The "single bullet" notion of causation has, in truth, always been predicated upon the far more complex systemic analysis and that has been increasingly the focus of peace psychologists, peace political scientists, peace sociologists and other intellectuals attempting to exegete how wars start and how to prevent them (Christie, 2006). Measuring what the former Shin Bet head called the gas fumes is at least as important as looking for the potential sources of spark.

Understanding conflict weariness, collective memory, and ripeness for peace is helpful as well. Dyrstad (2012) studied post-conflict attitudes and levels of ethno-nationalism in the Balkans examining data from 1989 and 2003; contrary to the expectations of some, levels of such nationalism sometimes decreased following the conflict. This may seem counterintuitive, since violence tends to produce strong reactions, but that has to be considered alongside the history of costs experienced by those surveyed. Are they unfamiliar with costs of violent conflict and thus have no natural brake on their identity outrage? Or do they understand that such violent conflict gains little at great cost and is ultimately seen as a sign of an inferior culture by much of the world? Since post-conflict is often pre-conflict, this is an important set of considerations. Unchanged levels of ethno-nationalism from pre-conflict to post-conflict do not indicate a drift toward war by themselves, but certainly show the lack of positive peace attained in any ceasefire, peacekeeping, peacemaking, or peace-building efforts—including development—following the conflict and thus a stronger likelihood that other events will reignite violence. Into this mix, already complex, research shows that some sectors of some populations may experience increased nationalism during and after armed conflict, e.g., Sinhalese Buddhist women in Sri Lanka, who found themselves with a public voice increasingly as the three decades of war with insurgent Tamil Tiger Hindus seemed to threaten their society, their culture, their religion, their autonomous separation from India and the cohesion of their nation (Samarasinghe, 2012). This new voice in a patriarchal culture might tend to reinforce destructive conflict and retributive settlements for a population— the Sinhalese Buddhist women—who had very little public voice prior to the struggle, thus changing the public discourse and regendering support for violence in special cases.

Applying the counterfactual—what would have happened if a particular war had not been preceded by some particular contributory driver?—can assist in imaging alternatives. Stoll (2010) has examined some of this logic in computer simulations. Can we learn to predict hot conflict, that is, shooting war, and take nonviolent conflict interventionary steps? We see the periodic love-hate relationship between Syria and Turkey (very hateful at this writing) and ask how collective memory might factor in this case? Turks were the seat of the Ottoman Empire before World War I. Birgül Demirtaş (2013, p. 112), International Relations, TOBB University in Ankara, notes that "Arab peoples were remembered as the ones who 'stabbed Turks in the back' during World War I, when they cooperated with the occupying countries and 'betrayed' the Muslim Ottoman Empire." This teaches the Turks what? To hate all Arabs, including Syrians, forever? To seek to woo Arabs for future ascension of a Muslim empire that will prevail next time? Both? Neither? This teaches the Syrians what? All the same lessons, mirrored? The long path to peace and friendship, so instantly reversed toward utter enmification, might indicate that all those lessons are in play at all times. Students of conflict can learn to keep analytical antennae up and sensitive to such variables, removing some layers of obscurity and confusion from the conflict forensics that can reveal potential paths for transformation.

Finally, stopping the violence should include stopping the structural violence, that is, devising and designing systems of nonviolently addressing the massive human rights violations that occur systemically rather than individually. When the life expectancy in sub–Saharan Africa is 45 years and is more than 80 years in Europe, this is structural violence that is arguably a greater violation of human rights than is the terrible torture of a suspected terrorist, or even a terrorist attack on a little girl in Pakistan (Douzinas, 2013). The next question then is which, if any, of these violations of human rights do we have an obligation to remedy? If we hear frustrated Islamic fundamentalists telling the world to ignore female genital mutilation because Western powers are not qualified to tell others how to live, should the people of the world simply ignore this form of abuse, of physical involuntary amputation of a portion of a girl's anatomy? Or should the liberal powers and peoples strive to end all human rights violations, including the massive arms flows from the Western powers to warlords who enable the extraction of cheap human and natural resources from places like sub–Saharan Africa? If we truly intend to end war, the approach needs to be both comprehensive and culturally sensitive, but nonviolently assertive.

Leadership Styles

Leadership is crucial, of course, to grievance reduction. Iranian women chafed and suffered under the draconian rollback of women's rights following the 2005 handover of the Iranian presidency from Mohammed Khatami—who had launched many reforms during his 1997–2005 tenure to the harsh theocratic Shari'a law so detrimental to women—to Mahmoud Ahmadinejad. Women tried under increasing autocratic gender bias to organize themselves. They were lucky enough during the latter Khatami years to have jurist Shirin Ebadi receive the 2003 Nobel Peace Prize for her roles in championing children's and women's rights in Iran.

Women challenged these discriminatory practices in many innovative and daring ways, from infiltrating a soccer match that they were forbidden to attend, to a woman illegally filing for her candidacy for president. Women sought an end to stoning—a punishment for adultery that heavily disproportionally affected women—and for other remedies to various biases in Iranian law, such as the inheritance laws, polygamy for men but not for women, and more. Thousands of women were being arrested each year for immodest dress (Beyerle, 2008).

Leadership that is violent is simply objectionable, even if people feel unable to object for a time. As soon as it is possible, brutal leadership will be confronted, either violently or nonviolently. Even when violence is used to oppose brutal leadership there may be a place for heroic nonviolence. In war-torn Syria, Kafr Nabl is known as the last bastion of nonviolent opposition—the "Conscience of the Syrian Revolution"[7]—and the formerly quiet town became so widely known for its witticisms and clever slogans that Syrians would wait for the latest from the town to begin using it. Of course the violent rebels found the town and are militarizing it, much to the great risk of the locals. The nonviolent activists of Kafr Nabl were keeping the focus of the revolution on the poor leadership of Bashar al-Assad, a focus that has tended to get lost as rebels jockey for power with their own violent leadership styles. Still, the resiliency of nonviolent activists in Kafr Nabl as they Tweet messages to the world demonstrates the deeper value of social media as a series of platforms from which to launch People Power campaigns challenging a despot. The old leadership is thus relegated to the cold columns in the ledgers of the old,[8] while the youth learn workarounds and unity-building communal tech. While social media can achieve transnational unity in a cohort it also provides a tool to achieve the same by terrorists who oppose any secular government, dictatorial or democratic. Jihadis in Syria can recruit Islamist jihadis from anywhere even as nonviolent Syrian youth use Twitter and other platforms to maintain their voice as much as is possible, hoping the corporations don't betray them. "To complicate matters further, states are catching up on social media, using them to gather intelligence and spread proregime propaganda. While state powers have some leverage over the companies, their infiltration of the platforms is another threat to activists" (Youmans & York, 2012, p. 316).

Systemic research on leadership changes in various forms of government as it correlates to ending war reveals that the most positive relationship to war termination is a leadership change in an autocratic government, usually then transferring negotiations to a more flexible and less culpable party (Flores, 2012). A great fear is that Arab Spring will result in the advent of a wave of Islamist governments (Fuller et al., 2011). While this may be the case, if nonviolence is the method used to bring the Islamists to power, the results will arguably generally be somewhat less hostile than if Western powers "help" militarily, and indeed, as Fuller (p. 39) notes.

> America cannot go on riding the tiger forever in the Middle East. We cannot expect to have "pro-American" forces in power in the Middle East when the publics don't like our policies. We cannot continue our endless interventions—out of fear that some states might emerge as anti–American. The world is sick

of such meddling. We have to deal with the causes of why populations have become anti–American. And all this comes in the context of the rise of new powers with their own interests and desire for clout in what they see as a new, emerging, multipolar global order. The costs are rising on our old patterns of imposing Pax Americana.

Corruption

To touch corruption, so to speak, is to simultaneously touch so many other social ills and injustices in society, from violence to poverty, human rights abuses, authoritarianism, unaccountability, substandard medical care and education, and environmental destruction.
—Shaazka Beyerle (2010)

War politics are based on lies. That is corruption. War economies are based on corruption—no-bid, cost-plus contracts that guarantee obscene profits to those who profit from bloodshed. Weapons are necessary to enforce structural violence, which is corrupt at its core, leading to a strong scholarship connecting corruption to the root causes of war (Beyerle, 2013). Domestic political violence is directly linked to protecting corruption. Corruption is at the heart of the radical shift in Gini Index to a huge base of poor and hungry and a hugely wealthy elite. Enough corruption, plus a sign of hope to the victims, leads to rebellion, and at that point the only question is what methods of waging conflict will be used.

When the decadent, opulent lifestyle of the Ben Ali family—rulers of Tunisia and clients of the United States—came to light via WikiLeaks, it was one of the primary contributory factors in the first launch of Arab Spring, in Tunisia. Judy Bachrach (2011) notes the most serious and damning cable, made public by WikiLeaks, was from the American ambassador, Robert F. Godec, to his superiors in Washington, detailing the sumptuous and extravagant lifestyle, featuring palaces and jet-delivered delicacies, while Tunisians grew more and more impoverished and victimized by imperious brutality all the way down to the police who spit on and beat 26-year-old college-graduate fruit-vendor, Muhammad Bouazizi, the man who finally desperately self-immolated on 10 December 2010. Al-Jazeera featured the cable and a TuniLeaks site was constructed. Tunisians have a very high rate of Facebook accounts—some 2 million out of a population of 10 million, and the coverage from mainstream media, coupled with social media, was ubiquitous. Ultimately, the embarrassment helped precipitate revolution, as noted by Bachrach.

And the very fact that this frank assessment of their arrogant leadership appeared in an American cable intended for an American government exacerbated a nation's embarrassment. Humiliating, the thought that Yankee infidels were passing judgment on a Muslim nation's conscious passivity, its submission and calm acquiescence in the face of undisguised corruption. Humiliating that the entire world now knew what these Americans had once quietly told each other. Humiliating above all that Tunisians themselves were not exactly ignorant of what the Ben Ali family had been up to—long before WikiLeaks had published a single syllable—and had done nothing about it [p. 37].

The costs of corruption may only occur on one side of the ledger for years, even decades, but are ultimately a serious contributory factor in the outbreak of public social conflict, even war. It is no wonder that officials in most governments everywhere were terrified by WikiLeaks and demanded the destruction of Julian Assange, precipitating an Interpol Red Notice on a man whose sole crime was engaging in sex without a condom with a woman with whom he was having an affair. No Red Notice ever appeared on many of the leaders of violent attacks that killed more civilians than combatants, oftentimes in countries foreign to them, yet nearly hysterical, shrill denunciations of WikiLeaks and Assange were issued from heads of state and their highest officers, with salient examples featured at the time of the Tunisian uprising in late December 2010–January 2011 that included the range from Moammar Qaddafi to Hillary Clinton. Fear of exposure of the corruption at the highest levels of nation-states became near pandemic amongst elites. Corruption is the gasoline soaking into the very floorboards of the social structure of a society; mass media of all sorts provide the sparks.

Syrians were certainly aware of the state terrorist regime that arrogated riches unto itself, and again the extent was really understood long before Arab Spring, but missing that mass exposure that challenged the core dignity of Syrian society. Indeed, in 2008, Transparency International found that the two most corrupt regimes in the MENA were Iraq and Syria (Borshchevskaya, 2010), on politically opposite sides of the geopolitical fence but each ruled with brutality enabled by foreign sponsors, the United States and Russia respectively. The floorboards had already burst in Iraq, bombed by the United States, and the new sponsor's own corruption was as highly ranked as the deposed dictator, Saddam Hussein's. It is very likely that violent overthrow of corruption simply paves the path for new corrupt leadership, less likely with mass nonviolent indigenous revolution.

Transparency

Dictatorial regimes and violent rebellions share an aversion to transparency; nonviolence can far more readily appear to be a true alternative to corrupt leaders when the nonviolent campaign is disarmingly transparent. The traditional assumption that it is more adaptive and safer to seek anonymity (e.g., Youmans & York, 2012) is not necessarily accurate. The image of the Guy Fawkes Anonymous character is tainted for many by the association with violence, however "justified" by the anonymous masked rebel—Fawkes was part of a 5 November 1605 Catholic "Gunpowder Plot" to blow up the House of Lords in order to assassinate King James I.[9] While there are times for hidden actions (hiding persecuted individuals from government thugs—"Jews in the attic"), those times are generally not what builds trust. Anonymity is often seen as suspicious, untrustworthy, and even threatening.

The reverse of this—open nonviolent defiance of corruption—seems risibly risky, but many intuit the truth, which is that if you apply prospect theory,[10] that will at times produce mass nonviolence, and even mass nonviolence without masks, as we saw in the Philippines in 1986, Serbia in 2000, in Ukraine in 2005, and in the Arab Spring uprisings in Tunisia, Egypt, Yemen, Bahrain, and, in the beginning, Syria—with some murmurings in Jordan, Saudi Arabia, and Algeria. Once corruption is faced and defied, the misery and violence that support and defend injustice and wealth disparity are part of the open public conversation, and "events don't move masses; discourses about them do" (Seigneurie, 2012, p. 485). Arab Spring spread a mix of discursive problem statements and a wide variety of possible solutions, but in almost all cases the literal target of protest was the authority figure at the top, propped up by external forces on the one hand (with military aid) and everyone at the bottom on the other (by their fatalistic compliance). Islamic extremism actually remained nonviolent—as was the case in Iran in 1979—and was joined in massive demonstrations by moderate Muslims, discontented Christian minorities, and practicing humanists, even some secular humanists and human rights activists. A discourse can emanate from a narrative frame or it can create one; events are made real and newsworthy by the journalistic frames imposed on them and, in the case of increasing citizen journalism, created by the citizens who also created the event. This can gain on mainstream media in some cases or be hijacked for nefarious purposes in others. The world watched in almost universal happiness at the end of both Ben Ali's regime and Hosni Mubarak's, two autocrats who jailed journalists and dissidents with impunity, and Mubarak's prisons in particular were known torture chambers. We were less sanguine when the enemies of the United States came under pressure from nonviolent civil society in Libya and Syria, not from any fondness for Qaddafi nor al-Assad, but rather from the destructive means ultimately chosen by the resistance in both cases—and indeed, we see the sad results in Syria, with a full-blown civil war claiming, at this writing, some 70,000 lives. The narrative was hijacked first and then the methods of struggle.

Media, the Hegemons, and the Opposition

Media is a nested concern; transnational news outlets favor some transnational views, as do national news purveyors, and so on through states or provinces all the way down to local media favoring certain local views. Just as elites are sourced much more often to tell us what to believe, elite nations are given much more global voice than are small unregarded nations (Galtung, 1965). Arguably, control of the media is one key source of power for the dominant elites, something that most of civil society understands at least superficially. The propaganda of the rulers can become a grievance itself. This was seen in Venezuela, for example, in 2007, when Hugo Chávez—certainly a fairly elected and popular leader—started to grow a more autocratic streak by interfering with mass media. Few rulers on Earth spend a great deal of most days expounding expansively on television; Chávez was the exemplar of the pontificating, preaching, wheedling, coaxing, blandishing and omniscient Jack (Hugo)-in-the-Box, constantly popping into everyone's living room, kitchen, motel room, barroom—anywhere with a television. Then on 27 May 2007 his government refused to renew the basic license of RCTV, a major channel that was not so favorable to Chávez or his party or policies. Students from a number of Venezuela's universities poured into the streets to nonviolently protest. They were met by violence, both from the government agents on duty and from the Chavistas (Chávez supporters) from civil society in particular, who fired at the students with live ammunition, wounding a number of them (Brading, 2012).

Students in Venezuela responded vigorously, proclaiming themselves nonpartisan, neither neoliberal nor socialist, just humanist and interested in pluralism and dialog. Indeed, the student sentiment grew from rejection of both sides in the failed April 2002 coup on Chávez, when leaders from both sides—the Chávez government and the opposition—called on the people to shoot each other. Nonviolence, symbolized by *Manos Blancas* (White Hands), meant to invoke an iconography of nonviolence and reconciliation, was the sign of the students. When they received outside help from USAID they became exceedingly vulnerable to attacks from the government Bolivarians and from analysts and academics who tended to defend Chávez's project, accusing the students of using destabilizing techniques from "Mahatma Ghandi's" [*sic*] playbook (Brading, 2012, p. 32). Key to the ultimate failure of the student movement was the failure to maintain nonviolent discipline when faced with violence in various cities, some of which featured students throwing stones, burning tires, and generally setting up a nearly Palestinian refugee–camp intifada-style resistance, thus justifying government crackdown. Another factor was the lack of oppression of the poorest Venezuelans, who knew the brutal grinding poverty of the neoliberal predecessors of Chávez and were not about to replace him because he shut down some television stations or jailed some judges. Chávez clearly was unafraid to use some despotic tactics because he did in fact radically improve the lives of the majority of Venezuelans, who had been both poor and powerless. The student movement had little to work with, ultimately.

One of the dangers of journalism is the tendency of the best journalists to be co-opted by the regime, to thread various journalistically sensitive ethical needles in a survival strategy that seems to present journalists in some countries a choice between success and possible complete failure, that is, loss of career, potential incarceration, injury or even disappearance or death. The ones who seek success and autonomy under some regimes cannot help but become recognized experts who rarely seriously ask the hard questions at the tough times. Noha Mellor (2009), Media and Cultural Studies at Kingston University, analyzed the memoirs of some 20 Arab journalists—primarily from Egypt, Lebanon, and Syria—and they generally claimed to have achieved autonomy, that they were highly regarded by the regimes under which they lived and worked, that they were not mere mouthpieces of those regimes, and that indeed they had generally contributed to the search for social reform. To the extent these claims were true, there is little doubt these journalists and others in the general expansion of Arab journalism in the last half of the 20th century figured into the emergence of Arab Spring. It is also likely that the Egyptian journalists enjoyed more influence and safety than did the Syrian journalists in the Arab Spring period and the time since.

Resource Conflict

Since November, a crisis of oil, money and history has been building in the semiautonomous northern Iraqi region of Kurdistan. Some 30,000 Kurdish soldiers face just as many regular Iraqi army troops, setting the stage for a civil war in a country that has already endured more than its share. Under these lands lie an estimated 66 billion barrels of oil, enough to shift the global market for crude and alter Iraq's economic fortunes—provided the resource doesn't tear apart the country first.
—Jay Newton-Small (18 February 2013), *Time*

Districts, states, provinces and other subnational territories exhibit conflict over resources, sometimes conflated with nonterritorial identity conflict (Ross, 2003). This conflation can mask conflict causation and make it appear to be instigated by behavior of another group when, in actuality, it is a conflict for power by an individual or a consortium of owners and other parties over control of resources. A dynamic of "war leads to jobs making war while destroying other jobs" can emerge, and war funding by resource capture is linked to that. Indeed, conflict reoccurrence can be strongly affected in this welter of vectors of conflict causation. Conflict researchers Rustad and Binningsbø (2012, p. 531) note that

> the effect of natural resources on peace depends on how a country's natural resources can constitute a motive or opportunity for armed conflict. In particular, three mechanisms may link natural resources to conflict recurrence: disagreements over natural resource distribution may motivate rebellion; using natural resources as a funding source creates an opportunity for conflict; and natural resources may aggravate existing conflict, acting either as motivation or opportunity for rebellion, but through other mechanisms than distributional claims or funding.

Oil is one major and obvious resource in contention both internationally and intranationally. Control over oil fields means great profits and development—for elites. It also means carnage and contamination for many and displacement of indigenous peoples in some locales—and in fact, some seasoned analysts are noting that in some cases, the misappropriation of the land from which resources are extracted can be even more devastating to the well-being of local peoples as a degree of actual physical violence (Le Billon, 2008). While Iraq, Iran, and other major holders of oil reserves are clearly in constant conflict, other oil countries are in permanent internal conflict in many cases. Syria is the extant exemplar of eruption of conflict that apparently has nothing to do with oil yet Syria actually has oil, and it is a subtext of the conflict. Nigeria is another example of a nation in conflict, not in war, and conflict that relates to oil and its effects on specific conditions for certain populations.

During the Cold War, as the field of conflict resolution emerged, many conflicts were framed as a struggle for geopolitical hegemony, and the specific resource capture was often obfuscated, especially by the "Second World," that is, the communist countries, and mostly the Soviet Union. This was actually mostly legitimate, as the overarching goals of the Soviet Union were far more linked to the creation of the entire Earth as a buffer zone protecting the Soviet Union from attack. The overarching goals of the First World, by contrast, were actually more entrepreneurial, naturally, focused on capturing resources for profit. The national psyche of the Soviets—that vast land so vulnerable to frequent attack from its Teutonic West—was simply paranoid. So the framing of the conflict was much more naturally cast as political and ideological than as simple brutal greed. The end of the Cold War changed that analysis.

Short years after the end of the Cold War, when liberation struggles could no longer find funding from the Soviets, they improvised, and those looking for profit took advantage. Soon the challengers were funded by kidnapping, drugs, and conflict resources (conflict diamonds, conflict coltan, conflict timber, conflict oil, etc.). The term resource conflict became normalized.

In the field of conflict resolution there was speculation on water conflict, usually regarded as a fairly unlikely cause of shooting wars. However, it is instructive to take another look, both at past conflicts which were not seen as water-related and new conflicts that are water-based in different ways. The subtopics include privatization of formerly public waters; flooding due to global climate chaos; increased water capture by upstream riparian nations for hydropower, irrigation and other growing uses; pollution, by many possible sources as a result of the actions of many potentially responsible parties; and many groundwater issues related to pollution, consumption, and aquifer depletion (Pearse-Smith, 2012). All these conflicts revolve around issues of rights and fairness.

When resource capture has become the funding source for insurgents they are committed to illegal actions to a level far more profound than is a civil society nonviolent insurgency. That can work to reduce their organizational effectiveness by a degeneration into looting thugs—e.g., the armed factions in Colombia, fueled by narco-income, the diamond-enriched Revolutionary United Front (RUF) in Sierra Leone, or the similarly blood diamond–driven actions of the Union for the Total Independence of Angola (UNITA). Alternatively, criminal enterprises can strengthen an armed uprising, as with the Taliban, the Tamil Tigers and others (Staniland, 2012). In any event, the violence may foster a scofflaw ethos, contrasted with a nonviolent uprising almost always highly focused on drawing a fine and bright distinction between illegal but obviously moral nonviolent resistance and the legal brutality of the state.

In Syria, the most jihadi foreign fighter groups, affiliated with al-Qa'ida, have seized the only oil- and income-producing provinces and are shooting their way to their version of control and power, killing Assad's soldiers, other armed rebels, and nonviolent civil society demonstrators alike (Sly, 2013). While temporarily controlling the primary source of income to the regime may afford these Jabhat al-Nusra fighters a way to cripple Bashar al-Assad's hold on power, it is unlikely that Syrians will long countenance such transnational hegemony over their economy and local autonomy. Indeed, in these northeastern Syrian provinces of Raqqah, Deir al-Zour and Hasakah the local tribal leaders are, at this writing, often defending against Jabhat al-Nusra and are killing Saudis, Tunisians, and others who have come to Syria to further the al-Qa'ida violent grab for power and control over the region's wealth. It is possible that the only serious errors—the fatal ones in the end for the al-Qa'ida affiliate—are killing locals and killing nonviolent civil society demonstrators. Earning the undying enmity of the people is more of a liability than seizing the natural resources is an asset, at least in the likely long run.

Sustainability as Conflict Reduction

There are studies connecting oil to conflict in particular and there are studies positing methods of reducing or eliminating oil consumption and importation. Sustainable energy—that is, energy generation from fuels that do not pollute, that do not contribute to the global climate chaos that is producing climate refugees, that are inexhaustible, and that do not engender conflict—may be considered as a strand in the fabric of nonviolent solution to civil war and resource conflict.

> *Climate change is upon us and is exacerbated, if not totally caused, by burning fossil fuels.*
> —Climate scientists Thompson and Kuo from a 2012
> *World Future Review* essay

> *The security implications of climate change are attracting increased attention, and for good reason.*
> —International Crisis Group

How does global climate change—now termed a "planetary emergency" by NASA climatologist James Hansen—relate to our choice of methods of conflict management? Arguably, there is no more important factor in mitigating the anthropogenic climate change than how we choose to manage conflict. The primary factors in this case are the use of fossil fuels by the militaries of the world—the U.S. armed forces in particular—and the increasing demand for increasingly scarce fossil fuels, which is producing conflict and even war. Added to this are exacerbating factors such as food and water shortages, climate refugees—innocent victims who then also contribute to the levels of conflict due to resource scarcity—and enormous expenses associated with more severe or enhanced natural disasters. These sorts of additional manifestations, and more, of climate chaos engender more conflict, and our choices of methods of management either slow or speed climate chaos itself.

Unless we change our methods of conflict management from violence to nonviolence we will finally succeed in finishing what we've been doing, which is to destroy our ecology and our economy. In short, our methods of conflict management are core to our societal systems, not peripheral, and in this instance, the choice is becoming urgent.

Violence and the threat of violence—the mission of the armed forces, after all—has a huge carbon footprint and a massive pollution impact in virtually all categories that turn our natural world into an increasingly hazardous unnatural threat to health, home, and economy. The same conflict management approach that is pumping massive amounts of carbon into our atmosphere and our oceans is drastically draining our financial resources.

The climate refugee problem is a conflict nightmare. Researcher Nathaniel Dorent notes in a 2011 article in the journal *Development,* "Water will be a quiet force that will infiltrate our cities progressively, due to rising sea levels. Today, 643 million people live in coastal areas of 'lower height' (less than 10m over sea level)." He asserts a scientific consensus on an escalation of people forced from their homes and even in some cases, their homelands:

> 144 million in China, 63 million in India, 62 million in Bangladesh, 23 million in the USA. Even at the current rate of climate change, we already know that by 2050 we will count more than 150 million.

This flood of internally displaced people and refugees will produce conflict at every turn.

The climate problems are not solely heat, fierce storms, rising seas and saltwater intrusion above and below ground. The oceans are also acidifying. "The ocean absorbs about 30 percent of the carbon dioxide we put in the air through fossil fuel burning, and this triggers a chemical reaction that produces hydrogen, thereby lowering the water's pH," according to a 2012 *Washington Post* article.

Are we leveling off in our carbon production? It's the opposite; humankind is growing its carbon footprint in an almost straight-line increase between the 21 billion tons of CO^2 emitted into the atmosphere from fossil fuel burning in 1990 to the 32 billion tons emitted in 2012, according to the International Panel on Climate Change (IPCC). The Goddard Institute for Space Studies (GISS) is clear that most of the Earth is warming dramatically from decade to decade, 2000–2009 being the worst.

The militaries of the world generally, and the U.S. Department of Defense in particular, are key players and core components of this set of problems. Indeed, the Pentagon is the world's largest single consumer of fossil fuel, and a DoD report observes, "Not only is DoD by far the largest energy user within the federal government, but it also faces unique strategic issues associated with energy." And showing that the U.S. military, while creating massive climate change problems due to their consumption patterns, is also attempting to blunt those problems somewhat, another Pentagon report asserts that Pentagon officials and policies are attempting to reduce energy consumption and use greener fuels: "For the first time, the Department of Defense (DOD) has published a strategy to transform the way it consumes energy in military operations." U.S. congressional Republican Senators were quick to draw and shoot themselves in the foot, however, attacking the DoD green-fuel purchases as irresponsible.

And while DoD research into and purchase of alternative fuels is a good thing, it is the methods of conflict management that are the foundational problem. Replacing fighter aircraft with a nonviolent conflict management system avoids attempting to replace the fossil fuels currently needed by the armed forces.

In a positive feedback loop of negative consequence, the race for the world's remaining fossil fuels will produce more conflict and require ever more fuel to win that race. Adam J. Liska and Richard K. Perrin underscore this problem for the Air Force. "In addition to domestic initiatives, the U.S. Air Force, the world's single largest consumer of petroleum, recently announced a plan to substitute 50 percent of its fuel use with alternative fuels, with particular emphasis on biofuels. Yet, biofuels will be able to supply no more than roughly 25 percent of motor fuel in the foreseeable future, so other regions where oil supplies are available will likely see greater military investment and intervention." The U.S. military has raced to command everything from the benthos to outer space, with more than 1,000 bases large and small in more than 150 nations (of the 200 on Earth), with its NORTHCOM, PACOM, EUCOM, SOUTHCOM, AFRICOM, and CENTCOM. With the growing scarcity of oil reserves the U.S. military has entered an Orwellian era of permanent war, with hot conflict in multiple countries constantly. It may be thought of as a giant raptor, fueled by oil, constantly circling the Earth, seeking its next meal.

In 2009, commissioned to think about this, the Rand Corporation produced interesting options. In their report, "Policy Options to Address U.S. National Security Concerns Linked to Imported Oil," Rand suggested three options each to three presenting problems.

Policies to Mitigate Disruptions in the Supply of Oil
Option: Support Well-Functioning Oil Markets
Option: Drawing on the Strategic Petroleum Reserve
Option: Improving the Resiliency of the Domestic Supply Chain

Policies to Expand Domestic Sources of Supply
Option: Open Access to Environmentally Sensitive and Other Restricted Areas
Option: Increase Supplies of Unconventional Fossil Fuels
Option: Increase Supplies of Renewable Fuels (Biofuels)

Policies to Reduce Domestic Consumption of Oil
Option: Higher Fuel Taxes
Option: Policies to Limit Oil Imports
Option: Raising Corporate Average Fuel Economy Standards

Rand apparently felt a change in conflict management methods was out of the range of imagined solutions. From a conflict forensics point of view, it is the only serious, sustainable option.

One aspect of climate change with unanticipated security impacts is the melting of the polar icecaps. The arctic ice is thinner and smaller than any time in recorded meteorological history, and this opens more of the polar seabed to oil exploration, already engendering conflicting claims of who owns which parts of that vast seabed previously sheltered by thick permanent ice—that is not, in fact, permanent.

These problems associated with our violent methods have historically been brushed aside as regrettable but unavoidable, as necessary evil. The formula—still promulgated by traditional stuck thinkers—is expressed as a question: Do you want to bomb someone or just do nothing? Fortunately, we now have what anthropologist and intercultural negotiation authority William Ury calls the third side, that is, an overwhelmingly strong case for nonviolence as the conflict management option that will radically lighten our carbon footprint.

Indeed, Ury is one of the original authors of a tiny 1981 primer, *Getting to Yes*, that gives us our essential method, called principled negotiation. From that simple four-pronged approach we can create a transformative method of conflict management that attenuates the destructive impacts of the adversarial method and enhances the constructive outcomes of conflict.

Ury and his coauthor Roger Fisher suggest that we separate the people from the problem, focus on interests rather than positions, insist on fair standards, and create options for mutual gain. Using this scaffolding we can build conflict management systems that are easy on our treasury, on our emotional sense of individual and collective identities, and on our environment. This method, coming out of the Harvard Negotiating Project, has been critiqued as being overly Western, but its roots are in turn reliant upon Gandhi's discoveries, which are decidedly pluralistic and essentially equally East and West (Cortright, 2009; Fischer, 1982; Gonsalvez, 2010; Hastings, 2002). If in fact we can assume that a desired conflict management system design prefers a nonviolent transformation from the potential violence of our current system, each step in principled negotiation is crucial, and the outcomes will be as nonviolent as the methods.

Nonviolence has a tiny carbon footprint and a far greater record of success, as we have learned in the best research done on these basic questions in the past few years. Erica Chenoweth and Maria Stephan have produced groundbreaking work with a massive database and validity-threat-proof methodology looking at the respective track records of armed uprisings and nonviolent civil society rebellion in 323 such cases. They found that violent insurgency succeeds about one-quarter of the time between 1900 and 2006 and nonviolence succeeds (that is, effects a regime change) slightly more than half of the time.

The Chenoweth & Stephan cases were all maximal goal—deposing dictatorships and other autocratic rulers. These are not cases of merely avoiding expensive lawsuits in courtrooms; these were cases of war and substitutes for war. The idea of nonviolence is never back down, engage in the battle.

> *Those who used nonviolent action in our stories did not come to make peace. They came to fight.*
> —Peter Ackerman & Jack DuVall

These results have been validated by others (e.g., a Freedom House study examining 67 regime changes in the 33 years up until 2005, showing significantly higher levels of success with nonviolence and finding stronger metrics of democracy, civil rights and human rights at least five years after regime change done with nonviolent methods) and yet are so counterintuitive that they have not properly registered so far in our political cultures. When we as a species understand that rising up with violence in opposition to the Bashar al-Assads of the world is a statistically poor choice—and that strategic nonviolence is the best choice—we will begin to diminish our carbon footprint from the challenger side of conflict. When nation-states begin to understand that we can in fact defend ourselves without massive arsenals, huge armadas, armies of tanks and Hummers, and without war jets and bombers, we will see a dramatic reduction of the carbon footprint in nation after nation, most importantly the United States. All the steps require reframing our assumptions.

The first assumption in need of reframing is that violence is power and that the power of violence trumps everything, when, in fact, the latent power in civil society is greater. Refusal to cooperate is something we are born with as a species, as the original nonviolence researcher, Gene Sharp, frequently pointed out. Babies cry until they are fed. It takes some time to train children to avoid so much noncooperation, and children are taught that only misfits do not cooperate; the rest of us who want to fit in all cooperate. Those lessons are learned too well, and our civil society power to nonviolently resist effectively—which relies on mass action—is thus counterintuitive. Teaching the generations that mass nonviolent civil resistance can work to oppose repression will produce a society predisposed to success in using effective nonviolence as a collective defense against all forms of injustice.

Learning to reframe our transnational struggles in terms of successfully reducing demand as opposed to successfully acquiring more is a crucial task. Thus each conservation effort becomes a declared victory, which raises expectations, and the social psychologists tell us that raised expectations are a strong recruitment instrument, thus beginning to start a positive feedback loop with positive, lifesaving and Earth-saving benefits.

Massive public pressure has produced historic attitudinal shifts for several of the most negative aspects of the militaristic approach to conflict. We as a species have outlawed and are working to rid ourselves of some bad weapons and bad practices. Most of humankind has agreed that we can no longer have biological, chemical, and buried booby-trapped explosive ordnance weaponry (landmines). We periodically express our desire to rid the Earth of nuclear weapons, and we are finally building down, generally (with the outlier exceptions of Iran and North Korea). This is a principle expressed by Charles Osgood, graduated and reciprocated initiatives in tension reduction (GRIT). This is a technique that can be used to disarm and to de-escalate conflicts. GRIT begins small, unilaterally, building trust. Pressure mounts to reciprocate. If the will is there, it can be the basis of a "peace race."

The myth that war is good for the economy needs reframing or it will continue to be a serious stumbling block to progress in changing our reliance on a massive military. It is critical to reframe every billion spent on the military as a job loss, and just as importantly, it is vital that we reframe the corporate contracts for war materiel as unpatriotic war profiteering. Arms transfers should be reframed as gunrunning rather than arming our friends or our clients or an insurgency that is shooting against a rival. Shipping arms produces blowback, something that continues to hurt everyone except the war profiteers. We have seen this in a major blow to the United States on 9.11.01 that stemmed in part from our support for various mujahedeen in Afghanistan in the 1980s as they fought the Soviets and in minor ways many other times. Another case is the ongoing quid pro quo to Egypt, U.S. arms for an agreement not to attack Israel, including a demilitarized Sinai, reaffirmed by Leon Panetta on 5 February 2013. Those arms are used against Egyptian civil society, generating hatred for the United States and making more military "necessary."

In the field of conflict resolution, we should reframe mediation as transformative only, not ever including so-called "mediation with muscle," that is, the mediator threatens military action if no agreement is reached. That is not mediation, that is thuggery. This is what makes so many conflicts so intractable and keeps all sides interested in rearming and arms races.

In summation, the connections between climate chaos and conflict management are many, are serious, and are subject to transformation if we can engage, educate, agitate, reframe and recommit to peace and justice by peaceable means. Dismantling the violent systems will radically reduce our carbon footprint and slow the chaos both in the climate and in our cultures and relationships. We can weather this together.

Individual Choices

Each human is a unit of consumption and impact. We can measure our carbon footprint online[11] and learn steps[12] to slowly or dramatically lighten that footprint. The short list would include—but not be limited to—turning down the heat, bicycling more, driving less, walking more, using mass transit, growing a garden, eating locally grown food, neither owning nor leasing a car, installing solar panels, eliminating the use of disposable shopping bags, mounting a wind electric-power charger in your yard or on your roof, reducing the floorspace you occupy, buying more used clothing and other goods from second-hand stores or sales, printing on already-used-one-side paper when possible, dressing warmly and reducing heat in cold months, using cross-ventilation and fans more than air conditioning in hot months, buying energy-efficient appliances and much more. We can do more and more with less and less if we focus and prioritize. None of us are too important to not engage in this self-assessment and daily effort. This is crucial for peace, justice, and the quality of life for children and those to come.

Poverty

Poverty is sometimes dismissed as a cause for violent uprising, and it is frequently pointed out that many of the leaders and followers of the most violent uprisings have been middle class, even professional. Che Guevara was a doctor. Many intelligentsia in jihadi movements are professionals. Hillel Cohen (2013, p. 107) explains the analytical distinction: "Economic status has more of an effect on non-ideological people than on those intensively engaged by ideology, for whom religious and national considerations trump personal and economic ones."

Jose Ramos-Horta (2001), 1996 Nobel Peace Laureate, points out to the Global North that the rest of the world is well aware of rapid advances in quality of life—medicine, computers, luxury autos, climate-controlled environments—for the rich countries, and they know they are not seeing that advancement. This cannot help but breed the growing grievance that feeds both insurrections and terrorism.

Poverty is a more certain predictor of civil war than is religion (Fish, Jensenius, & Michel, 2010, p. 1,337). Cerván (2010) examines the role of development—or lack of it—in the likelihood of war, especially in countries that have experienced war relatively recently. An armed violence reduction and prevention (AVRP) approach stresses that poverty mitigation is war prevention, human rights protection is conflict reduction, and sustainable development is far more important to peace than is nonrenewable resource extraction.

Political scientists Zeynep Taydas and Dursun Peksen (2012) examined data correlating civil conflict to civil war to public welfare spending to spending on the military to corruption. Their findings are clear.

The prevention, management, and termination of civil conflicts necessitate, first and foremost, a clear understanding of the complex dynamics of armed conflicts. Although the existing literature has already identified a number of factors that influence the risk of civil conflict, the importance of the state's ability to provide public goods and welfare policies has been largely neglected. In this study, we offer an empirical analysis of whether welfare spending by the government reduces the probability of civil conflicts. Our findings indicate that welfare spending lowers the risk of civil conflicts and that the redistribution of state resources contributes to the maintenance of civil peace [p. 284].

Taydas and Peksen warn that aid from third party nations is a significant factor; military aid meant to quash civil unrest usually exacerbates it, reversing the nominally intended effect. Foreign aid that is strictly humanitarian and monitored rather than just given without strings to a "friend" is more likely to accomplish the stated goal of peace and prosperity, of peace-building or development. When I guest-lectured in Colombia the effects of U.S. largesse over the years were obvious to the casual observer; military and police crawled everywhere in the capital, Bogota, and crime was high. I was advised which streets to walk on in broad daylight and which might result in something negative. Sidewalks were frequently broken and streets had major potholes. Clearly, the funds were all for the military and none for civil society. Excluding the wars in Iraq and Afghanistan, Colombia[13] has received more military aid from the United States than any other nation except the benefactors of the original Camp David Accords, Israel and Egypt. Reconfiguring foreign aid from the United States alone would have major potential for promoting peace and preventing civil war in Colombia and many other places. This transition will be impossible as long as the conflict industry—the arms manufacturers and other war profiteers—control the narrative, control the public discourse, and control Congress. Indeed, this aspect of war prevention probably requires the deepest commitment and involvement from civil society in the United States and other aid-giving nations. Without massive insistence from the citizenry, this pattern will continue and the results will not vary significantly. The latest example of this sad choice at this writing is the decision announced by U.S. Secretary of State John Kerry to fund and offer "non lethal" aid to the Free Syria Army (AP, 2 March 2013). Back when Assad was being terribly brutal toward a mostly nonviolent opposition, Iran criticized him. The foreign minister of Iran, Ali Akbar Salehi, told Assad to recognize the legitimate voices of Syrians, and even Ahmadinijad said the crackdown should stop (Anderson, 2011). Thanks to the justification provided first by the FSA and now by the USA, Iran has closed ranks and is attacking the United States. This is actually blowback from the mere announcement of the military aid.

The country most intrinsically involved is, clearly, the United States, and in the United States the income gap has been widening steadily, overall, and is now the greatest disparity since the Great Depression, and it is due mostly to the astronomical rise in corporate executive pay (Whorisky, 2012). Can a culture tolerant of this juxtaposition of wealth and poverty in its own borders be expected to develop a consciousness and adaptive policies that will account for the far more desperate poverty in other lands? Will changing U.S. public policy to ameliorate global poverty and arms availability be possible? While the 2013 public discourse seems to slightly favor taxing rich people a little bit more to avoid cutting medical services to poor elderly, the progress is not promising to date.

Infectious disease is often related to poverty and, as Kenneth Letendre, Corey L. Fincher, and Randy Thornhill describe in their 2010 study (p. 669), is related to intrastate war:

> High intensity of infectious disease leads to the emergence of xenophobic and ethnocentric cultural norms. These cultures suffer greater poverty and depriva-tion due to the morbidity and mortality caused by disease, and as a result of decreased investment in public health and welfare. Resource competition among xenophobic and ethnocentric groups within a nation leads to increased frequency of civil war.

The excellent work being done to eradicate infectious diseases is then much more than "mere" humanitarian work; it is peace work.

Peace Tourism and Citizen Diplomacy

A small but interesting subset of poverty reduction is the notion of peace tourism, that is, the more citizens travel to another nation, the less likely it becomes that war erupts between those nations. Some call it citizen diplomacy. The practice is ancient, but naming it is recent. First suggested by physicist and president emeritus of Oberlin College, Robert Fuller,[14] this general notion has been contemplated and critiqued, including an analysis of this idea vis-à-vis the 1994 peace accord normalizing relations between Jordan and Israel. While that agreement lowered barriers to crossing the Israeli-Jordanian border, and while traffic radically increased, evidence suggests that was successfully spun to the Israeli citizenry as just another security threat (Hazbun, 2012). This points to the need for much more investigation into border-screening effectiveness and a general commitment to creating and defending the image of the tourist/traveler as an emissary for pluralism and peace. The idea may be a sort of "soft power" that acts not in traditional national interests of power over others, but rather in a transnational soft power for peace, for the enlight-ened self-interest of all (Eastwood, 2007). In this approach, the leaders are led by civil society, and civil society takes no backseat in terms of expertise nor diplomatic skills. A healthy skepticism is adaptive when transparency is the exception in official international relations and we see so much corruption and duplicity from possibly the majority of nation-state officials, if the revelations of WikiLeaks teach us anything.

Indeed, there is a U.S. Center for Citizen Diplomacy, and in 2009 it reported that in the United States alone there were then some 300 nonprofits with explicitly international missions and a total of approximately 5,000 nonprofits with some international component (Cherbo, 2009). Some 120 of these nonprofits are in coalition to support the CCD.[15] The applications are innumerable, from artist exchanges to technological conferences to student travel to infrastructural assistance and much more. John Paul Lederach (1997) posited that the unofficial transnational professionals might offer the most productive communicators for constructive conflict resolution, since they were neither the grassroots citizens who were impacted existentially by conflict (and would thus be more prey to extreme fear and hatred) nor were they the visible elite negotiators who needed to show their mettle and belligerent attitudes toward others. The notion of citizen diplomats is intriguing and offers another track that Lederach noted could more easily and honestly communicate to both elites and average citizenry. In addition, he noted, professionals and others tend to think in terms of transnational collaboration and knowledge sharing, not in terms so much of destroying others or conquering them. They also tend to respect competencies and best practices from others no matter national or cultural identity.

Enable Anti-Corruption Civil Society Movements

A concomitant to poverty, especially in exacerbating conflict to the point of violent clashes and even potential civil war, is corruption. Often associated with resource conflict, it can also be a post-conflict phenomenon that, conflated with poverty, enrages citizens and precipitates factional power struggles. This was the case in post-liberation Timor-Leste, even with reasonable amounts of international development aid and a slow process toward stability (Kingsbury, 2007; Kingston, 2006). It is arguable that, absent the ascendancy of Jose Ramos-Horta, whose orientation toward integrity, tolerance, and democracy gave many more citizens the idea that their poverty was not going to be permanent, Timor-Leste might have descended into civil war. Even without such charismatic and stable leadership, these sorts of situations can be mitigated by development aid that does not feed corruption, nepotism, and one-party rule—which was the perfect storm brewing in Timor-Leste and one that is not entirely uncommon in a globalized free-market world (Kingston, 2006). In the case of East Timor (Timor-Leste), a responsible United States would have given special aid and support, given its key role in enabling the 7 December 1975 Indonesian invasion and slaughter of East Timorese, facilitated largely by the machinations of then–Secretary of State Henry Kissinger, for which he has been nominated as a war criminal and accused of crimes against humanity. Approximately one-third of the *entire population* of East Timor was murdered in the terror of 24 years of occupation by the U.S.-backed Indonesians. At the least, the United States should have entirely ceased arms transfers to all parties in the region. While revolution by machete is possible, it is the rare exception; the flow of arms almost always precedes the flow of blood. In the aftermath of the referendum that mandated independence for East Timor, Indonesian militias went on a scorched-earth rampage, murdering at least 1,000 and destroying some 80 percent of the civilian infrastructure. Despite East Timorese civil society preference for accountability, these war crimes from the ruffian perpetrators to the heads of government ordering or allowing these atrocities have gone untried and unpunished.

Ramos-Horta suffered an assassination attempt on 11 February 2008 by a breakaway armed faction, was shot twice, nearly died, and spent two months in treatment in an Australian hospital. Upon his return he negotiated the surrender of the remaining armed rebels and publicly forgave them (Kingsbury, 2009). This, coupled with judicious application of relief and resettlement funds for both internally displaced people and a large number of former soldiers with deep grievances, was the breakthrough that kept Timor-Leste from descending into the category of failed state and civil war. The one-time payments to two civil society/former military groups, done in the immediate aftermath of Ramos-Horta's huge popular homecoming reception, jolted a nation into a new condition that presupposed fairness instead of corruption, paving the way for real social, political, and economic recovery.

In sum, the investment in compensation to large numbers of civil society has worked far better than has a woefully inadequate juridical response to a quarter century of atrocities, and development assistance tied to integrity has worked far better than arming security forces in the case of East Timor. Sometimes the solution to poverty, given the competencies, capacities and cleverness of civil society, is to simply distribute a large enough one-time payout that can put smart and skilled people back on their feet and give them a chance. "The way to stop insurrection is to give 'em something to lose," said Al Opsahl. As soon as East Timorese felt their government had integrity and as soon as many of them received a lump sum assist, conflict began to appear much more like normal democratic loyal opposition than a series of anarchical drives toward collapse.

Democratic Aspirations

Syrians who watched well what took place in Iraq "in the name of democracy" and what is taking place now in Libya are well aware that violent change to exert reform is not the way forward.
—The Rev. Haroutune Selimian, President,
Armenian Protestant Community in Syria (2011, p. 9)

Few in Washington doubt that we can occupy Iraq within a few weeks' time. Then comes the difficult task of moving Iraq toward a government that is democratic, peaceful, and respectful of the rule of law. Fortunately, smart officials in both the Defense and State departments have been doing serious work planning for that eventuality for over a year now.
—Michael Barone, *US News & World Report*
(2003, before the Bush invasion)

The imperious arrogance of analysts and pundits as their empires wane is painful to witness. Michael Barone of *US News & World Report* is hardly unique in his smug assessment of the small problems that other recalcitrant nations might offer a clearly superior United States. At that time, in early 2003, journalists in mainstream corporate media in the United States were generally dismissive of doubts about the necessity, morality, and success of the Bush-Cheney plan. Spreading democracy was their easy rationale, democracy by any means, anywhere, at the discretion of the overwhelmingly powerful United States military operating under the control of the Father of All Democracies, the United States. The United States, in the name of giving voice and representation to others, denied it and imposed its own brand of "Answer to U.S." democracy.

Peoples who are not represented and who see others with representation tend to escalate their conflicts until they have what others have, and seeking democracy can produce civil war; indeed, war for democracy is more common than religious war (Fish, Jensenius, & Michel, 2010, p. 1,337). There are those who associate the emergence of democracy anywhere as a result of war. From James Woolsey (2003, p. 10):

Eighty-six years ago, in the spring of 1917, when America entered World War I, there were about 10 democracies in the world: the U.S., Canada, Australia, New Zealand, Britain, France, Switzerland and a couple of countries in Northern Europe. It was a world of empires, kingdoms, colonies and various types of authoritarian regimes. Today 120 out of 192 countries in the world are democracies.

The evidence is that democracy is more likely to result from a nonviolent struggle (Chenoweth & Stephan, 2011; Karatnyky & Ackerman, 2005), but many are wedded to an intellectual path dependency that shapes their intuition and ends their capacities to question, think critically, and remain open to new evidence and new paradigms that may prove more adaptive for humankind.

Of course, parsing the grievances isn't always simple; Arab Spring struggles—both violent and nonviolent—have varying levels of both sorts of issues, and it is unclear whether the removal of one crop of strongmen from the helms of some Arab countries will lead to armed skirmishes that result in another set of such dictators, a full-scale regional war to establish some variant of an Islamic caliphate, or a peaceable—if fractious—emergence of actual Arab democracies (Abbasi, 2012; Parker & Salman, 2013).

Preventing civil war, then, from the point of view of the aspirants, is simply choosing nonviolent methods of escalation of conflict, seeking more power-sharing by nonviolent means of coercion and persuasion. From the point of view of the monarchy, military regime, communist dictator, or other undemocratic ruler, one prevention strategy might include what Kriesberg and Dayton (2012) call noncoercive inducements, or unilateral carrots. Giving civil society greater and greater measures of democracy in the hopes of retaining power, if continued long enough, results in the very state the rulers fear, only without the beheading or torturous mutilation that they fear even more.

A recent germane example of the success—actually a win-win outcome—of this strategy is the less known Arab Spring revolt in Morocco, which had salutary results for almost all concerned. In response to the February 2011 uprising there, King Mohammed VI promised reform and ratified it in September of that year, and elections were held in November, giving Moroccans what they wanted and avoiding the instability of regime change (Kriesberg, 2012). Indeed, noncoercive inducements are a good tactic to incorporate into any nonviolent strategy for avoiding a transmogrification into destructive conflict. For Kurds seeking democracy in Syria for many years, the use of noncoercive inducements was actually being met in-kind in a small measure by the Assad regime in its early days. So, for example, nonviolent demonstrations that had more than 200 Kurds in Syrian prisons were followed by partial releases by the then-new regime of Bashar al-Assad in 2005 (MacLeod, 2005). Similarly, when new oppressive laws that would degrade women's freedom were introduced in May 2009, Syrian women began a nonviolent movement in opposition. This nonviolent movement won (Fouda, 2011). Sadly, this dialectic cannot easily survive any instance of violence and, without enormous discipline in the nonviolent movement, will unravel and reverse quickly, as we have seen. Military discipline is key to military success—it is discipline that keeps a fighting unit operating as a collective instead of ineffective fighters. Nonviolent discipline also keeps a movement operating as a far more effective unit, and when it breaks down, that often spells losses for the movement. The lack of discipline in Syria triggered massive brutal suppression, easily predictable.

As the Reverend Selimian observation above notes, the entire region of MENA is well aware that violence will not tend to produce democracy; can we infer that those groups using violence are less desirous of democracy than they are of gaining or keeping power over others? This is not an unreasonable assumption in the light of how we see coercive Islamists seeking power on the one hand or violently suppressive tools of Western powers scrambling to retain power on the other—and, at times, the intersection of the two, as we see in Libya. Is nonviolence a guaranteed easy path to full democracy? Clearly, not, and no serious activist nor social-conflict scholar ever made that claim. The research simply shows that metrics of democracy are more likely to follow and be sustained by a nonviolent uprising than they are after a violent regime change (Karatnycky & Ackerman, 2005). This is not to discount the daunting pressures, internal and external, on nascent democracies in the MENA in particular and in Egypt specifically, which not only include long sectarian and other identity conflict internally, but a constellation of external tensions, including but not limited to hydropolitical issues with Central Africa and distrust of the new leadership by Arab strongmen leading other countries in the region as well as the fears of Israel, which is by far the most heavily armed and isolated nation-state on its borders (Sarquís, 2012). To handle all these overwhelming challenges and find sustainable democracy is a nearly insurmountable challenge to Egypt, and that it did not in fact have a violent revolution is at least one mitigating factor giving it a better chance of success, but to predict that democracy is either doomed or assured in Egypt is, at this writing, a precipitate proposition.

Secession

For various reasons, there are those philosophically in support of secession, generally, and those who treat potential secession struggles as best served by federalism (O'Leary, 2012). This matters for many reasons, not the least of which is the state of transnational support for those indigenous actors and parties in the nation-states so affected.

Some who favor secession in general do so out of sympathy or identification with original sovereignty before the colonial era. For example, in an era before Europe violently created colonies in Africa, Asia and the Americas, each linguistic group, or ethnic group, had its own complete sovereignty. Yes, the definition of its boundaries was often much more flexible than today's mostly gridded globe, but that was part of its sovereignty too. A return to a precolonial state of sovereignty—or as close to it as is possible in our radically changed world—is often a sentiment shared by those who support secession.

Those who seem to favor federalism—a continuation, generally, of our nation-state system with greater autonomy for groups seeking independence—may support tweaking the status quo rather than tossing it all up in the air, but it may be difficult to determine motivations for this seeming support for the status quo. Is it to favor a legacy of colonialism or is it to mitigate political, financial and general disruption?

The Gandhian view of this is interesting, as is the tribal view. Gandhi did not want India broken up and others did. The result was two, then three countries, mixed into the largest refugee communal migration in history, full of violence. Was Gandhi correct? Are the tribalists correct? Or does that matter compared to simply helping whatever choices people make about their ends, their outcomes, their aims and goals, less relevant than their choices about methods of conflict management?

Scotland and the United Kingdom have been in ongoing struggle over Scottish independence for centuries, and the key problem in many instances historically has been Scottish internal division between those who wished to keep or regain the independent Scottish nation on the one hand, and those who preferred to enjoy the benefits—and lack of certain freedoms—that came with becoming or remaining a part of the UK. This has resulted in various sorts of wars over these centuries, including interstate wars, intra-empire wars, and intranational Scottish wars. Now, at last, in this era of decolonization, Scots are able to work this out via voting, which means their internal conflict is political, not featuring violent insurgency. The slow civilization of both Scotland and the British empire has made all this possible and, in 2014, the Scots will again vote on independence.[16]

Neither civil war nor, in fact, any civil war are attributable to just one cause. We will be confounded if we make no conflict map taking all causes into account. For example, most analysts point to many factors in the long decades of war in Sudan, and Smith (2011, p. 169) notes this, adding that the "causes for conflict in Sudan have thus been pegged to the legacy of colonialism, ethno-religious divide, Islamist terrorism, a resource war, state failure, regional conflict concatenation, genocide," and more. The synergy of such conflicts is powerfully creative when it is nonviolent and eliciting dialog amongst peoples, but is synergistically disastrous when destructive methods are in play. The total of two atrocities is far greater than the sum of its parts. Poor methods of religious conflict can result in a mass killing, and the retaliation is often worse. Then, those who might profit from destructive conflict in resource extraction can use the atrocities to justify more brutal efforts to gain access to cheap human and natural resources, even though they may have been unable to accomplish those power plays before religious violence gave them the opening. There is no cynic greater than the one who will expropriate rationales for violence and misapply them to conduct more violence for personal gain.

When enough causes for violence have been successfully added to the mix, an uprising can become a full-on war, and if the cleavages are along fairly clear lines geographically, the worsening violence and additional resolve that accretes to every act of violence may precipitate into a war of secession.

In southern Africa the racialism from the colonial era is arguably the worst example on Earth, with the Boer notions of white superiority contaminating virtually all struggles, trumping other identity issues but also leaving strong justification for other abusive practices by the revolutionaries who overthrew the apartheid regime in South Africa or ended the white rule in former Rhodesia, giving us Zambia and Zimbabwe. Interestingly, the sustainable implications and correlatives show the most nonviolent of these revolutions (Zambia) has produced the nation-state with the least stated identity grievance and the lowest level of documented corruption, two major African complaints from country to country. The most violent revolution (Zimbabwe) that toppled the colonial regime has shown a strongly contested and brutal ethnocracy even engaged in genocidal practices against one of its minority regions (Ndlovu-Gatsheni, 2012). While an African-wide study and a global study of this series of post-colonial factors and results would show a stronger picture of these correlatives, it is likely that nonviolent methods of waging conflict would prove to be generally far more likely to produce respect for autonomy, if not complete sovereignty, for minority ethnic groups who were stitched into a nation-state formulated by colonial masters during that period.

This is to suggest, then, that the methods of waging secessionist struggle or struggle for federated autonomy are in fact far more important than the particular indigenous choice in that matter. The means are the ends, as Gandhi claimed, and sustainable success is linked far more to that than to separate questions of unity, inclusivity, nationalism or irredentist tribal land and liberty claims.

Working toward a vote of some sort, then, is by far the best way to avoid civil war due to secessionist or autonomy goals of the stakeholders. That right to choose is one that identity groups can more easily prosecute when they use nonviolent means, even in (or perhaps especially in) the face of repression so brutal it crosses the red line of genocide, as when the ethnically Shona military of Robert Mugabe's Zimbabwean armed forces were sent to terrorize the Ndebele peoples who aspired to independence. Some 20,000 civilians were slaughtered by Mugabe's Fifth Brigade in a 1982–1987 campaign of state terror, ultimately documented by Genocide Watch (Ndlovu-Gatsheni, 2012). Mugabe's regime has virtually no credibility worldwide except amongst ultra-leftists who relish violent revolution and seem purblind to its sequelae.

Identity Conflict

All these merely whetted the appetite of the beast of intolerance, to
whom a superficial loss of face can only be assuaged by a loss of lives.
—Wole Soyinka (2003, p. 23), Nigerian Nobel Laureate for
Literature, on the growing violence that ultimately drove
the Miss World Pageant from Nigeria to London

Identity conflict is ubiquitous in human life—gays and heteros, women and men, young and old, black and white, Jew and Muslim, workers and bosses, Bantu and Zulu, American and Russian. Identity conflict is persistent; it can operate intergenerationally—indeed, identity as a member of a particular generation can be the basis for conflict with a member of the same culture but different generation—and can cross the world, erupting in communities in diaspora at a geographical and temporal remove (Tint et al., 2013). Only a few identity conflicts rise to the level of precipitating civil war, or invasion and occupation, and our values are a predictor of both our behavior and what behaviors we tolerate from our governments (Michaud, 2013). Studying the case histories and ascribing causation to various sorts of identity can be difficult indeed. Is the conflict boundary across much of Africa a fault line between lighter-skinned and darker-skinned Africans, between Arabs and black Africans, between Christians and Muslims, between corrupt elites and impoverished masses, or between tribal groups? These are all identity conflicts, all real on the ground, and also contaminated in many cases by resource conflict underneath the nominal divide-and-conquer identity groupings. In reality, what makes a group take umbrage so fiercely they are prepared to kill others?

Is the identity, and are related conflicts, of Israelis related to recent memories of the European Holocaust and instant conflict at the founding of the modern nation-state of Israel, or more a result of the ancient collective cultural memories of the genocidal campaign against the Persian Jews in the Book of Esther or the Exodus from Egypt (Greenstein, 2012)? How can Israel learn that occupation of Palestinian land—even if Palestinians are, in a modern sense, a self-created people spun out of a non-nation-state and areas seized by a victorious Israeli army in 1967—will fuel an endless drive for Palestinian sovereignty? How can Palestinians accept Israeli identity and learn that being gracious and respectful of searing memories like the Nazi genocide of Jews is key to coexistence?

As in so many other aspects, nonviolence is the alternative not merely to violence, but to its concomitants. With nonviolence, serious efforts are undertaken to form unprecedented civil society coalitions, therefore working to unite identities, not separate them. With most nonviolent civil society conflict, religious and ethnic identities are united in opposition to injustice against any identity. Indeed, these basic frames are typical in their radical differentiation, and in the end can help to explain the stronger success rate for nonviolent insurgency than violent uprisings. Had the Arab Spring in Syria remained nonviolent, it may have been possible to reconcile the Alawites, Sunnis, Shi'a, and Kurds. But with the tragedy of the civil war, those sectarian and ethnic fault lines are opening and promoting destruction. Indeed, at this writing the forces of Bashar al-Assad are regaining ground lost to violent insurgents (Sly, 2013b). The intuitive choice to use the tried and true method of violence, the "fast" method and "the only method that works with dictators" certainly must look profoundly and tragically unwise to anyone using objective analysis more than two bloody years since the first nonviolent demonstration in Syria. Yes, there are problems in Tunisia and Egypt, and Syrians who can think critically must envy the Tunisians and Egyptians dealing with their problems. Violence is proving again and again to be the most maladaptive choice of conflict management methods for the mass of civil society and again and again the only logical choice for those who profit from deadly conflict in the three categories of the conflict industry: money, power, and status.

Ethnic Conflict

A primary sort of identity conflict, modern ethnic conflict is often a legacy of the colonial era, when a handful of marauding European powers invaded, occupied, and redrew borders that have settled into our current world of approximately 200 nation-states that, precolonial, were at least 800 distinct territories sovereign in every way except unrecognized as such by the colonial powers. Thus, with the end of the Cold War, ethnic conflicts once again manifested themselves in hot wars trying to regain some semblance of original territories. Ethnicity exists, history exists, and collective memory exists. The psychology of ethnicity is as crucial as the perceived ethnic differences, even if those differences are invisible to an outsider.

This is particularly cloudy to outsiders attempting to understand conflict in the resource-rich regions so coveted by East and West in the Cold War era, regions in which the governments were recruited into one camp or the other during the Soviet Union-United States contest for armed and political superiority. Strongman governments beholden to one power or the other were the norm, and those strongmen usually brutally suppressed ethnic, religious, and diasporic nationalist identity within their own borders. This haunts conflict today. Jon Lee Anderson, writing in the *New Yorker*, reports, "Damascus feels as if the Cold War had never ended. Russia has been Syria's primary sponsor for decades, and the city's policemen wear Soviet-style peaked caps and shoulder epaulettes" (27 February 2012, p. 58). Visible and far more deadly manifestations of this sort of legacy are found in the militaries of former client states around the world.

Scholars who study ethnic conflict frequently look to fear, hatred, resentment and other triggering emotions, as well as structural issues that might include disproportionate access to resources, manipulation by elites to gain power and wealth via such conflict, and lack of positive and sustainable development in roughly equal and adequate levels in competing communities, even if those communities are presently commingled, as, for example, Hutu and Tutsi in Rwanda and Burundi or Kurds inside Syria, Turkey, Iran and Iraq. All force vectors are two-way; for instance, elites are well known for influencing and steering masses, though some seem to ignore the effects that civil society can exert on elites (McDoom, 2012). Imagine a nuclear explosion in Pakistan likely traceable to India, even though India might deny it. Could a rational Pakistani leader avoid a nuclear retaliation even if she wanted to? Or would a victimized Pakistani populace force a leader into commensurate, if disastrous, retaliation?[17] Much ethnic conflict is similarly self-fueling once begun.

The rational nature of extreme emotions or the irrational nature of calm dispassion are usually invisible, but can be present outside the vision of the casual observer of ethnic conflict. Rwanda is a startling example; how could Hutus hack Tutsis to death with machetes in the most blindingly fast episode of genocide in modern history? How irrational. How primitive. Savage.

Imagine, however, a society of hundreds of years of colonial favoritism for one ethnic group over another, and one group is offered more and better employment both in the colonial era and in the globalized era of predatory capitalism, even though the majoritarian underprivileged group has gained power in the democracy. Then imagine the majority of the relatively powerless group is illiterate and impoverished, with radios for their news rather than the written word. Further imagine an armed group of the historically privileged group amassing in a neighboring nation-state, threatening to invade. This is a powder keg. Now imagine an incident in which the leader of the nation—a member of the historically oppressed group—is assassinated, followed by incessant radio broadcasts objectifying the privileged group and warning, they are coming to kill you and your family. They are coming, they are coming. Prepare to die or defend your families.

The fear and hatred thus became actionable, and Hutus attacked Tutsis as though their lives depended on it, which they thought was the case. Were they rational or emotional? Yes. Yes to both. Therein lies the danger of untreated ethnic distrust and unreconciled pain from the past.

Countering this sort of hate messaging is possible using willing and able civil society organizations, even those externally funded. In Nigeria, for example, the Nigerian affiliate of International Physicians for Social Responsibility decided to produce radio spots that would bring violence research to the public, presenting science in laypeople's terms. When these Nigerians surveyed Nigerian listeners, 92 percent reported that they felt they learned about violence and 84 percent responded favorably to the radio programming (Onazi, Valenti, Swomen & John, 2010). Messaging is only one variable, but that variable can go toward causing—or preventing—more hatred, more violence, more war.

In its essence, arguably, identity conflict is about sovereignty, which is tied to notions of respect. In his study of the African American sociologist St. Clair Drake, Andrew Rosa (2012) notes the thematic thread of Drake's studies of struggles for sovereignty for Africans in diaspora, wherever they have immigrated and whatever communities they form. Drake strove to incorporate a philosophy of nonviolent conflict management into his approach to attaining and retaining sovereignty, linking his work to Quakerism for decades, both as a scholar and as an activist working during and after all periods from the Great Depression onward, until his death in 2000. His nonviolent activism, based in Quaker philosophy, was a strand of pacifism that preceded the U.S. civil rights movement, certainly informing part of it and demonstrating the ongoing linkages between identity-based grievance in the United States and the early nonviolent methods of Quakers in working to resolve injustice using nonviolence.

Stopping civil war that stems from a variety of factors including ethnic conflict has many successful nonviolent examples. The russification of Ukraine helped produce the sort of ethnic conflict that is also laced with invader-resentment, fear, genuine disdain for the other ethnicity and religious involvement—indeed, the religious role there helped keep that ethnic conflict from turning violent (Filiatreau, 2009). Sourcing the strands of nonviolence in any aspect of identity—religious, historical, philosophical—and harnessing them into the extant struggle is how many successful strategic nonviolent campaigns have effectively substituted nonviolent civil society struggle for civil war.

Many conflicts that are clearly ethnic are couched in religious terms and some conflicts over resources are also lumped into the religious conflict category. It is not easy to parse the parts and ascribe proportionality of conflict causation in these complex cases, but it is helpful to note as many variables as can be found.

Religion

Some religions appear to be more prone to outbreaks of violent conflict than others, and some religious groups may be more prone to identify their nominal cause of war or social violence as religiously related. The assumption in the early 21st century is that Islam is such a religion, just as Christianity was in England under Henry VIII, when his break with Rome ushered in an era of heterodoxy that ultimately featured "the" Civil War (Wort, 2012). However, "Islamism is implicated in an appreciable but not disproportionate amount of political violence" (Fish, Jensenius, & Michel, 2010, p. 1,328). Specifically, these scholars found that intrastate war was not disproportionately associated with the percent of a nation-state that is Muslim, though the identified extreme rationale for political violence in those nation-states is often religiously identified and so stated. Just as definitively, the authors warn that "despite enormous public interest in the issue, scholarly investigation is in its infancy. Empirical treatments are scarce, and the data available to us make a statistical evaluation of hypotheses difficult" (p. 1,328). After explaining correlating data sets that include Gini coefficient (wealth/income disparity), percent Muslim population, deaths by conflict and by percent of population, the authors conclude, "The soundest conclusion we can draw is that we find no evidence that Muslims are more inclined than non–Muslims to large-scale political violence" (Fish, Jensenius, & Michel, 2010, p. 1,339).

Nonetheless, we can observe the stated cases of intrastate violence, including terrorism, associated with calls of "God is great!" in Arabic (*Alua Akbar*!), and we can easily see that invoked Islam is an important factor in much of the outbreak of social conflict in the Middle East, Central Asia, various Pacific Rim nations such as Indonesia and Philippines, Africa, and Europe, even though the sacred texts of Islam may be interpreted alternatively as condemning and condoning violence (Etzioni, 2011). Many of the incidents of hot conflict in many of these nation-states are not part of a civil war but are instead acts of patterns of terrorism. Nonetheless, terrorism includes actions meant to inspire civil war for some, perhaps most, of the terrorists. Further, terrorists can achieve many deaths and perhaps push a nation-state into a state of real civil war. Certainly the violence of jihadis within Syria, and especially jihadis who flooded by the thousands into Syria beginning in summer 2011, have helped push a nonviolent Arab Spring uprising that could have succeeded by a concerted and disciplined majoritarian oppressed Sunni civil society into a tragic, bloody disaster. The Alawite minority ruled for four decades and is guilty of engendering what Eyal Zisser (2013) calls a peasants' revolt of the Sunni periphery.

Although the thrust of this review is the causal factors in civil war, it is noteworthy that Henne (2012) finds that in interstate clashes, "conflicts involving religious–secular dyads are more severe than those including other dyads" (p. 755). One of the factors in that intensity is the mutual threat perception by each party—the basic fear of the extremism and immorality perceived by the leadership and often broad swaths of civil society in each nation-state as they view the other. This dynamic might be replicated in any state that is decidedly officially one orientation with a sector of civil society or a region of that nation-state holding the opposite orientation. A secular state and a religious rebellion is particularly volatile, as we have seen in the Philippines, Indonesia and elsewhere. Defusing that is sometimes made much trickier when the perception (and perhaps the reality) is that the majority are suppressing the minority, which has the added detraction of skewing the opinion of the persecuted minority against democracy if, in fact, the regime in question calls itself a democracy. Will the extremists who call for Shari'a law be able to muster much support if in fact the society in question shows high tolerance for religious freedom, or, conversely, will the government be able to defend itself against charges of minority persecution if, in fact, the religious minority is essentially persecuted? Democracy is more than two cats and a mouse deciding what's for lunch. Can we find amongst the many who are calling for Shari'a law those who favor a nonviolent, even democratic, system and oppose terrorism? Yes, says International Relations scholar Amitai Etzioni (2011):

> Hence, to the extent that the West makes the rejection of violence its criteria as to who can be a reliable Muslim partner in building a new Middle East (and more generally a stable world order), it can readily find major Muslim texts in support of such a position. It can find highly influential Muslim authorities who strongly reject terrorism and the use of force more generally but do not and will not support a liberal form of government. These can be considered "illiberal moderates."[18]

A factor in the intersectionality of civil war and religion in our era is the support for a religious faction of fighters from externals. Those external parties could be religious organizations, theocracies, individuals, or nongovernmental organizations. For instance, the governments of Saudi Arabia and Qatar are supporting the most fundamentalist fighters, the jihadist wings of the armed rebels, in Syria.[19] Is that because of religion or because those U.S. clients have been instructed to do that? The threat and power of sectarianism is abundantly clear throughout the MENA (Denton, 2012). The ruling Alawite sect in Syria is, at most, represented in 20 percent of the Syrian population. Is that an explanation of why Bashar al-Assad is so willing to bomb civilian areas he knows to be majority or nearly entirely Sunni? It seems tragically likely that when the "normal" violence of the average Arab ruler was met with a violent uprising in Syria in particular, we see the horrific result of a minority-sect dictator in abject fear of the rage of the majority, lashing out wildly against broad sectors of his own people—whom he clearly does not regard as his own people. Indeed, Bashar al-Assad and his father made at least as many successful overtures to the Shi'a state of Iran as it made to the Sunni state of Saudi Arabia. The Assads have long attempted to maximize support from both (Szanto, 2013).

The questions that surround external party support are complex and few universal findings are applicable, though some general principles can be suggested.

One, when external parties set up their own agendas, often using the scale and character of their support for armed rebels as a political tool in their own societies, the benefits to the populace in the conflicted country can be outweighed by the costs. Syria is an example. It began as an Arab Spring nonviolent revolt for reform or regime change and, as more violent elements began to use violent tactics—very probably influenced by the transition from nonviolence to violent "success" in Libya—the government of Bashar al-Assad responded predictably in kind. The external powers began vying for victory for their favorite future allies, supporting them with arms. The U.S. supported factions they decided might be more secular and Western-oriented, providing intelligence and "light" arms through military aid to Qatar in particular, promoted by some in the name of fighting terrorism (e.g., Spyer, 2012; Totten, 2012). Indeed, other externals, more oriented toward extreme jihadism, supported those armed elements on the ground. The cumulative result has been the brutal suppression and marginalization of the only actual alternative, nonviolent civil society factions, even though the U.S. State Department authorized ongoing training of those parties by some of the world's foremost scholars in strategic nonviolence, including Dr. Maria Stephan—aid which is both documented and derided by some Western journalists.[20] Stephan did not initiate any intentionally nonviolent sector of Syrian civil society; that was active and persecuted for years, with a blossoming of the "Damascus Spring" for a few heady months in 2000, following the death of Hafiz al-Assad, the brutal dictator who had ruled with an iron fist since his 1970 bloodless coup, which followed the Ba'athist military coup of 1963. Despite pushback from civil society, Assad simply crushed the opposition, including a massacre in Hama in 1982 that left tens of thousands dead and the city in ruins (Dahi & Munif, 2011). When Bashar, his son, began his rule, there was hope that the young Western-educated leader would be much more liberal and enlightened. That hope is now replaced by a hope that he will topple. South African anti-apartheid theologian Allan Boesak (2011, p. 11) wrote of the initial promise of the Arab Spring in Tunisia, Egypt, Yemen, Bahrain and Syria,

> I saw the determined, yet fragile, militant, nonviolent resistance despite unremitting pressure and almost unbearable provocation, and the contagiousness of courage. I saw the faces of the women, men and young people standing up for freedom and justice; and I saw the children on the shoulders of their parents, the woundable hope of a nation displayed in gap-tooth smiles and waving little hands.

A flowering of public intellectual outcry for human rights, civil rights and increasing measures of democracy bloomed and then was crushed, as Assad the Younger ordered the end of such challenges, and many of the intellectual leaders were rounded up, summarily convicted of bogus charges such as "weakening national sentiment" and imprisoned for periods of many years, even as the leaders "agreed on a program based on nonviolence, democracy, opposition unity, and political change" (Alvarez-Ossorio, 2012[21]). These intellectuals formed the nucleus of civil society opposition to the Assad regime from 2000–2011 but never achieved much national messaging capacity and never galvanized the masses of Syrians. Their contribution was to construct an analysis, open a national conversation to the best of their abilities under repression, and serve as a beacon for the later uprising.

Tunisia and Egypt achieved regime change with very few mortalities; Syria, it was revealed, leaped from hundreds to thousands to an estimated 25,000 by the end of 2012, and the UN determined those estimates were quite short—Syria has lost more than 80,000 at this writing . The armed intervention in Libya by the United States has long-lasting implications, both for Libya and for the United States, where the Republicans threaten a "Watergate or Iran-Contra"[22] scale investigation into all the decisions and events resulting in the murder of U.S. Ambassador J. Christopher Stevens and three other Americans in Benghazi in 2012. The price of violence is often paid many times by many parties, some utterly innocent and some at a geographic or temporal remove.

Religion can also be a dampening force upon the potential of civil war, as we have seen in the cases when nonviolent civil society toppled dictators and thus saved a nation from civil war and that nonviolent uprising was fueled or made more successful by some aspect of involvement of religion, such as the Philippines in 1986, when nuns were very instrumental in training civil society in nonviolence leading up to the overthrow of Ferdinand Marcos, and indeed they essentially convinced Cardinal Sin to broadcast the plea to the people to interpose in what was clearly about to be a civil war between two factions of the military. The cardinal did his call on Radio Veritas, the Catholic service, and it was key to the outpouring of Filipina/os into the streets.

Just as a minority of civil society participants are pacifists in most nonviolent success stories, the times when religions have been peace or pacifist are a minority, even when those religions have played a key role. Indeed, in times of instability and frequent government violence, it is often far harder for pacifist sects to go unpersecuted, since they are perceived by most violence-prone governments as a danger to the legitimacy of violence (Kisala, 1999). Looking to religion to help avoid civil war rather than contribute to civil war is not an exercise in identification of pacifist sects, but rather a strategic evaluation of the potential to harness values held strongly by civil society that overlap with values held by adherents to a religion.

Historically, other religious conflicts have turned violent, but in our era, in the 21st century, a great deal of political violence is associated with Islam, a religion that is on the upward curve of growth on Earth and happens to be the dominant religion in the most oil-rich region of the world, the Middle East. This brings us to resource conflict.

Cross-Border Spillover War

Syria's government warned neighboring Jordan on Thursday that it was "playing with fire" by allowing the United States and other countries to train and arm rebels on its territory. Jordan, Washington's closest ally in the Arab world, has long worried that Syrian President Bashar al-Assad's regime could retaliate for support of the rebels.
—AP (4 April 2013)[23]

War can cross borders and ignite new wars. The ultimate cross-border spillover war is a war that not only spreads to another nation but that ignites nuclear war. The fear of this distinct possibility after the first use of nuclear weapons in 1945 helped move the field of conflict resolution in two key directions, and helped eventually to make peace psychology emerge as quite distinct from the individual therapy-based psychological study or industrial psychology it had been. We are barely beginning to see the emergence of peace political science—indeed, political scientists who researched peace were rare and their findings ignored for decades.

It was during the Cold War, with its jingoism and xenophobia backed by nuclear saber-rattling, that peace professionals began to emerge from various fields as challenger intellectuals, opposing the mortal threats that were implicit in so many governmental policies of the United States and Soviet Union. The United States and Soviet Union vied for regional and geopolitical hegemony and clumsily negotiated red lines, beyond which all expectations of rationality and proportion vanished existentially. Recognizing that it was now crucial for intellectuals to move from clever support of the state to more selfless (or enlightened self-interested) contestation with any policy that might prompt mass incineration, and knowing since observing Germany and Japan in the 1930s and '40s that governments left unattended by independent scholars were entirely capable of excruciatingly poor judgment, growing numbers of academics began to think for themselves and for humankind rather than continuing to think for the benefit of elite rulers (Christie, 2006).

Eventually, this academic output found specialized vehicles, such as the

Journal of Conflict Resolution, starting in 1957, and slowly other disciplinary and transdisciplinary journals were launched to provide needed platforms for this growing level of scholarship designed to explore causes of war and methods by which it could be prevented. Understanding how to keep the nuclear line bright and unacceptable to any politician tempted to cross it became an increasingly rich corpus of literature. As the Cold War eventually ran its course all the factors have become notable in their own right, not only due to the roles they play in a potential nuclear holocaust. Understanding and preventing cross-border spillover wars is one of these areas of study.

Some cross-border war is the product of a civil war, either in a failed state or a divided society in extremis. The presence of other or additional factors is illimitable, including counterinsurgency strikes by powers that seek to end—or in some instances widen—the violence (Böhmelt, 2012). For those who wish to work to stop all wars, and who might focus on the current nature of civil wars in particular, stopping cross-border spillover violence is imperative. Sovereignty is a limitable philosophy and even emotional factor only when it is most respected, thus making this particular area of war prevention and violence cessation particularly problematic. Legal considerations are both innumerable and in evolution (Bhatt, 2012). Mediation-based approaches have newly researched intricacies that require tough choices and deep analysis (Böhmelt, 2012). Humanitarian aid is potentially an influence toward nonviolence but can also feed violent parties and their search for more power and more resources, hence, the care of design of sanctions is crucial.

At this writing, the most likely transmogrification of civil war into interstate war is under way in Syria (Ayoob, 2012; Cannistraro, 2011; Greenberg & Dehghanpisheh, 31 January 2013; Khashan, 2013).

Khashan (2013) analyzes the chances of a cross-border spillover war in Lebanon as a result of the civil war in Syria, arguing that such a war is unlikely but needs to be monitored. While actual cross-border war may be unlikely in that particular conflict, cross-border violent attack has happened, and porous border migration of fighters and refugees is prevalent and massive at this writing, with other transnational identity sovereignty threatening national sovereignty. Indeed, some analysts believe interstate war is becoming more likely (Alpher, 2012). Being an Alawite or a Sunni is not a nation-state sovereignty question; these are transnational identities with a different set of sovereignty issues that ignore, despise, or work around nation-state borders with relative ease. There is an influx of "foreign" fighters into Syria, most of them entering to join battle on behalf of sectarian loyalties, not in an attack on or in defense of Syria as a nation per se. Indeed, the Arab Spring–turned–civil war now has Syria on the verge of collapsed central government and the likely end of the 40-year Assad dynasty of Hafiz and then son Bashar (Zisser, 2013).

Syria has a long history of meddling in the internal affairs of Lebanon—they were at times all part of one sovereign nation in the long written history of the Middle East, leading to irredentist claims, counter-claims, and pockets of powerful cross-border loyalties and animosities. Religious sects, Hezbollah, the fading but still sparking Cold War relationships and rivalries, all work toward that bloody possibility as Syria descends further into anarchy and near-collapse (Ayoob, 2012). Unhelpfully, the United States supplies arms to the armed uprising and Russia sends arms too, but to the Assad regime, with all that history of cross-border allegiance and hatred. The best hope for mitigating the arms flow in the Middle East or anywhere is American civil society insisting on a ban on arms transfers from the United States, the world's largest supplier of arms. The new small Arms Trade Treaty[24] (AP, 1 April 2013) may or may not be invoked to curb the flow. At this writing, Bashar al-Assad is warning that supporting armed insurgents is very likely to lead to cross-border war (Cumming-Bruce & Arsu, 5 April 2013),[25] and indeed, Israel has responded to relatively small incursions of Assad's forces into Golan Heights with massive airstrikes on targets in and around Damascus (Barnard, 2013).[26] Refugees—some 350,000 in Turkey alone—whose camps are hotbeds of violent insurgency organizing and staging—are not just peaceful victims biding their time until return. In austere times, they are a drain on hosts—at this writing, Turkey alone has spent more than $300 million on hosting Syrian refugees, Turks themselves are not receiving some government services, and Syrian refugees are violently protesting conditions in the camps, even abducting Turkish police (Egin, 2013). While all major players in the Middle East seem wed to violence, the individual foreign nations have no right to intervene with violence—that is the province of the UN, if in fact it is the province of anyone. As historian David M. Wight (2013, p. 177) concludes upon reviewing newly declassified papers from the Ford administration that shed light on U.S. interference in the civil war in Lebanon in 1975,

> This tendency in U.S., Israeli, and Syrian foreign policy in the region to seek to marginalize, often violently, major groups with whom they do not agree, has been a significant factor in perpetuating Lebanese and Palestinian factions who espouse tactics of intransigence and violence. Relying on force and imposed isolation has not curbed Lebanese and Palestinian resistance or violent opposition to U.S. and Israeli policies; Hamas and Hezbollah are proof enough of this. It was Kissinger's efforts to marginalize the PLO and the Lebanese Left that led him to ultimately support Syria's intervention in Lebanon. Kissinger and the Ford administration bear responsibility for the bloodshed and mistrust generated by their marginalization efforts.

Syria had no right to interfere in Lebanon—but its history was so deeply enmeshed that it certainly had more right to be there than did any party from any government from the North American continent. Henry Kissinger, Gerald Ford's inherited (from Nixon) secretary of state, is now revealed to have cynically turned Hafiz al-Assad against his natural allies in the Lebanese civil war—the predominantly non–Christian "Lebanese Left." Lebanon, capable of generating its own problems, descended into collapse and massive violence, thanks to irredentist Sunni-Shi'a sectarian violence exacerbated by Israel-created Palestinian refugee rage and U.S. arms flow to belligerents. The welter of influences is highly complex and fraught with danger, as we see with just one nation-state, Saudi Arabia, which steered the Yemen Arab Spring, prevented it in Jordan, suppressed it in Bahrain, crushed it at home, and supports the armed opposition in Syria (Alpher, 2012). Iraq and Lebanon have Shi'a majorities and generally support the Shi'a minority (Alawite) rule of Bashar al-Assad, but also may harbor Sunni arms flow to rebels in Syria.

Part of the problem of cross-border spillover conflict is the root issue of the creation of many of the borders themselves, often a product of the colonial era, when a few European countries arrogated unto themselves the privilege of drawing actual national boundaries and usually did so for strategic reasons in the national interest of whichever European nation-state was hegemonic enough to get away with it. Looking at the MENA in particular, political scientist Raymond Hinnebusch (2012, p. 18) notes, "Europe literally made the contemporary Middle East states system." When a European cartographer at the behest of European politicians draws lines on a map that become lines in the sand, indigenous belligerents may not hesitate to cross those lines, as we see at the time of this writing at the Syrian borders with Lebanon, Israel, Turkey, Jordan, and Iraq in particular—each with different reasons to support opposition to al-Assad. Turkey's growing rivalry with Syria is nearly as dangerous as the bitter enmity with Israel (Alpher, 2012; Aras, 2012). Refugees from Syria into neighboring nations exceed a million and ratchet up all tensions as they are not ciphers, but rather highly affected victims with appropriately strong opinions—some of them fighters who defected from the Assad army—leading to even more conflict in these host countries in particular (al-Gharbi, 2013). Colonizing nations drew lines that divided indigenous groups in order to better pacify them, or drew lines that included rival indigenous groups into one nation-state despite wishes by the various indigenous groups to retain discrete sovereignty. These machinations have made it much more likely that national borders in many formerly colonized regions are considered illegitimate and an ongoing affront to many who are naturally influenced by their collective memory—passed down through the generations—of former territorial, cultural, political, and economic sovereignty.

Indeed, the repercussions are evident and serious, even with nonviolent success, such as the first two instances of Arab Spring in Tunisia and Egypt, which have not only produced more uprisings that have been hijacked into violence, but have destabilized the region in general and have interfered or ended some friendships, such as the Turkey-Israel rapprochement (Panayiotides, 2012; Robins, 2013). Of course, it is highly unlikely that such excellent relations would have been adversely affected by a solely nonviolent series of uprisings in formerly undemocratic or autocratic nation-states; violence has a pattern of contaminating many primary and secondary relationships from the transpersonal to the transnational. Ethnic conflict is forever, or at least until an ethnic group with territorial aspirations regains some homeland—and even then, because of our migratory species, our long history, and our overcrowded planet, we see more conflict, as in the case of Jews driven from Europe, getting a tiny homeland, and ever since being attacked and opposed by all neighbors. In short, as long as violence is the conflict-management method of choice, ethnic conflict will continue to threaten and to destroy the peace. At this writing, for example, the rebellion in Syria is essentially the Sunni majority opposing the Alawite rulers, a religious sectarian contest, but the Syrian Kurds being pushed into Turkey threaten to ignite ethnic conflict as well, and Turkey is becoming increasingly nervous about a cross-border war as well as another Kurdish uprising, with escalating bitter rhetoric from Prime Minister Recep Tayyip Erdoğan and Foreign Minister Ahmet Davutoğlu (Aras, 2012; Krajeski, 2013). Indeed, Kurds—a special case of divide-and-conquer, having been sliced into bits as the victors in World War I dismantled the Ottoman Empire and left Kurds in Turkey, Syria, Iraq, Iran and Armenia—are both a transnational party to conflict and the largest ethnic group without its own land. Many hold a dream of Kurdistan, which augurs a great deal more conflict. Syria cynically sponsored the Kurdistan Workers' Party (PKK) in the early 1980s, a group with which Turkey had done armed battle for decades, earning Syria yet another poor neighborhood relationship (Aras, 2012). This is just the sort of external support for an otherwise just cause that can risk a cross-border spillover war with consequences disastrous for all. Kurds who were attracted to violence have failed repeatedly, and the reality now is Kurds used, once again, as an excuse for more violence in the region, with Iran and Syria supporting armed Kurds fighting for nationhood carved out of Turkey, a direct result of the armed insurrection in Syria, which is spilling over into Israel, Lebanon, and now Turkey (Egin, 2013).

Turkey's AKP Foreign Minister Ahmet Davutoğlu made a concerted effort to mend all relationships with all nations bordering Turkey, a new focus that supplanted the increasingly frustrating efforts by the successive governments of Turkey to accede to European Union membership. Davutoğlu called his policy "Zero problems with neighbors," and he set about repairing the relationship with Syria, including a history of problems over water, territory and

Syria's past support for Kurdish rebels in Turkey (Phillips, 2012). Entering this rabbit hole, however, set Turkey on a destructive path in its relationships to the United States and EU, as well as Israel. Once Arab Spring began, however, this deteriorated for Turkey as the Assad regime grew more brutal, and Turkey joined many others in the late summer of 2011 in calling for Assad to step down, but by then Turkey was also hosting FSA units, which had led to Syria gunning down a Turkish military jet in June 2011, killing two and threatening to ignite a real regional war. The competition to curry favor with whomever succeeds Assad in Syria is a bidding war toward more war; Saudi Arabia and Qatar are shipping large amounts of arms to the most radical Salafist Islamist factions of the FSA, and Turkey is becoming yet another hub in arms transfers, virtually guaranteeing a higher level of bloodshed first in Syria and then in the region as those arms fuel hot conflicts in places they were not intended to go. Ironically and predictably, the arms being delivered by Saudi Arabia and Qatar straight to the most violent and extreme Salafist units of the FSA all come from the United States. Here, then, we see the conflict industry—those who profit from hot conflict—fueling all sides and reaping the profits while others pay the prices in blood and treasure.

Failed States

There is a mutually reinforcing dynamic between war and collapse of a nation-state, as we see in the failing state of Syria as its civil war worsens and threatens the 40-year reign of the al-Assad dynasty (Zisser, 2013). In some regions this is related to certain other precursor grievances, such as cross-border spillover of war—e.g., Sierra Leone, Liberia, and Côte d'Ivoire in West Africa (Abu, 2012). In some cases a failed state is simply a legacy of past colonial border creation—e.g., Eritrea, Ethiopia, Somalia and Somaliland in the Horn of Africa, where borders were drawn through the territory of some tribes, around more than one tribe, or across pastoral nomadic lands that provided commons to all. The nature of each failed state is a product of the legacy and current factors, leading to a fractured, impoverished, and unstable government, usually then unsupported by external powers or even eroded further from lack of external support. Most of all, internal cohesion is so lacking that civil society has little or no enthusiasm for retention of governance from a central source.

A civil-society structure that supports a nation-state is not a given. When the nation-state makes demands and cannot offer services because it lacks resources or capacity, suspicions of corruption emerge—true or false—and the quality of administration is negatively affected. This feedback loop can send a nation-state toward and finally into collapse. A failed state produces a power vacuum, into which rush entrepreneurial players, almost always with guns, and the dynamic descends further and embeds itself mercilessly. There is no more salient example of the claimed validation of the Hobbesian dogma of our human condition defined as a war of all against all. Failed states are normally portrayed as dominated by powerful warlords jousting over borders between and amongst them, and sometimes this is not far from accurate.

The Fund for Peace Failed State Index[27] parses out the factors in its 2012 edition, pointing at Africa, Asia, the Middle East, the Pacific Rim, and somewhat at Latin America as places of concern. Indeed the only listed sustainable nation-states are Greenland, Canada, Australia, Sweden, Norway, Finland, Austria, Ireland, Luxembourg, and Iceland. Others, including the United States, are listed as stable but not sustainable, or in some decline toward failure.

Implications are considerable. In Syria, as a current example of a threatened state, some note the possibility that the state will collapse into religious enclaves, with Christians fleeing to Lebanon, Sunnis migrating toward a merger with Anbar province in Iraq, and Kurds uniting with other Kurds in Turkey and Iraq (Alpher, 2012).

Conflict Early Warning

What if? What if, at the first outward sign of ethnic conflict, or religious clash, or tribal hatred, or conflict based on gross inequality—or in fact any social conflict with any history of past violence—what if there were some early warning system that could flag these harbinger events, these grievance manifestations, and trigger a response from a committed and respected third party neutral? Not a military threat, not an invasion of troops, but efforts by a party with skills? Perhaps such a party would be UN-developed, or regionally created, or of some unknown nongovernmental origin. If such an Early Warning and Response (EWR) system could stop one war per century, it seems like a worthy endeavor for humankind.

This has been a dream in the field of Conflict Resolution since the late 1950s, and, theoretically, some regional and subregional but supranational organizations have adopted EWR systems. However, in a study by Herbert Wulf and Tobias Debiel (2010), they found that the African Union, the Economic Community of West African States/Economic Community of West African States Monitoring Group in West Africa, and the Intergovernmental Authority on Development in East Africa—all of which have established variations of EWR mechanisms—the organizations themselves have been too weak and internally divided to deploy effective responses. Further, they found that models that would assist in understanding tipping points or threshold lines are not well understood, making it difficult to use EWR in countries with moderately stable histories and apparent conditions. They note that in a welter of potential causal variables it is difficult to respond effectively—e.g., in a moderately stable but ethnically divided "country with high infant mortality, a hybrid regime, and state discrimination" (p. 539) how can a third-party neutral with limited resources respond effectively? Or, what levels of specific contributory causes trigger sufficiency and thus hot conflict, given other levels of causal variables? Intervention is poorly understood. To better construct effective EWR, they recommend that EWR "be based on the 'subsidiary' principle; that is, in a bottom up approach, the lowest level should be the starting point, entrusting the next higher level only when the local authorities are not capable of handling the conflict" (p. 539). Research and response design should not granularize at the nation-state level but rather at the local and aggregate later into patterns and projections in order to improve accuracy of remedial intervention methods. This would bridge and even eliminate the gap between information and action, especially if local actors are citizen partners with agency, not merely objects of intervention.

Post-Conflict Is Pre-Conflict

Since the majority of wars and hot conflicts are reignition of old fights, paying attention to how conflict is ended and how the parties are treated in the post-conflict environment is a key component to preventing the next war. A number of factors need attention, beginning with the agreement that stops the shooting. Kegley and Raymond (1999) studied European peace agreements and elapsed time between reoccurrence of war from the Napoleonic wars through World War II and found a clear correlative between harsh treatment of the losing party and faster outbreak of the next war. A generous peace accord is likely to produce more years of peace.

Other systemic factors can roll waves of influence over old conflicts for better or worse. One might argue, for instance, that the end of the Cold War produced a willingness by Arab powers to talk peace with Israel, as they did in 1991 at the Madrid Conference, in part at least because the old system of military support from the Soviet Union suddenly evaporated with the dissolution of the Soviet Union (Olmert, 2011). One might even speculate that the terrorism that arose following those initial talks with Israel related to the heresy implied in such conversations. Recognizing that Israel even exists is almost impossible for Islamic fundamentalists, and suddenly, in 1991, there was nothing resembling military symmetry any longer, so the obvious courses were either realistic peace talks or radical asymmetric warfare, terrorism. Genuine peace has long been the chimera in the Middle East, with all sides claiming that is all they want. One example is that Abba Eban concocted and solidified the myth that all Israel ever wanted was peace and that it was most clearly demonstrated by Israel offering a generous peace to Egypt and Syria just nine days after the rout of the 1967 Six Day War, when Israel not only rebuffed an attack but took territory—the Sinai Peninsula and Golan Heights. Eban claimed that the resolution offering both territories back to Egypt and Syria, respectively, was passed by the Israeli Cabinet (true) and transmitted via the Americans to Cairo and Damascus (false, according to newly obtained documents) (Raz, 2013). What is the upshot of the failure of organized, overtly nation-state violence against Israel and its usurpation of Arab lands in 1948? After all, Arab states have consistently failed to militarily achieve anything (except one stalemate by Hezbollah in the 2006 July War in Lebanon, with the usual ratio of dead on either side, that is, far more Lebanese than Israelis, and part of Lebanon rendered uninhabitable due to widespread indiscriminate use of Israeli cluster bombs[28]). The "solution," if violence is the assumed method of conflict management, must then be asymmetric warfare of attrition, and that leads to terrorism, which necessarily puts Palestinians on the front lines, since they are the people in diaspora with the largest grievance against Israel and the world powers that decided to create Israel where it is. Post-conflict is permanent pre-conflict in the Middle East as long as Israel, the Palestinians, and Israel's neighbors continue to regard violence as the only realistic path. A student of strategic nonviolence, gauging the track record globally, may well predict about that pre- and post-conflict between Israel and Palestinians: First one to use and exclusively stick to nonviolence will win.

Smaller factors are illimitable but generally predictable through the lens of restorative justice, compassion, and care for both victims and perpetrators, seen in practice and in rhetoric of some leaders of emergent nonviolent liberation struggles, such as the movement to nonviolently free Burma, marked by the galvanizing speech given 24 August 1988 at the Shwedagon Pagoda in Rangoon by Aung San Suu Kyi (Palmer-Mehta, 2009). Johnson, Asher, Kisielewski, and Lawry, (2012), all medical doctors, studied the screening and care of combatants from the civil war in Liberia and found that those with traumatic brain injury (TBI) of any kind (also the "signature injury" of U.S. troops from both Iraq and Afghanistan wars) were more likely to commit violence and were more recruitable back into future armed conflict. Screening is simple and treatment is crucial. In Liberia's case, as many as 21,000 child soldiers saw combat, and the TBI rate is estimated at 20 percent amongst soldiers not wearing helmets in any given combat environment; the child soldiers had no helmets, so the decades of increased risk of new hot conflict are increased by failure to treat and maintain treatment of these combatants.

Child-Soldier DDR

Using children under 15 is a war crime under international law. This enables the international community, as well as domestic actors, to remove child soldiers from combat or from any other armed forces association at any time, even during conflict. This means demobilization, disarmament and reintegration of those particular soldiers is not only ongoing, but is meant to last after the DDR for adult soldiers is complete. Nigerian peace scholar Oluwaseun Bamidele (2012) notes that the complexity of DDR for children— and the UN definition of a "legal" child soldier is one aged 15–24—requires far more sophisticated and thus expensive and lasting services and support than most war-torn countries can afford, necessitating a great deal of external support for a long period of time. This is not only one of the most effective ways to keep a current conflict from erupting afresh, it can help stabilize a nation seeking to build a peace culture from the ashes and chaos of war.

The common image is of a young boy carrying an AK-47, the one instrument that made child-soldiering so very possible, since it is a far lighter weapon and is reliable even after being banged about and dropped in the mud. The other typical image is of a harem of young girls coerced into sexual slavery. While these images are accurate, they are not complete, as girls and boys alike sometimes join the irregulars willingly rather than be alone, orphaned, without protection and without any means of survival in the hell of generalized war. Girls often play many other roles ranging from virtual pack-porters to camp commanders, sometimes developing a complement of logistical skills and authority, depending upon the situation and war culture of the forces in which they find themselves. The organizations and personnel who conduct DDR must be clear on all these factors and many more in order to competently help each individual child and the particular society recover, repair, and transform toward a lasting peace.

The tragedy of young people coerced into violence is matched by the inspiration of young people volunteering in youth-based or youth-launched movements in many locales. Otpur, the Serb youth group, was instrumental in toppling Slobodan Milosevic. Huge numbers of youth helped precipitate and participated in Arab Spring movements in Tunisia, Egypt, Yemen, Bahrain, Syria, Saudi Arabia, and even Jordan. From religious persecution to war to environmental destruction and climate chaos to educational system failure to hunger to lack of jobs, youth are on the front lines globally, and are responding (Jeffrey, 2013). The challenge for parents, educators, and civil society in general is to guide youth to refuse to participate in the problem of violence and to participate instead in the solution of nonviolence.

Decaying and Failed States

Bah (2012) exegetes the conditions and trajectories of three West African nations that experienced state decay, failed or nearly failed states, and civil war, suggesting that the place to begin to prevent this slide was in the political arena.

Aftermath of War of Occupation

In Iraq—a nation that lived in fear under a strongman, Saddam Hussein—civil society was unfree and subject to the tyranny of the minority. Sunnis like Hussein formed the favored-identity ruling group. The only way to make matters worse was exactly what the United States did—invade, occupy, and let loose the grievances that had been festering so badly. Now, in 2013, as predicted by peace and conflict analysts and by many nonpartisan, independent military and political analysts, Iraq is an ongoing bloody war between religious sects, ethnic groups, and various powerful and armed groups (Ghazi & Hauser, 2012). The terror of Saddam Hussein is receding in collective memory, replaced by the successive terrors of U.S. invasion and occupation and pullout. Democracy installed at gunpoint by an invader is inauthentic, foreign, not an indigenous solution to indigenous problems, and generally predictably on an ongoing path of violence until some new strongman replicates the rule of Saddam Hussein in many of its signature aspects.

Kurds have been disfavored by Hussein and the Ba'ath party and favored by the United States, which may augur ill for their abilities to maintain their relative prosperity in their oil-rich areas in northern Iraq. As the United States pulled out the tensions rose, with the majoritarian Arab Iraqis "deeply hostile" to many of the advantages enjoyed by Kurds and by Kurdish focus on security, which includes border checkpoints with fellow Iraqis and registration of all non–Kurds entering their region of Iraq—and that English is preferred to Arabic in what Kurds call Kurdistan (van Wilgenburg, 2013, p. 50). After the genocidal practices of Saddam Hussein and his armies, this is natural Kurdish concern, and the challenge is to process all those factors properly in order to avoid civil war following invasion and occupation, which itself followed a long and bitter no-fly zone enforcement, which itself followed the false hope felt by Kurds immediately after Hussein invaded Kuwait in August 1990 and the United States in turn drove Saddam out the following winter. Kurds believed they could finally declare independence, that it would be backed by the United States, and they were again slaughtered by Saddam's men while the George Bush the Elder administration watched. This itself was preceded by chemical war on the Kurds by Saddam's henchman, "Chemical Ali." Clearly, Kurds have reason to worry about the possibility of the neotonic Shi'a government of Nouri al-Malaki.

Media

So, Slobo dies and he's at the pearly gates. St. Peter says, "Where do you want to go?" Slobo says, "What are my options?" St. Peter puts a disc in the Heavenly Computer and it shows wistful-looking angels sitting on clouds slowly plucking on harps. He takes it out and puts in a second disk, showing wild dancing and debauched partying. "That's where I want to go!" exclaims Slobo, pointing at the screen. St. Peter nods and beckons him to the elevator. They get in, go plummeting down and down, and Slobo's feet are so hot by the time they come to a halt he is hopping from one foot to the other. The elevator opens and St. Peter nudges him out. Slobo looks, aghast, at poor souls chained to the rocky walls, in flames, screaming in eternal agony. He turns around and shouts at St. Peter, "That's not what you showed me!" As the door is closing and the devil's imps are descending on Slobo, St. Peter shrugs from inside the elevator, "State television."

—Gallows humor by Erick Torch[29]

Media is at times almost a direct grievance. While Josef Goebbels carried it to an extrapolative absurd end, propaganda is met with outrage at times and shrugs when it gets commonplace. Still, it has an effect, as we see so painfully in North Korea and elsewhere. In more subtle forms, war journalism is also propaganda-based. War journalism has slowly made room for a growing amount of peace journalism, though the predominant style of reportage and editorial content is still delivered as war journalism in many societies.

War or peace journalism generally may be characterized by a hermeneutic array of frames, language, assumptions, orientations and gatekeeping (see Table 2). In a hot conflict, peace journalism can frame stories to explain opportunities for nonviolent conflict transformation, thus enabling a potential or an extant peace process (Jan, Paracha, Sultana, Sherazi, & Ali, 2011). Each serves an agenda, or complex of agendas. Each serves interest groups; war journalism serves elite special interests and peace journalism serves the public interest. While it may not be possible or even desirable for any particular journalist to promote peace by stated opinion, it is ethically incumbent upon journalists to seek sources who can explain opportunities for nonviolent conflict transformation rather than just focusing on a blow-by-blow account of damages and threatened retaliation (Lee, 2010). When this journalism ethic is more widely understood it will afford opportunities to pressure media outlets to practice it.

Table 2: Characteristics of War and Peace Journalism

Characteristic	War journalism	Peace journalism
Dichotomizing (moral judgment toward one side)	x	
Dichotomizing solutions (a or b)	x	
Assigning blame (who started it)	x	
Here and now (devoid of historical context)	x	
Elite orientation	x	
Emotive language	x	
Sources elite adversarial conflict experts	x	
Oriented toward zero-sum victory over enemy	x	
Serves elite special interests	x	
Multiparty orientation		x
Nonpartisanship		x
Avoidance of emotive language		x
Historical contextual balance		x
Exploration of range of options		x
Sources civil society nonviolent leaders and transformational conflict management intellectuals/researchers/practitioners		x
Oriented toward win-win, reconciliation		x
Serves the public interest		x

Table 2: War and peace journalism characteristics. Sources: Galtung (1992); Jan, Paracha, Sultana, Sherazi, & Ali (2011); Lee (2010); Lynch & McGoldrick (2005a); Lee, Maslog, & Kim (2006); Buller (2011). Note that, in actuality, peace journalism is not only more objective, it is far more comprehensive, and it is logical to assert that peace journalism is simply good, professionally ethical journalism.

One of the most pervasive and bare-naked practices of war journalism is the overt banning of uncontrolled journalists from a conflict zone. Various powers practice this in different ways. The government of Syria is obvious, practicing state terrorism in almost every fashion, including torturing and disappearing journalists and their interview subjects (Galperin, 2012). The United States is generally more subtle, experimenting since the Vietnam War—when free-range journalists reported many upsetting stories that hurt the legitimacy of the United States—with press pools and embedded journalists. The underlying principle is simply that states greatly prefer to control all messaging that may have anything to do with the image and thus the legitimacy of their violent control of everything possible, and the outbreak of any violence gives them permission and justification to exert total control. The message supporting banning foreign journalists from Syria by the Assad regime is nearly identical to the message supporting the protection of embedded journalists and the corresponding abandonment of independent journalists in a conflict zone. The latter message may be more subtle, but when independent, non-embedded media personnel are hit by missiles launched by the United States, the claim of mistake can look flimsy at best.

Empowering independent journalism, protecting investigative journalists such as Julian Assange—the most extensive whistleblower in history—and working to promote the practice of peace journalism in societies that are not officially at war but which suffer from violence (Biazoto, 2011; Jan, Paracha, Sultana, Sherazi, & Ali, 2011) are all part of war prevention.

While peace journalism may be somewhat rare, it does occur. In her commentary in *Newsweek* 8 March 2013, Janine di Giovanni writes about the tragedy of the failure of nonviolence in Syria, and how it was both internally inspired and externally augmented by Srja Popovic, one of the youth leaders of the nonviolent revolution in Serbia in 2000. Before Popovic and the Otpur youth group became active, the uprising in the former Yugoslavia had generally been violent—with the exception of the Kosovars under the leadership of Ibrahim Rugova, who worked with Kosovar Albanians to nonviolently become independent from the autocratic Serb minority rulers. In that generally violent break-up of what had been Yugoslavia, suddenly Bosnians were shooting at Croatians shooting at Serbs, and the vicious infighting was brutal and bloody with a violent end, once NATO just began bombing and imposing military rule—though it could not achieve much in Serbia itself, and Milosevic looked impregnable—until Serbs like Popovic began themselves. The hope for Syria is in fact the hope that they can draw from the Serbs and Liberians and others who stopped hot civil wars in their homelands using only nonviolent people power. Giovanni notes the similarities, that it "reminds me of Bosnia in the way people used to call themselves Syrians and now are saying they are Druze or Shia or Sunni or Alawite or Christian."[30] Giovanni advises rebels to stick to nonviolence, to eschew armed uprisings, which is certainly peace journalism, especially in a conflict supported by arms shipments from the United States and others.

Similarly, in the March 2012 *Atlantic Monthly*, also a mainstream media outlet in the United States, Liel Leibowitz profiled Popovic, simply titling the piece "The Revolutionist," and described the journey Popovic took from being a young biology student with an interest in politics to a youth leader in the uprising against Milosevic—then winning decisively and totally nonviolently in 2000—and his eventual travels all over the world, training others in nation after nation in the art of people power, of civil society organizing, mobilization, and victory.[31]

From Leibowitz:

> Still, for all his method's success, Popovic feels that those who should be paying the most attention—academics, politicians, journalists—instead continue to view politics largely as a game played by governments and decided by war. "Nobody, from very prominent political analysts to the world's intelligence services, could find their own nose when the Arab Spring started. It is always

this same old narrative: 'It happened in Serbia by accident. It happened in Georgia by accident. It happened in Tunisia by accident. But it will never happen in Egypt.' And this is the mantra we keep hearing—until it happens."

Popovic, of course, is aware that he is changing that narrative, and that others are also working on this. Slowly the evidence collects, the news finally is seen in its patterns, and journalists actually begin to source those who understand alternatives to war—hence the journalists sourcing Popovic, Gene Sharp, and Erica Chenoweth upon occasion. When peace journalism is the norm, war will be history, but to help relegate war to history, peace journalism is needed. Thus we slowly spiral toward an end to war.

More research is needed on the problem of media presenting inaccurate, incomplete or even fabricated information to the public, the public recognizing it, the media apologizing and correcting long after the damage is done, and the public then trusting the "transparent" media that then does precisely the same thing again. We see this from war to war, and perhaps social psychology will explain this public forgiveness and restoration of trust—something most people would likely not do in their personal relationships. So, for instance, the expatriates who were featured in the Bush administration's narrative justifying the invasion of Iraq were telling lies about WMD, were caught later in those lies, admitted to those lies, and the media that reported those lies in the first place then reported that this mistake had been made. Now we hear from Syrian expatriates who attribute all civilian deaths in that civil war to the Assad regime, and many media outlets are reporting these views, seeming to justify sending arms and possibly engaging militarily in the civil war on that pretext (al-Gharbi, 2013). We are also learning from other media—primarily unofficial, citizen journalists on the ground in Syria—that rebels are killing many noncombatants. Neither armed side is waging their war in a fashion consonant with international law, rules of warfare, or in keeping with the UDHR.

Media Mimesis

When Egyptians watched Tunisians rise up using massive civil society outpouring and protest gathering against the conditions produced by decades of oppression, they reported that seeing what Tunisians were doing made them believe they too had hope (Salti, 2012). Hope that comes from seeing others cast off oppression is a powerful, dangerous, wondrous thing, achievable by the new rampant, instant-upload-and-download imagery captured by millions of citizens with cell phone cameras and small, lightweight video cameras. The potential of viral nonviolence or viral violence as a product of media mimesis is a tantalizing and an awful prospect. Both rumors and rumor control are more easily accomplished using social media, another demonstration of the two-edged sword of high technology. Confronting a corrupt official in Kenya with the almost certain knowledge that one is going to be beaten and arrested is now accompanied by Twitter—29-year-old Boniface Mwangi has 33,000 followers, and he seems determined to use them to bolster his ability to dissent (Associated Press, 10 May 2013). Would he take those risks without his ability to Tweet?

Aside from testimony in interviews, observers of photographic and video-graphic images of demonstrations in Syria, for example, reported signs with slogans clearly borrowed from Egypt and transplanted to Syria. Probably the most amusing to students of nonviolence was the photo of an Egyptian woman in hijab in Tahrir Square holding a banner with the Serb youth group icono-graphic clenched fist of Otpur! (Resistance!).

With more platforms for delivering an unprecedented synthesis of news and entertainment, the new priority for some of the research is to address the historical gaps in knowledge of how the "soft," or cultural side of media—entertainment—affects war and peace (Burston, 2003). Any casual search for news and views on almost any conflict will reveal a new explosion of such cul-tural confluence, from Facebook to Twitter to YouTube, from cartoons to posters to short videos to mixed media creativity. This can promote war or peace and, to the extent it is founded in the enlightened self-interest of average people rather than demagoguery, represents a new hope for stronger public discourse toward peace.

The traditional concern has been about the lack of objective media or dissenting media and the corresponding lack of public opinion dissenting from a governmental point of view. This is seen most overtly in autocratic nations present and past, currently the subject of research in China, North Korea, and, in particular, Iran (Klein, 2012). The nimble ability of masses of people to devise workarounds to government technical blocks on social media and Inter-net access is important, although not dispositive. From private mimeograph machines in the Civil Rights era to phone trees in many campaigns to samizdat press in many other movements, people find these various vectors when they decide to seriously look. And if they haven't found them, they create them. The challenges are not overwhelming once enough people develop raised expectations.

PART 2

Promote Nonviolent Conflict Management

Ending civil wars is nonviolently done by civil society. All the principles Chenoweth and Stephan (2011) identified apply. Recruit. Build coalition. Encourage defections from warriors to peace activists. Erode the pillars of support for war. Is this news? Not to Gandhi, whose *swadeshi* campaigns of local self-reliance drew support away from the dominating colonial paradigm of pauperizing indigenous populations by making them producers of raw materials and consumers of value-added products, and not to theoretician case-study scholars Kurt Schock (2013) or Gene Sharp (1973), but "many scholars assume that the absence of violent conflict means that no conflict exists at all" (Chenoweth & Cunningham, 2013, p. 272). If nonviolence were merely overlooked by scholars, that would be a non-issue, but it's often similarly ignored by journalists and therefore missing, generally speaking, from both the educational and media subsystems, from which we obtain most new information. The handful of historic peace traditions are not widespread enough to counterbalance this lack of study and knowledge production, and thus the many nonviolent success stories are not only missed, but the citizenry is led easily to believe that the violent option is the only reasonable alternative when under duress. Those who dismiss nonviolence as a European church oddity tied to quaint women in bonnets and men in frocks or those who wave nonviolence aside as an artifact of nude Jain monks or minor begging-bowl Buddhist mendicants are now themselves in the outdated category. Increasingly, the very subdiscipline of the study of nonviolence is developing many strands that have only begun to be braided into an interdisciplinary tapestry. Much more can be done along these lines, and the practice can best be moved forward by the dialectic of research informing that practice and the practice informing the research (Schock, 2013).

One of those pillars is the near deification of the violent warrior, a sacralizing project that seems both subtle and buck-naked obvious in mainstream media as they tenderly, cloyingly report on soldiers, Marines, and their longing to be home even as they courageously obey the patriotic call of duty to defend ... a political and economic hegemonic agenda that profits the elite owners of war-contracting corporations? ... a perfervid sect of violent fundamentalists driven by hate? ... nationalist mercenaries who slaughter civilians at a much higher rate than they kill terrorists? Indeed, close watchers of media from a variety of nations or transnational associations who are engaged in war see this historically common phenomenon almost panculturally. It is time to stop war and to stop worshipping warriors of all stripes, colors, religions, identities, ideologies and national origins.

Nonviolence is the method of conflict management that has historically received little meaningful research aside from that done by one political science scholar, Gene Sharp. This is finally changing, and slowly, with that change, comes a change in the rhetoric, in the persuasive skills necessary to explain the research so that it becomes usable, a sort of synthesis of evidence and oratory required to advance both knowledge and acceptance of that knowledge (Jasper & Young, 2007). Activists who promote nonviolence now know many more case histories and they know the numbers. Sharp, who began the process of cataloging the case histories and providing analysis, deserves credit in any advance in the cases of the use of nonviolence, though he credits the actual players, not himself (Pal, 2011). Many others have joined in describing case histories and offering analysis, but only two major studies to date have taken a quantitative approach alongside their analysis: Peter Ackerman and Adrian Karatnyky in their 2005 Freedom House study, and Erica Chenoweth and Maria Stephan in their 2008 study. They know that strategic nonviolent rebellion succeeds twice as often as does violent insurrection and that the least effective method of rising up against a government is terrorism. They can cite the 2005 Freedom House study, How Freedom Is Won, and they increasingly discuss the 2008 Strategic Studies article by academics Erica Chenoweth and Maria Stephan, "Why Civil Resistance Works," and their 2011 book by the same name. As the ideas and findings from this new research become known, change can accelerate. Not only is civil society becoming self-aware—understanding that adopting nonviolent methods will give them better metrics of civil rights, human rights, and democracy—but they are slowly beginning to understand that it is in all our enlightened self-interest to stop spending ourselves into permanent debt and deficits preparing for the same interstate wars our grandparents fought. The future fight is with nonviolent civil society forces.

To be clear, the idea of nonviolent resistance is different from nonviolent opposition and simple political action—and it's one of many versions of conflict transformation, that is, the art of helping morph a destructive or potentially destructive conflict into a constructive, usually creative, conflict (Lederach, 2003). Part of what helps us understand the actual reality of the concepts is to stress the civil society orientation of nonviolent efforts, even though that doesn't incorporate all instances of approaches. For example, the theory and practice of Consensus Organizing creates and exploits the potential and real collaborations between civil society and more powerful, even elite, external parties. Perhaps the greatest example of such an approach is the International Campaign to Ban Landmines, which focused on—and achieved—"international ban on the use, production, stockpiling and transfer of 'anti-personnel' landmines" (Villacampa, 2008, p. 519). The organizers, starting with Jody Williams, approached any leadership in high places they could contact and involve in every possible country to argue for this ban. As they were doing so, they built a massive coalition of civil society organizations globally to produce the wind that could effectively help the elites to decide to join the effort. The model was so successful it resulted in the first global treaty entirely produced by grassroots action.

Within that model was a phenomenon sociologists call diffusion, that is, the quicker and quicker spread of actionable movements, based on the observations of apparent success elsewhere. This phenomenon has been evident historically, including the 1968 global eruption of social change, antiwar, and revolutionary movements, and of course the Velvet Revolution sweep of regime change from Hungary to the Baltic States to the dissolution of the Soviet Union, from 1989–1991 (Kriesberg, 2012).

Philosophically, there has always been a counter-current of thought, from the ancient Stoics who eschewed violence and especially revenge, to various religions East and West, most of whom had nonviolent sects or at least those with allegiance to the nonviolent teachings in each religion. Just as no law is written in a vacuum, no philosophy of expressed nonviolence was made without the prompt of violence to help formulate it. Lisa Curtis-Wendlandt (2012) examines the contributions made to the thinking about rebellion and violence by political philosophers Elise Reimarus and Immanuel Kant. Both opposed the precepts offered by John Locke and Thomas Hobbes, thinkers who constructed what amounts to a secular approach to Just War doctrine during the Age of Enlightenment. Some assert that, whether considering religious or secular philosophers, and whether considering interpersonal or group-to-group violence, the keys often revolve around moral disengagement, that is, a suspension of normal values in order to justify acts that are otherwise unjustifiable. This moral disengagement may be

> euphemistic labeling of violent acts, distortion or minimization of the consequences of violence, dehumanization of its victims, justification of violence for higher moral ends, displacement or diffusion of responsibility for violent acts,

and advantageous comparison of outcomes (e.g., arguing that a violent act is necessary to prevent worse suffering) [Howard, Shegog, Grussendorf, Benjamins, Stelzig, & McAlister, 2007, p. 560].

These psychological, cognitive processes may be inherent in humans, and we leave it to the moral leadership to either endorse our most base instincts with ornate and eloquent reasoning, or to challenge us to remain true to our inner altruists. Certainly we see these conflicting tendencies in the contesting philosophies of Locke and Hobbes on the one, justifying, hand, versus Reimarus and Kant on the more rigorous, challenging other hand. These moral structures are not built in a vacuum. Certainly all four of these philosophers were responding to the violence of their day, both overt and structural.

Reimarus, for example, constructed her essay, "Freedom," in 1791, in an atmosphere of violent insurgency throughout Europe and North America, including in her hometown, Hamburg, Germany. In that piece, says Curtis-Wendlandt, Reimarus first repudiates violent rebellion as virtually always worse than the oppression it is meant to relieve, and then offers her (pre–Gandhian) alternatives, loosely tapping into the potential for civil society working through a discourse and remedy, anticipating Immanuel Kant in some respects and certainly building her ideas from a social-contract philosophical tradition that generally supported a "right to resist." It is this long struggle of the mind away from violent uprising that helped lead, ultimately, to Gandhi and then his theoretical and practical successors. Simply, Reimarus had some limited faith in even the worst legal system to do a less harmful job than a violent revolution would do, but more importantly, she had a strong faith in the emerging moral advancements of society, coupled with the overwhelming desire of the new intellectuals to lead honest, open, reasoned public discourse, which would lead to endless reform. The other salient point about Reimarus in particular is that she is one of the most bold, innovative and brilliant political philosophers of her era and, like most women of that time, mostly lost to history. Efforts to reexamine that era through a gender lens have uncovered a trove of French, British, and German women who were significant in the development of several crucial strands of thought. Drawing from the dialogic model of Socrates, Reimarus posits a dialog between cousins considering the uprising, the conditions producing the grievances, and the alternatives politically and morally. While it is fashionable to leave morality out of discussions about methods of rebellion, perhaps it is time to resynthesize the notions of ethics and effectiveness. Reimarus had none of the practical experience of Gandhi and therefore lacked the options of nonviolent civil resistance, but her early political philosophical attempts help us see some of the roots of our current strands of thinking about means and ends.

From classical constructs of the Just War doctrine until today, there have been strands that have proceeded toward a nonviolent alternative to war and those that construct new theories accounting for new facts and new trends. With the advent and application of human rights law, this has now come in the new packaging called Right to Protect (R2P), and new rationalizations for more war have followed (e.g., Davenport, 2011). These determined theorists keep justifying war even though far less costly and far more effective options exist. It is hoped that, eventually, these analysts will transform their own calculus of conflict costs and begin to excuse nonviolent resistance to oppression rather than armed uprising or intervention. Indeed, says Gene Sharp, the proven success of nonviolence has rendered the Just War doctrine obsolete (Flintoff, 2013).

One of the mutually exclusive dynamics that is finally being challenged is the dual role of any nation trying to both export arms and negotiate peace. The United States has arrogated these roles unto itself for decades, keeping its role as peacemaker high in its rhetorical profile and its role as massive arms supplier very low, even obscured. Nonetheless, people who see various weapons used against them labeled "Made in USA" know very well that someone is profiting from their suffering. Trust in those who are in fact benefitting from bloodshed, that is, from the continuing conflict, is usually nonexistent. Yes, the leaders of people who are hurt by U.S. weapons are seldom open about the destruction of trust, but it is the basic default setting and contaminates every process.

Is nonviolence crazy? Ghaemi (2011) makes the case that both Gandhi and Martin Luther King, Jr. were mentally ill, but in a good way. They suffered from bouts of depression that, in their cases, asserts Ghaemi, resulted in leadership featuring extraordinary and inspiring and adaptive empathy. The empathy these leaders exhibited in turn evoked empathy for their followers, first by external actors and then even by the people who were their opponents.

The costs associated with violent methods of waging civil war are also a list of grievances that tend to exacerbate contributory factors that drive more war, thus clearly changing the equation of advantage of one method or another.

An example of how that happens is that the use of violent insurgency can lead to the cycle of revenge that tends to protract the conflict, harden the positions of the parties, widen the war across borders to affect other nation-states, further suppress democracy, escalate ethnic and religious conflict, and drive groups of refugees on a collision course with previously unaffected groups. The use of nonviolence may widen the conflict, but it generally does not cause new grievances as it does so; nonviolence simply provides an outlet that can make those grievances more actionable. So, for example, the nonviolent methods used in Tunisia in late 2010-early 2011 spread the conflict to Egypt, but not because new grievances caused that migration of the conflict. Rather, those nonviolent methods made it seem possible for another civil society to act with hope of improvement, and they began to do so. But the violence of the uprising in Syria caused new grievances in Turkey and Lebanon,[1] new acts of cross-border destruction and death that added more reason to engage in further violent conflict, revealing a highly dangerous positive feedback loop that damaged peace and justice across the region. Violence tends to deepen suspicion for long periods, an erosion of trust that makes this feedback loop more powerful and sustainable in its destructive effects. The responses of the parties to a huge bomb blast in Beirut, Lebanon, on October 19, 2012, shows this. The al-Assad regime denounced the bombing, and the Syrian rebels joined international analysts, many of whom blamed the Syrian government (Barnard, 19 October 2012). The blame was made more credible to many when it was revealed that a Lebanese intelligence officer, Brigadier General Wissam al-Hassan, was one of those who died in the blast, as he had just claimed to have uncovered a Syrian government plot to cause upheaval in Lebanon. It is hardly conceivable that this particular attack—whoever is to blame—would have happened if the Syrian uprising would have been nonviolent in the Tunisia model rather than the "normal" violence.

Justifying the competing acts of violence is frankly easy. Even preemptive violence presents few serious ethical obstacles for those who use the shopworn Just War doctrine (e.g., Buchanan & Keohane, 2005). The justifications cannot prevent the negative results of the positive feedback loops of destruction and causation, revealing a consequentialist flaw in that doctrine, which is already highly suspect in any deontological sense. In other words, the Just War doctrine seems to produce more war, less justice, and immeasurably higher costs even at the same time it ignores a moral obligation to protect innocents by the most secure and least reckless manner. The Just War doctrine was never going to satisfy basic criteria attached to the ethics of virtue, that is, the moral character of the party who promotes the war, especially when one views that history of the development of the doctrine in the millennia past. All official efforts to spruce up the idea of war have thinly masked rationales for waging wars of bloody aggression, from Augustine—tasked with constructing a churchy version of excuses to conquer—to Aquinas—given the job of coming up with reasons to attack Islam, consolidate national power, and acquire land without saying any of that and instead acting as though Jesus would have approved.

What possible hope does nonviolence have in preventing civil wars? The strongest reason to place faith and vigorously promote nonviolence in this regard is that statistically it is far more likely to succeed than is violent insurgency. Indeed, nonviolence has directly halted civil wars that have either begun or were widely predicted to be inevitable. What follows is an annotated set of potential nonviolent strategies to avert, mitigate, prevent or stop civil wars.

Claiming credit for acts that are deeply unpopular is unlikely for any party in any conflict. Much more likely is that the acts for which credit may be claimed are claimed by all parties, and all blameworthy acts are attributed to the other side. In violent conflict that is often simply a matter of saying it and citing previous analogous behavior. The Free Syrian Army is an example. Since they employ violence instead of nonviolent civil society methods, it is easy to smear them as the party responsible for firing mortars into civilian areas.[2]

It is worth noting that a naïve nonviolent philosophy is not immediately adaptive in some cases, especially if no concomitant nonviolent force is applied. Thus, once the dynamic of violence has been established and the trajectory is clear, avoidance of the violent parties for a time is at times the most adaptive civil society strategy (Barter, 2012). While a precise set of evaluative metrics cannot guarantee results in any specific scenario, leaders are best advised to use caution in the face of likely violence or any credible violent threat. Shane Joshua Barter cites the examples drawn from experience in the Liberian civil war when some local leaders tried to transform advancing rampaging soldiers in Charles Taylor's army. In one described incident, village elders met the soldiers with offers of peace, cows as gifts, and invitations to enjoy the hospitality of the village. The soldiers executed more than 300 of the villagers and laid waste to it. Other villages fared better by fleeing into mangrove swamps. Discretion can indeed be the better part of either valor or innocence. Nonviolence is the best option, but it may need to be done strategically and judiciously in order to protect civil society as much as possible under threat. The analog in interpersonal threat is that waiting to confront an enraged and out-of-control individual holding a weapon until the obvious rage is somewhat reduced, is adaptive and advised. Timing in the application of any strategy is key.

Association is also crucial. Armed civilian militias are considered combatants, and those in their company risk the same status, which is usually far more dangerous than simply being unarmed civilians in the path of violent forces. Indeed, any stated loyalty to any armed faction in any conflict is partially protective and partially elevated risk. This is a dangerous calculation for any local leaders in any potentially violent locale.

Strategic Nonviolence

People power is catching: The more often it works, the more often it will be used.
— *The Economist* (19 January 2006)

Strategic nonviolence or nonviolent resistance is defined "as the application of unarmed civilian power using nonviolent methods such as protests, strikes, boycotts, and demonstrations, without using or threatening physical harm against the opponent" (Chenoweth & Cunningham, 2013, p. 271). Other scholars of strategic nonviolence seem to define it similarly, while those who also include a philosophy or religious mandate of pacifism usually add that component. Chenoweth and Cunningham seem to use the terms *nonviolence* and *pacifism* interchangeably, whereas this author and others seem to differentiate *nonviolence* as in need of the modifier *strategic* to indicate an instrumentalist approach or *philosophical* (or *religious* or *principled*) to indicate an engaged pacifism. Arguably, it is simply most helpful to know that the vast majority of those who engage in strategic nonviolence are not, in fact, pacifists, but simply see the strategic advantage of nonviolence. While it's true that the pacifist logic is "If everyone were a pacifist, all necessary changes would occur," it's also true that pacifism is not synonymous with social movement creation and development (Schock, 2013). Strategic nonviolence is about winning and nonviolence is merely the most advantageous tool, though certainly some of the leadership of some of those campaigns also subscribe to a nonviolent philosophy.

The use of strategic nonviolence to turn likely war to peaceful change is possibly the greatest hope for averting the destructive method of violent insurgency. When nonviolent civil society struggles are undertaken with training, planning, unity and discipline, the nonviolent insurgents have a far greater chance for success (Chenoweth & Stephan, 2011; Filiatreau, 2009; Karatnycky & Ackerman, 2005; Stephan & Chenoweth, 2008). "Our findings show that major nonviolent campaigns have achieved success 53 percent of the time, compared with 26 percent for violent resistance campaigns" (Stephan & Chenoweth, 2008, p. 8). And while these authors researched only "maximal goal" (regime change) struggles, the long list of strategic nonviolent victories in many other categories clearly marks a line of sight to ending our pathetic and tragic reliance on arms.

Arguably, each of these nonviolent regime changes was an instance of preventing civil war—that is an impressive record when we consider it in that light. But there are many more occasions when, in all likelihood, civil war was also prevented by nonviolent action. In 1991, for example, civil war in the disintegrating Soviet Union and then the reconstituting Russia was decidedly possible as a serious coup d'état occurred. Russians formed a "Living Ring" of interposition between the belligerents and very likely stopped a civil war, which could have been long and bloody or short and bloody, and those nonviolent Russians from their civil society halted a coup d'état-in-progress, saving their democracy (Taylor, 1994, 2011). In truth, although antiwar activists don't possess this perspective—yet—nonviolent civil society has already shown how to stop civil wars. It is very possible that, indeed, strategic nonviolence has already stopped civil wars or secession wars at various moments in Ghana, Zambia, Tanzania, Benin, Cape Verde, Ethiopia, the Gambia, Madagascar, Malawi, Mali, Côte d'Ivoire, Mozambique, Senegal, Uganda, Philippines, East Germany, Hungary, Poland, Czechoslovakia, Latvia, Lithuania, Estonia, Serbia, Bangladesh, Guatemala, Indonesia, Mexico, Nepal, Nicaragua, Peru, South Korea, Taiwan, Georgia, Ukraine, Mongolia, Lebanon, and Kirgyzstan (*Economist*, 2006), not to mention Tunisia and Egypt. "In all these cases, people power opened the vise of arbitrary rule by disputing its legitimacy, escalating the cost of its operations, and splitting the ranks of its own defenders" (DuVall, 2007).

Central to all these considerations is that nonviolence is the strongest, most successful method to address a problem often embarrassingly missing from standard theories and practices of Conflict Resolution, the problem of asymmetry between and among parties to a conflict (Dudouet, 2013; Stephan & Chenoweth, 2008). Many commentators—most of them from the group considered relatively powerless—have critiqued the practice of Conflict Resolution as one which makes no usable nor particularly relevant allowances for the disadvantageous power position of the oppressed at the negotiating table. Is this fair? Of course not. Are there remedies? Yes, and they primarily center around strategic nonviolence. Is there a guarantee of victory? Again, of course not, but at the very least, nonviolent action usually creates previously unavailable space, politically and socially, in which to organize the next steps of correcting the power imbalance (Mahony & Eguren, 1997; Norman, 2013).

It is also patently clear that with nonviolence, the costs are far less, and the two factors are related. All violent insurgency justifies the violent suppression by the government forces, making the rebellion more and more costly and eventually driving away participants who cannot afford to commit their entire lives to violent revolution. Sooner or later, civil society increasingly hates the insurgents almost as much as they hate the government, since the government crushes civilians alongside rebels. This is exactly what happened in Syria as rebels seized towns, only to have them bombed into rubble, killing far more civilians than fighters, ruining civil society in a rain of destruction that the government justifies in the name of fighting "terrorism."[3] In early October 2012, the town of Maarat al-Noaman was "liberated" by Syrian rebels fighting to overthrow Bashar al-Assad. "On Thursday, jubilation turned to horror as government airstrikes sent fountains of dust and rubble skyward and crushed several dozen people who had returned to what they thought was a new haven in a country mired in civil war" (Barnard & Saad, 18 October 2012). The results are part of that predictable dynamic of tragedy and loss, from the same story in the *New York Times:* "That dynamic—rebel gains, army crackdowns and ensuing resentment against rebels as well as the government—has played out again and again, including in Aleppo, Syria's largest city. Rebels last month began what they said would be an all-out offensive there. But the result was to spread fighting into previously peaceful neighborhoods and damage the city's beloved historic center, leaving many residents as angry at the rebels for bringing the fight there as at the government for its harsh response."

Strategic nonviolence is almost always predicated upon planning and prior training. Ad hoc uprisings may begin nonviolently but succumb to violence once tested by a brutal regime. In both Tunisia and Egypt, for instance, civil society had been organizing, planning, training, and preparing for a serious social challenger movement whenever conditions permitted, and activists from those nation-states were also studying the methods of other successful uprisings, including the overthrow of Milosevic in Serbia (Kriesberg, 2012). This was less seen in other Arab states, and the reversion to violence was sadly more predictable. Resisting the natural temptation during the heat of struggle to adopt violent methods is very hard if oppression and violence become too great. This is precisely the time to renew nonviolent discipline and commitment. Sliding into violence will raise costs and frequently delay success. Desmond George-Williams (2006, p. 111), scholar at the University for Peace Africa Programme, notes,

> In the cases of the South African and the Ogoni peoples, casualties increased after the ANC went underground and when militancy rose in the Ogoni region after clashes with ethnic neighbours and when the security forces stepped up repressive measures. In Madagascar, casualty figures rose when clashes erupted between the rival supporters of Ratsiraka and Ravolomanana.

In addition to reducing costs in blood, treasure, and the environment, nonviolence tends to produce stronger post-conflict metrics of democracy (Steger, 1999), civil rights, and human rights (Karatnycky & Ackerman, 2005). This should not be mysterious. When a civil war occurs the insurgents who succeed with armed forces claim all power, claim the success, and brand themselves as the vanguard of the revolution, arrogating an entitlement to a lifetime of power unto themselves. This is usually mutually exclusive to honest democracy, the American mythos notwithstanding. The basic notion that a relatively small group of armed revolutionaries were completely responsible for victory and are the true champions of the people is ubiquitous and never needs to occur in a nonviolent takeover, since civil society clearly provides the power en masse, even with a charismatic leader or two. Simply, democracy tends to flow from democracy; this is not only a drawback of violent insurgency but of the more anarchic varieties of nonviolent insurgency (which almost never succeed except rarely in local struggles, and are thus much harder to research meaningfully).

Examples can help us reframe intrastate conflict and take hope for a new way forward.

Philippines

In the mid–1970s various groups of Filipinas and Filipinos began to organize grassroots nonviolent opposition to the increasingly martial law despotism of Ferdinand Marcos. Nuns began training cadres of nonviolent actionists, essentially strategically preparing civil society for nonviolent revolution. At one point, they told Cardinal Sin to be prepared to address the nation when the time was right. That time came in February 1986, as a civil war began. The people interposed between two armies of tanks in a remarkable four-day nonviolent mass action. They stopped an emerging civil war, rescued their democracy, and did all this with zero mortalities. It stands as one of the most remarkable episodes in human history, demonstrating many basic principles of nonviolent success and offering lessons to civil societies everywhere.

Nonpartisan Assistance to Nonviolent Civil Society Movements

Can the world become a nonpartisan supporter of civil society when enough manifestations of grievances show that a repressive regime is facing at least some nonviolent resistance from its own civil society? Indeed, external parties have provided support for indigenous struggles. Both the United States and the EU supplied Serbs with computers, funds for printing bumper stickers, and other requested material support. Worldwide Catholics supported the civil society struggles that toppled Ferdinand Marcos in the Philippines and the communist dictatorship in Poland. Peter Ackerman and Jack DuVall (2005, p. 47) suggest this can be more effective and engender less suspicion if regularized through some international effort.

> To protect and expand this assistance, and to insure it does not serve any government's agenda for "regime change," an international institution or new international foundation should channel aid to civilian groups that choose peoplepower strategies. Such an institution should be independent and adopt new international norms for dispensing help. For example, assisted groups should commit to nonviolent action, democratic self-rule, and the standards enshrined in the Universal Declaration of Human Rights.

While some will forever find fault with any external aid to indigenous opposition coalitions facing violent regimes—certainly many ultraleftists oppose any criticism of Hugo Chávez in Venezuela, the theocracy in Iran, and even the militaristic cult communists of North Korea—it is the opinion of civil society worldwide that might matter in this regard. Routinizing aid to nonviolent civil society struggling against a violent regime seems like a positive evolutionary step for humankind.

Imaging Work

> *Without a vision, the people perish.*
>
> —Proverbs 29

We will either build the images of the society we wish to live in and then develop a plan to get to those images, or we will live in someone else's vision of the world they want. Elite war profiteers have already done this quite well; if civil society decides to engage independently in their own visioning instead of waiting for elites to construct a self-serving vision and treat it like received wisdom, civil society will create hope instead of having tolerance of intolerable conditions imposed on them. Till Förster (2012) describes how the violent insurgents in Côte d'Ivoire hold ceremonies expropriating nationalistic components of the very government against which they are rebelling, but clearly are in control of a different future, allegedly for the benefit of all but they are always the ones with the guns. Celebrating that sort of future is allowing the armed rebels to legitimate their hoped-for seizure of power by strengthening the claim that it is done in the name of the people. But nonviolent movements could do the same and better if they chose, which is partly why Elise Boulding developed her imaging workshops.

Inventing a future together is how a strategic coalition of civil society organizations can become unified, purposeful, and strategic. The visions that come to people have historically propelled them to persistent attempts to reify those visions—this is why visionaries are regarded as leaders, or at least inspirational figures. The easy, epiphanic work is conjuring or allowing the vision, though that seems hard for most of us stuck in the present and shackled by "realism." The hardest work is selling that vision to enough people to set its actualization into motion. The work lies in transforming a fantasy or dream into a vision by also developing and promoting a realistic plan to achieve it.

Glenn D. Paige was a young warrior in the Korean War, and his dissertation in Political Science parsed out some of the preparation for that war, looking favorably at the decision-making process. Then, in 1974—mid-career for this academic—his vision came to him, "straight up through me, giving me just three words: No More Killing" (interview, December 2011). Paige began to construct a philosophy and cross-disciplinary perspective around that simple but seemingly impossible inner directive. He is founder of the Global Center for Nonkilling. He explains that nonkilling is a society in which no humans kill each other and no humans threaten to kill each other, thus hold no "hardware" of killing (e.g., handguns) and do not have armed law enforcement, but rather a society that creates other ways of managing human needs and human conflict (Paige, 2000, 2009). This is the sort of organized effort that can clearly push the envelope far past stopping a particular war or even stopping war in general, since Paige contemplates a society without a military at all—and he does so in one of the most militarized academic disciplines, Political Science. Visions can change the discourse. Powerful visions can produce lifelong persistent, resilient, determined promoters of another way of being, making our "mere" intent to stop invasions and occupations and civil wars seem moderate and possibly achievable. Paige may be reductionist in his constrained opinion that a large advantage of nonkilling over nonviolence is that nonkilling is measurable and nonviolence is not, but he is working with a discipline that wants clear, measurable quantifiable data—the same discipline that helped the CIA miss the fall of the Berlin Wall and Arab Spring, so Paige has a fair point in this regard. If the desire is to end civil wars, invasions, and occupations, a nonkilling scholarship and policy approach is helpful. The vision is being explored, as Paige hands off his work to younger scholars, including Joám Evans Pim of Spain, who has now edited a series of books focusing on the nonkilling theme through the lenses of different disciplines, taking Paige's vision far beyond Political Science. This scholarship is a fine supplement to a growing corpus of peace and conflict literature in the expanding field.

Whether formally in the Elise Boulding Inventing a World method or less formally, creating a shared vision can assist in changing the quality and characteristics of a conflict. Hillel Cohen (2013) theorizes that the creation of a shared vision of bi-communal life in Jerusalem by the Palestinian Fatah group and various Israeli peace groups has begun to transform at least part of the ongoing conflict over Palestinian statehood and Israel's identity in general and Jerusalem in particular. Fatah still wages conflict including an armed wing, but does not seem to be attacking civilians, only military personnel and military sites. While this is not an end to civil war or anti-occupation violent insurgency, it is at least along the continuum toward transformation. If creating a shared vision can save children and other civilians, that is a positive step. Creating opportunities to dialog toward more shared visions for the future of Israel and Palestine—not mere dialog just to talk, but to talk with a purpose, as though citizens have agency—seems adaptive.

Strategic Nonviolence and the Theories of Conflict Resolution

> Not the winner, but in the category of "Honorable Übermenschen," we
> give our Pyrrhic Victory Award to ... violence.
> —Al Fresco, the Outdoor Satirist

As the field of peace and conflict studies grows in theory and practice, undertakes more research and develops rigorous testing, we can use these theories and practices to greatly strengthen the effects of strategic nonviolent conflict management (Dudouet, 2013; DuMont & Noma, 2013).

At the core of conflict resolution is the notion of respect, dignity, or face (Wilmot & Hocker, 2007). Framing all actions, all practice, in that way can help develop strategy, goals, media work, liaison work to armed forces/police/politicians/corporate officials, and generally assist in more effective persuasion and recruitment. While some (e.g., Hallward & Shaver, 2012) believe the field of conflict resolution assumes symmetry and strives to maintain the status quo, the strand of conflict resolution researchers and professionals who advise on becoming a more effective party, how to become assertive, when to escalate, and how to level the playing field, is now perhaps closer to the mainstream professional practice. In one provocative paper, peace psychologist Laura Taylor (2013) argues that maintaining dignity in the face of almost certain death by genocidal murder is an act of pure nonviolent resistance—to evil, to dehumanization, to false victory, to the superiority of violence, and to the ethos of might makes right. She essentializes peace and conflict to a core value of maintaining respect, something that indeed allows for transformation under any conceivable circumstances.

Understanding the basic notion of assertion cf. aggression cf. apathy is also crucial to developing a strategy and properly implementing tactics as a campaign is planned and executed. Apathy is what happens when fear is too high to overcome and populations do not become involved, which means the nonviolent movement fails. Apathy may not necessarily indicate that people do not care about an issue, but they may feel they need to risk too much in order to join. This is often the case when the insurgency is violent; it is hard to imagine being only a little bit involved in a violent revolution. You are in or you are out. That is why low- and no-risk nonviolent actions are such solid recruitment actions as long as other factors have engaged the interest of civil society. Apathy may also be a result of a combination of most of civil society having a lot to lose, no general grievances that are clearly expressed, and an image of the resistance as far too risky to join. This was the case with the Occupy movement, which lacked skills and thoughtful planning, according to analyst Gene Sharp (Pal, 2011). When middle-class America looked at the media images they saw no clear message, no discernible goal, and behavior that was alienating at best. The conduct of Occupy might have made a case in a nation with a poverty and unemployment rate far higher than the United States in 2011, but Occupy addressed too many people with too much to lose in ways that looked feckless and a poor wager, considering the sort of cost/benefit analysis available to the average American. Complaints about the media coverage are interesting and irrelevant; a movement is effective at messaging or it is not. Occupy was not.

There are examples of doing some of this quite effectively. Anika Locke Binnendijk and Ivan Marovic (2006) describe the processes in both Serbia in 2000 and Ukraine in 2004. In both cases, activists strategized in advance—something literally foreign to most U.S. activists. Further, they developed clear plans to handle relations with police and soldiers that would be maximally assertive—never backing down and never showing disrespect, much less violence, in their interactions with these security forces of the state. This resulted in a significant reduction in brutality, in arrests, in incarceration, by armed forces jaded by a decade of bloody attacks on civilians (in the case of Serbia). It ultimately facilitated a complete defection of police, gendarmerie, and soldiers away from the dictators/election thieves, which signaled victory for civil society in both cases. Activists who do not believe they can induce such loyalty shifts only hamper their own efforts. When, for instance, Tunisians achieved this by 10 January 2011 and the military signaled it would not crack down on the street protesters, it was a swift path to the fall of Ben Ali and a very large change for relatively low costs, with the military simply stepping aside in favor of relatively orderly civil society reinvention of the government (Dalacoura, 2012). Security defections like this have been more key than activists generally understand, and hostility toward police and soldiers attenuates the progress toward success of the nonviolent uprising, or even reverses it. If the lesson from Egypt—where too much authority was happily ceded to the military during the nonviolent uprising—can be instructive, future nonviolent rebellions will seek to engender loyalty shifts and defections from the regime without in turn handing over the reins of power to the armed forces.

Benefits of blunting the possible harms done by security forces to any civil society movement are numerous, and none so important as stopping war by keeping the insurgency nonviolent. A movement that is attacked by security forces often escalates into violence or dissipates and is defeated or badly delayed (Sharp, G., 1973). Attenuating the actual antipathy of security forces to a challenger movement is key to eroding that main pillar of support for any sort of autocratic regime (Ackerman & Kruegler, 1994; Hastings, 2004; Helvey, 2004; Sharp, G., 1973). Doing liaison work—direct, official contact and formalized meetings or more personal back-channel meetings—will make this possible when done in tandem with excellent education and training of movement leaders and members. At the "line of scrimmage," that is, in the streets under duress, police or soldiers may well attack. It is the conduct of those in the movement at that point that is critical. It is the test of any movement's discipline and resiliency. A movement that remains assertive and neither afraid nor aggressive will not only likely reduce future violence against it by security forces but will also rapidly gain sympathy and eventually recruits from amongst the rest of civil society in that country and beyond. Understanding the implications of a commitment to assertive nonviolence is therefore crucial. Most movements get that test at some relatively early juncture. The manner of answer will give an advantage to one side or the other. In Burma, for example, a nonviolent general strike against the military dictatorship first occurred on 8 August 1988 (8 8 88—famous symbolic code in Burma), and the regime responded with live ammunition by day and targeted killings at night, totaling more than 1,000 dead (Palmer-Mehta, 2009). The response was mixed, and thus the state violence was "justified" to some.

Heavy-handed overt monitoring is a tactic used by authoritarian regimes or agencies. Indeed, in the United States, FBI memos have, at times, called for just such clumsy, visible "spying" on civilian organizations to produce the impression of a ubiquitous federal intelligence presence (Hershberger, 2004). In the old Soviet Union, dissidents under surveillance would joke that if they pulled up any window shade there would be a KGB agent looking in, and one such activist told this author that when he left his home the agent or agents would be literally fewer than five feet behind him at all times.[4] With highly disciplined nonviolence, activists can welcome such a presence and engage personally and persuasively with the agents. The transparency of nonviolent activism is disarming and liberating. It tends to diminish the adversarial nature of oppositional activism by inviting agents of the state to come into meetings, to learn more about the organization, to meet members, to hear cogent stories about the grievances driving the protests.

In the Philippines in 1986, in Serbia in 2000, and in Ukraine in 2004, fraudulent election results were met by massive nonviolent opposition, taking a different form in each of the three nations. In the Philippines the masses were summoned to the streets by Cardinal Sin on Radio Veritas and the hundreds of thousands interposed between two factions of the military, one loyal to Ferdinand Marcos and one supporting Corazon Aquino, the actual winner of the election. In Serbia, a general national strike culminated in a nonviolent takeover of the parliament building while the security forces stepped aside. In Ukraine a long winter encampment led eventually to a reassessment of the judicial ruling on the election and a declaration of the true results.

Each society and each campaign is unique, of course. In Iran in 2009, the Green Revolution did not succeed in overthrowing the Ahmadinejad government, partially because the vote was actually too close to be too obvious to the majority of Iranians. In Burma in 1990 the vote went overwhelmingly to the New League for Democracy, Aung San Suu Kyi's party, but the military regime apparently used the elections to identify all the leaders, who were then rounded up and charged, subjected to show trials, and imprisoned (Kyi & Clements, 1997). In Mexico in 2008, again, the election fraud claims were vociferous but not dispositively credible, and Manuel Lopez Obrador's backers did not maintain nonviolent discipline, giving the Calderon regime the excuse it needed to quash the protests violently. It is far more important to the success of a campaign that it focuses on the behavior of its own people than on anyone else, including police or counterdemonstrators. From Binnendijk & Marovic (p. 415):

> In Ukraine, avoiding provocation was particularly important during Orange Revolution's three-week mass standoff. In order to avoid altercations between protesters and police or between Yushchenko and Yanukovych supporters, *Pora* and Our Ukraine volunteers formed human "buffer zones" between police and the crowds, and between rival tent camps. Trained volunteers patrolled the tent camps and crowds, looking for and diffusing potential disturbances. Pamphlets were distributed, saying: "Remain unprovoked. We will win. We are strong because we are calm."

In addition, like South Africa, the Ukrainian church helped justify and even enforce that nonviolent stance (Filiatreau, 2009). In sum, there are four ways to keep a movement assertively nonviolent and thus strategically growing and on a track to victory. One, constant training, at least as rigorous as any armed forces.' Two, steady strategic iterative management, using frequent debriefs, anticipation, and adjustments. Three, robust liaison work to any and all security forces to reassure them repeatedly of the campaign's nonviolent intent and ability to deliver. Four, media work that is so vigorous in its nonviolent framing that civil society learns to expect to hear and see that the movement is invariably nonviolent under even the most challenging circumstances. When these factors have been combined well, civil wars have been averted but victory has been achieved.

Truth and Reconciliation Processes

The myth of peace is powerful. A moment of joy is the common assumption; we have signed an agreement to never fight again, as long as the grass shall remain green! Time to dance! Let's all sign and sing! "And the paper they were signing said, they'd never fight again."

Meanwhile, back on Planet War, someone blows up a bus full of children and the war is back on. Someone tries to disarm the irregulars, and instead a crime wave erupts in a frantic effort to feed families once supported by the war machine. Old grudges fester, and peace just makes it an individual thing, not so much an organized collective of killers under someone's command. Peace accords are sweet, but without some sort of truth and reconciliation process, they may become mere scraps of paper. Development is seen as a panacea, but it may be impossible under conditions of ancient hatreds and recent atrocities. War is traumatic for each society that suffers it on its soil, producing higher levels of overall mental illness related to that trauma and making the society thus more vulnerable to resumption of shooting wars. The background rate of serious depression in the United States, for example, is between 6 and 10 percent any given year, whereas in post-war Lebanon it has been about 40 percent (Abbyad, 2012; National Institute of Mental Health[5]).

It is widely accepted that "conflict environments give rise to 'otherizing' dynamics between competing groups" (Millar, 2012, p. 717). In the post-conflict environment—which is exactly when most conflicts break out afresh—measures that deconstruct and dismantle that objectification process are key to preventing more hot conflict. While TRC processes are associated with post-conflict, they are one of the tools available to try to blunt or transform the vestigial destructive conflict tendencies from war that has taken place, toward peace by positively manipulating the interlinking notions of identity, memory and political practice (Clouser, 2012). The most adaptive TRC path is one taken proactively, as Desmond Tutu demonstrated, before a war breaks out, as a preventive measure, to promise healing in order to make war avoidance more possible. Even the "reconciliation to forget" model may achieve a de-escalation of violence, while the "reconciliation to forgive" model might produce a more sustainable peace (Satha-Anand, 2002). We can take lessons on the transformative possibilities and limits of this constellation of approaches as attempted in a variety of locales under many different post-conflict conditions.

Sierra Leone

Following the 11-year civil war in this West African nation, one during which more than 50,000 lost their lives, more than half a million were displaced or became refugees, many child soldiers were in combat, many women and girls were raped, and many noncombatants lost limbs, the Sierra Leone Truth and Reconciliation Commission operated from 2002–2004.[6] The SLTRC was a condition of the Lomé Peace Accord reached in 1999.

South Africa

This pioneering effort at restorative justice was led by Anglican Archbishop Desmond Tutu and is widely regarded as making it possible for the transition to democracy from the minority white rule of apartheid South Africa. The healing aspects of the TRC were stressed by Tutu, but a primary purpose was simply to make it possible for white South Africans to envision a survival of transition from their position of political exclusivity and legal impunity into a society that recognized the civil and human rights of all. Any other path out of the brutality of apartheid may well have led to civil war of staggering destructiveness, making this TRC image a key heuristic toward the otherwise unimaginable nonviolent solution. There is no doubt that the interlocking aspects of nonviolent measures prevented the widely predicted "inevitable" bloody South African civil war—one augured by communal violence and other indices and then one which shockingly and wonderfully did not materialize.

The Balkans

In the former Yugoslavia there has been a sort of competing set of transitional justice models, coming from external players and powers like the UN and EU on the one hand, and from more national or even local origins on the other. It seems as if the more indigenous methods of transitional justice will likely result in more sustainable progress, although in the Balkans there are inherent issues with the borders of the new states carved out of the former Yugoslavia now separating many of the formerly somewhat homogenous populations (Jeffrey & Jakala, 2012). Certainly, however, uncorrupted transitional justice emerging locally will have more credibility and less pushback and rejection than imposed transitional justice, and the questions then revolve around how or whether to assist from the outside. There are red lines seeming to require external involvement and yet sovereignty is key; can there be an effective global civil society cultural movement that finally establishes long sought universal minimum standards by which we treat each other?

Transform Conflict Industry

In the Soviet Union, capitalism triumphed over communism. In this country, capitalism triumphed over democracy.
        —Fran Lebowitz, American commentator[7]

In her book *Shock Doctrine*, Naomi Klein describes a piece of the conflict industry and how it contaminates decisions and democracy. The war in Iraq, a product of a conflict industry prepared to harvest opportunities to make money on conflict, was waged as a short-term bonanza for war profiteers—a taking so cynical even the producers of bottled water overcharged the taxpayer. Competing narratives about the reasoning—it was an imperialist motive by the neocons, it was for cheap oil, it was to satisfy some revenge impulse of the prodigal son for Saddam Hussein plaguing Bush the Elder—may be true in part or temporarily, but the simple ability to shift the wealth from the taxpayer to the corporate profiteer is sometimes overlooked. At this writing in 2013, China is now actually gaining the most energy security from the new Iraq oil boom, something so perversely opposite of the Rumsfeldian/Wolfowitzian (Scheer, 5 June 2013) reassurances that the invasion wouldn't cost the U.S. taxpayer anything once Iraqi oil could be tapped to pay for the invasion, it amounts to a *surrealpolitik.*[8]

In some conflicts, one or more parties benefit in some fashion from the continuation of the conflict and thus may work to sabotage resolution, transformation, or transcendence. Perhaps one of the parties gains financially, or in status, or in power. That party will often fail to support the good faith efforts to reduce or eliminate a conflict that benefits them, or may even actively work against such efforts. Conflict practitioner-scholars Steven Daniels and Greg Walker (2001) called those parties members of the conflict industry.

In some arms-exporting nations, the conflict industry simply makes all the conflicts on Earth more likely to become or remain violent, since arms are a lucrative industry and exports are sought, not merely passively ordered. The United States represents the apotheosis of that conflict industry, exporting more arms than any other nation, and even the arms transfers that are gratis are a direct benefit to the elite conflict industry–weapons manufacturers. In that case the U.S. taxpayer wealth is shifted from workers to weapon-corporation owners. The politics at each level is affected by the conflict industry.

In the U.S. example, it is well understood that the relationship amongst Pentagon contractors and politicians pushes more money and more jobs toward states and congressional districts that in turn support the politicians who vote for more such funding. This sets up a dynamic that tends to disfavor honest voting and favor politicians who vote to spend more on projects that generate massive profits for the elite owners of corporate contractors. Reinforcing this dynamic, American Legislative Exchange Council, or ALEC, monitors federal and state legislation to push for more votes favorable to more corporations, usually to the disfavor of the taxpaying public. ALEC not only lobbies for or against certain pieces of legislation, it writes model legislation that is highly favorable to weapons manufacturers and unfavorable to labor unions. That legislation is then picked up by corporate-friendly legislators and introduced in the United States at the federal level or versions at the state level in one or more states (McIntire, 2012). While ALEC is focused more broadly at corporate welfare in general than war profiteering in particular, it is a powerful tool that institutionalizes the conflict industry at the expense of the average voter, the average taxpayer, the average worker, and at the expense of a peaceful and unprovocative U.S. foreign policy. ALEC is a nonprofit 501 (c) 3 organization, yet

Lisa Graves, the executive director of the Center for Media and Democracy, which teamed up with *The Nation* magazine to publicize a cache of 800 ALEC model bills last year, said that as of last August, all but one of 104 leadership positions within the organization were filled by Republicans and that the policies ALEC promoted were almost uniformly conservative [McIntire, 2012].

In some periphery countries, the conflict industry is quite simple; a client ruler accepts military hardware and training, and the center nation's corporations are guaranteed cheap human and natural resources. This tends to favor the elites who gain in power, status, and wealth on all sides, but it tends to produce more conflict, more bloodshed, and a theft of resource income from the average citizens of the periphery nations, thus feeding directly into the grievances of poverty and ruined environment. Confronting the conflict industry in each nation-state is key to slowing and stopping civil wars.

Examining intrastate conflict is certain to reveal such parties, either in obvious instances or more subtle forms. Often the most perduring, intractable conflicts feature those conflict-industry representatives in key roles, able to erode or even "blow up" the process toward resolution. The violent revolutionary may seem like a champion, but many cannot envision themselves actually running any sort of government, responsible for fixing potholes and making the sewage system operate properly. They get the status, power and funding from violence and from ongoing conflict, not from resolution and not from successful negotiations.

Colombia

Colombia, with a civil war of nearly half a century at this writing, is clearly an example. Every time peace talks are attempted they are subverted by those from the government side and the rebel side whose empires of power and wealth are threatened by peace. During the Cold War, the right-wing government fought communists and received a great deal of military aid from the United States to do that, while the left-wing rebels were supplied with arms and funds by the Soviets. Indeed, the left-wing insurgents—never powerful enough to actually overthrow the central government completely—controlled huge portions of the country.

During the post–Cold War readjustment, the Revolutionary Armed Forces of Colombia (FARC), the communist insurgency, switched their financing methods from external arms-and-ideology aid from superpower Soviets to kidnapping ransom and drugs. Colombia is a massive exporter of cocaine, bringing in commensurately massive profits to the kingpins of that trade, including the FARC, who can use the profits to buy the arms that the Soviets used to supply free. The Cold War was always hot in Colombia and simply switched over to the War on Drugs and, handily, the Global War on Terror. Some years the rulers of Colombia were given more military aid from the United States than any country except Israel, thus strengthening the influence of the military, another member of the conflict industry. Indeed, this is at the very crux of transforming hot conflict everywhere; militaries of governments and irregulars alike have a larger and larger mission if they are engaged in a shooting war. It's the Goldilocks Syndrome; the conflict industry prefers a certain level of destruction—not too cold, not too hot. For them, some death and loss is Just Right.

Peace talks failed three times in the 1980s as the Cold War raged. Now the FARC has finally agreed to talk, and it's obvious to all that their control of some areas and much wealth is threatened enough to come to the negotiating table, but the question is, will their leaders relinquish power and wealth for the peace that Colombians want and need? Doubt is strong[9] (Neuman, 2012).

Iraq

The analysis of the U.S. invasion and occupation of Iraq is commonly viewed as a big blunder based on bad intelligence, since no WMD were found. This is received wisdom in the U.S. public discourse, enabling policymakers to safely ask for more funds for intelligence services—thereby feeding that malfunctioning portion of the conflict industry and never interfering with the other portions.

A deeper analysis ascribes motivations such as neoconservative desire for global hegemony, an acquisition of U.S. military bases in Iraq, and the wish to transnationalize the Iraq economy (e.g., Stokes, 2009).

Certainly elements of this sort of "rational" goal-setting existed in the Bush administration, but the ultimate goals of the conflict industry are to gain in status, power, and money. If some policy that is making an attempt to gain in status or power or both also makes a great deal of money for the power players in the conflict industry, they cannot lose. It is the perverse, elite-benefitting version of a Gandhian dilemma; any move is a win for the conflict industry. So, to finally break through this dynamic, the first step is to reframe all these factors to expose the goal-setting and strategic planning of the conflict industry. In the case of Iraq, few were noting that. Most analysts assert that no one gained anything from the invasion and occupation of Iraq (see, for example, Fawcett, 2013), but that is not quite accurate.

For example, what of the "secret" goal of the elites to build new bases in Iraq and thus control that country? It would have indeed served the neocon dream to dominate the economy and political environment of one of the key oil-producing nations, one that had been so inconveniently recalcitrant under Saddam Hussein. But much more foundationally, the invasion was less concerned with building those bases in order to assure U.S. hegemony in Iraq than to simply increase spending to generate massive contracts for war profiteers. This was visible on a day-to-day basis in Department of Defense press releases of the contracts awarded on that day, always in the hundreds of millions of dollars. The bases would have worked out well to somehow extend U.S. rule, but the real guarantee was met—huge shifts from the working and middle-class income in the United States to the contracting corporations. The bases were always disposable—it might be understood as the Jay Leno "Doritos Paradigm": "Crunch all you want. We'll make more."[10] Viewing military expenditures more like snack food than a serious attempt to tyrannize the world reveals the most massively open secret since the construction of the pyramids. That is, yes, where these sorts of power and resource grabs work, that is best, but if they can be framed as legitimate long enough to generate record profits for the corporate elite who own the war profiteering companies—and this literally includes snack food, not just weapons and ammunition and the bally-hooed flak jackets—then the underlying interests of the conflict industry have been served again, to the detriment of everyone else. Those who bore the costs include the taxpaying moderate income Americans, the injured and killed soldiers on all sides, and civil society in Iraq, who lost so many lives and suffered through the rampages of Saddam, the United States and its allies, as well as the sectarian violent forces. Only—*only*—the corporate elite conflict industry benefitted, plus some higher-ranking U.S. military officers who gained during that fiasco.

Nuclear Nightmare Normal

One of the most insidious examples of the conflict industry gone mad is the nuclear threat to all of life on Earth. Nuclear weapons have been around, at this writing, for 67 years, not even an eyeblink of time in the history of humanity, let alone the entire Cambrian Period to now, of life on Earth. That anyone should think nuclear deterrence is sustainable or in any sense wise is astonishing. And yet, year after year, the United States continues to pour $billions into upgrading and modernizing the most unusable arsenal ever constructed. This conflict industry consists of the classic military-industrial-congressional complex, with the capital-intensive, often no-bid and/or cost-plus contracts flowing to the industries who best support the members of Congress who best support those industries, and the Pentagon/DoE/NASA complex simply absorbing all the U.S. taxpayer dollars redirected to them by Congress, and in turn redistributing it to the elites who own and operate the contractors. Part of this is examined routinely by the Center for International Policy in reports[11] (Hartung and Anderson, 2012). Preventing nuclear war is perhaps the most important task peace and antiwar civil society can accomplish. Allowing this conflict industry to continue indefinitely is unconscionable—indeed, the likelihood of a failure and nuclear-weapons launch and attack is more likely every year, not less, since the complexity of systemic problems is overwhelming. We have seen a tiny foreshadowing with Chernobyl and Fukushima. What will it take for humankind to rise up and finish off this threat before it finishes off humankind?

Sanctions

The general view amongst activists who think about sanctions as an instrument of change is path dependent, trending toward acceptance and advertising of sanctions when one form of them is used to help liberate people—e.g., the economic sanctions on the apartheid government of South Africa in the 1980s—and then moving toward dismissing sanctions as merely a tool for oppression when another form of them hurts people—e.g., the sanctions on Iraq in the 1990s. In fact, peace researchers have developed much more nuanced understandings of the relative merits of sanctions.

George Lopez and David Cortright (2000, 2002) looked at sanctions in the aftermath of the U.S.-led UN sanctions on Iraq, sanctions that Arnove (2000) and many activists condemned both specifically and increasingly generically. The typology of sanctions, however, is complex, as are the questions. Who is harmed by sanctions, the elites or the peripheries? Whose behavior is targeted, elites or peripheries? Are sanctions that are conducted by civil society more legitimate than those conducted by nation-states? Are supranational organizations (e.g., UN, OAS, EU, ASEAN) or regional power blocs more or less justified in designing and implementing sanctions than are nation-states?

Each case is unique, yet, in the interest of stopping civil wars, sanctions can assist, if designed and implemented well toward that end. Further, sanctions can push rogue nation-states toward negotiations that mitigate poor behavior, as is evident in the case of Iran, a target of U.S.-led sanctions with the express purpose of keeping it from developing a nuclear arsenal. While the government of Iran will likely not announce that the sanctions worked and it will now capitulate and end its program of nuclear weapons development, in fact that is likely to be the understood outcome eventually. Certainly the relationship of the sanctions to Iran's willingness to begin negotiations is more than circumstantial, complicated further by Israeli and U.S. threats to bomb Iran.[12]

Sanctions in a multi-nodal world are becoming less likely to emerge from a UN Security Council that has transitioned from its World War II victor/Cold War/U.S. unipolar path (Vines, 2012). While the UN can still use sanctions to attenuate the factors that might contribute to the outbreak or continuation of civil war, sanctions are not the sole province of political institutions. Certainly individuals can conduct small sanctions and, if done in mass numbers, can affect the likelihood of civil war via civil society initiative.

Peace and Conflict Education

[Conflict resolution education] *CRE has usually been introduced into schools through external channels and treated as add-on programs rather than integrated into ongoing curricula, classroom activity, and everyday operation of the school.*
—Jennifer Batton (2004, p. 271)

We should be examining the penchant for studying war to the exclusion of peace. This is a serious problem. It is as though medical school studies disease and not the cure. Instead, I believe, we should study conflict management. War should be seen as the failure it is, and the methods of attaining and maintaining peace should be what our children, our teens, and our adults learn. Instead, we are only taught that conflict is synonymous with violent force, and we are supposed to leave that to the experts and to the military. It is learned helplessness. And then, of course, anyone who doesn't want war is "girlie" and "doesn't have the stomach" for what needs to be done, and therefore should be quiet and let the real men handle it. Our Second Amendment is virtually conflated with the Word of God. And we wonder why our men are mentally ill and prone to entering grade schools, houses of worship, or movie theaters and opening fire on innocents. I guess they "had the stomach" for it. Any challenge in the United States to the Second Amendment is met with rage and dismissed out of hand; apparently the school children who die in a hail of bullets are simply acceptable losses to these people.

On the other hand, if we can manage to educate our children that humans don't do that either as individuals or as groups, and then teach them the methods of conflict management that involve both carrots (e.g., friendliness, generosity, inclusivity, love) and sticks (assertive opposition, earnest confrontation, steady insistence, withholding of labor, escalating refusal to cooperate, peaceful disruption of business as usual) and also teach our children to support each other in these struggles, we would build a culture of peace that would get along in the world. We would change the world.

Since the 1980s select schools in the United States and elsewhere have been teaching children some of the methods of constructive conflict management. CRE programs are part of the curriculum in some 15,000 or more of the 85,000 public schools in the United States. The U.S. Department of Education recognizes CRE as a component of the 1994 Safe and Drug-Free Schools and Communities Act. While there may be few correlates between CRE at the level of peer mediation and the most egregious violence—e.g., rape and murder—studies and meta-studies of the many CRE programs in thousands of United States schools do show measurable improvement in many categories of social and emotional well-being in students exposed to CRE (Jones, 2004). Teaching CRE in any culture is going to push that culture now and in the future toward peace and away from the cognitive dissonance that arises when children are taught peace and shown war.

At the very least, we have quite a long way to go worldwide and in most countries in basic K-12 conflict resolution education (CRE) (Batton, 2004). Infusing CRE into basic competency education throughout the K-12 system in more regions of more countries is one of the most certain components of humankind's transition from violence to nonviolence. The norm is often to only offer CRE as a special one-off during occasional in-service days to skill up teachers who might be interested, or to offer specific activities to select students, such as peer mediation. This usually keeps CRE marginalized and too often only available to more well-funded schools. Nonviolence is often a once per year mention around the birthday of Martin Luther King, Jr., in the United States—or Mohandas Gandhi's birthday in India—if that. This maintains the notion that peace education is a special exploration of a historically anomalous phenomenon rather than preparation for the wave of the future.

Law

Written laws are like spiders' webs; they will catch, it is true, the weak and poor, but would be torn in pieces by the rich and powerful.
—Anarchis, sixth century B.C.E.

When the President does it, that means that it is not illegal.
—President Richard Milhous Nixon[13]

Is the law nonviolent? Arguably, no. If I am arrested in the U.S. town where I live, the police officer is wearing a gun. This implies a threat of violence and that threat is executed frequently. On the other hand, except for Northern Ireland, I would generally not face an armed police officer in the UK.[14] In a sense, the law itself is not violent, but enforcement of it can be. It is entirely conceivable—and indeed accurate in some societies now and historically—

that enforcement of the law could be entirely nonviolent, involving many other elements, such as restorative justice, shunning, economic sanctions, interposition, mediation, truth and reconciliation, removal of privileges, opprobrium and other NCI measures.

The effectiveness of both violent and nonviolent law enforcement is limited. While violent and often retributive law enforcement in some instances correlates to higher rates of certain criminal activity, it also has the reverse result in others, acting as a deterrent to some crimes and a preventive to some crimes in other situations. Nonviolent enforcement has its strengths and limitations as well, tending to enhance chances for reconciliation, restitution, and restoration, but also failing in some cases to satisfy those who want criminals punished and held accountable.

The law itself is promising when those who suffer in wars feel as though they can hold elites accountable—those who profit financially, in status, or in political power from war—though there are some who argue that this approach is "hard human rights law" and somehow takes the focus off the victims and onto the power elite who have ordered the brutality (Riga & Kennedy, 2012). While the perpetrator focus may not be restorative justice, it does serve as a minor deterrent to some dictators and as a beacon of light and hope to some of those who have been hurt or who are under threat. So the deterrent value of the combination of the International Court of Justice (nation-to-nation case law) and the much newer International Criminal Court (victims of any status and individual defendants, often high-ranking politicians or military officers) is one factor, as is the sense that the law is evolving to redress grievances in cases of violations of human rights laws and rules of war no matter how powerful the defendant. Still, in the application from case to case, victims are often less satisfied with the outcomes than they were with the idea of bringing the alleged perpetrators to the bar (Kent, 2012). Further, the laws that have really barely begun to protect human rights—the very laws cited by invading countries often to justify their invasions and occupations—including the Universal Declaration of Human Rights, are now being clouded by the interstices of failed and failing states, asymmetric warfare, terrorism, insurgency and counterinsurgency (Bhatt, 2012). Once again, the struggle from the nonviolent side is to hold the violent parties accountable, starting with the top commanders on the powerful side. This is a battle in the legal arena, the political sphere, and for the hearts and minds of various publics. Requiring this is insisting on the fair standards that are precursors to mediated agreements in all these mapped regions.

So the evolution of the law that protects those on the far side of the shield of sovereignty proceeds on a woven path involving the creation of new and better laws on the one hand, but more importantly, new and better nonviolent enforcement mechanisms. Unfortunately, the world's most powerful nations continue to claim sovereignty above the laws of human rights and conflict conduct (rules of war). Crimes against peace and crimes against humanity continue to be essentially victors' justice. It is true that the corpus of international law protecting human rights and peace has grown enormously in the past 150 years, and that erstwhile powerful figures have been held to account, but the powerful nation-states ignore or dismiss charges against them still (Ackerman and Glennon, 2007). While it is natural to view the birth of an international law and the development of its enforcement much like the birth of a human baby—that is, toothless and helpless for a time—it is also demonstrably possible to design some laws with serious enforcement mechanisms, once the global political will to do so emerges.

Civil society can have an impact, both within its own state borders and transnationally. In 1967, philosopher Bertrand Russell convened the International War Crimes Tribunal in Stockholm (Hershberger, 2004). A great deal of testimony from Vietnam War victims—civilian and military—as well as witnesses, moral leadership, and experts in international law produced enough international political pressure to change some practices and certainly to give pause to both military and political war planners in future conflicts.

More quotidian are the transnational civil-society organizations who offer educational workshops and trainings in nonviolent social change methods (Ackerman and Glennon, 2007). These capacity-building efforts can spread knowledge and experientially based theory from grassroots to grassroots. Conferences in neutral nations can bring together those who are resisting both autocrats and democratic but militaristic practices in nations both weak and powerful. Activists from weak Zimbabwe facing dictator Robert Mugabe and activists from powerful America facing a scofflaw government that invades, occupies, and assassinates anywhere it chooses, can cross-pollinate, learn from each other's successes and failures, and seek stronger and stronger civil-society transnational coalitions with a growing grassroots capacity to enforce the laws of war and the human rights law.

Suspicions that nonviolent training and education is secretly funded by those foreign powers seeking geopolitical hegemony are nearly risible; such trainings have been provided by most such nongovernmental organizations (NGOs) to activists from almost everywhere on the political arc—to those seeking to nonviolently overthrow both friends and enemies of the United States, for instance, and even to activists inside the United States working to undermine U.S. foreign policy that inflicts violence or violates international human rights law or rules of war. Indeed, this author has sought and received such trainings inside the United States, and the activists who received the workshops were mostly U.S. citizens challenging U.S. policy, though we were happily joined by three Vietnamese activists who were generally working to undermine tyrannical communist rule in their homeland. Skilling up nonviolent activists from everywhere is how we help power slowly precipitate downward from elites to the streets, from the upper branches of government and corporations to the tangled mass of grassroots.

When Strategy Meets Principle

> *Nonviolence includes not only the refusal to engage in lethal activities but it also presumes a commitment to strive for conditions of fairness, justice, and respect in human relations. Nonviolence presumes a commitment to speak to the conditions that often give rise to warfare. Therefore, nonviolence is not centrally about the things one is opposed to, nor even about the actions one refuses to participate in. Nonviolence implies an active commitment to social changes that would ultimately result in a fair distribution of world resources, a more creative and democratic cooperation between peoples, and a common pursuit of those social, scientific, medical, and political achievements that serve to enhance the human enterprise and prevent warfare.*
> —Daniel L. Smith-Christopher (2007, p.10)

Each element of this religiously inspired and morally based assertion about nonviolence has strategic implications, revealing the potential for the integration of strategic and principled or philosophical or religiously mandated nonviolence. Smith-Christopher approaches nonviolence from an interfaith perspective yet addresses many of the drivers to war in his claims about the values and utilitarian worth of nonviolence. Understanding this synthesis and utilizing it with equal focus on each perspective provides a strong base for any movement or campaign able to operate from that ground.

When a movement is intentionally nonviolent it is often the case that the leadership in general has no particular affinity for pacifism beyond its practical superiority, but there are often one or more central leaders who are, in fact, philosophical or religiously motivated pacifists who tend to give the movement leadership a tilt toward a more robust, committed, and therefore trustable code of behavior. At times an initial commitment to strategic nonviolence can eventually convince a leader to adopt a principled philosophy of nonviolence— this is the case for this author, and I have observed this in others. The reverse is true as well; pacifists who study and engage in movements will at times become convinced and committed to nonviolence as the most effective strategy. When these conversions happen, that norm can spread via those players in both directions and indeed, at times, has, in my direct observation and experience.

Section II: Ending Invasions and Occupations

Young people who had not yet had a chance to enjoy and experience life were sent off to die—by old people who decide that there will be a war.
　　　　　—Linus Pauling, at age 90 in 1991, about the poor process leading to Gulf War I (1998, p. 249)

The questioning of God regarding the suffering of the innocent lies at the heart of faith.
　　　　　—Daniel Berrigan (1998, p. 203)

While most wars of the new millennium are civil wars, the invasions and occupations are significant and require transformation from destructive conflict to constructive conflict also. Traditionally, the means and methods of resisting occupations are "theoretically problematic" (Carrington, 2013, p. 4) and not much researched. The nonviolent methods by which this can happen are a complementary collection of internal opposition from within the invading nation and opposition from external parties, including the opposition from civil society of the nation that is invaded. The connections and cross-fertilization points of these nonviolent challengers are complex and will be noted, but organizationally this section will primarily address them in separate sections while noting the various strategic approaches to connecting these oppositional forces.

Strength is crucial; nonviolent efforts based upon moral witness or ethical superiority have a relatively poor win-loss record, but strength that results in stronger resolve to resist is merely a different form of weakness. Thus, while the kinetic capacity of U.S. Marines to sweep into an area, conquer it physically, and hold it with armed troops is quite high, that sort of short-term victory almost invariably leads to several consequences, all related and all tending to unwind any victories. One, resentment at invasion and occupation will produce resistance, even if quite asymmetrical. Two, whether in urban warrens or thick jungles full of caves, insurgent fighters can last essentially forever and only await moments of weakness or an exit due to new policy from the invading country. Three, loyalty of civil society to insurgents (sometimes damaged by the practices of insurgents, but strong at certain points). This is not to discount the effectiveness of invasion and interposition by military forces with no agenda, including UN peacekeepers, who do have a variable record of actually helping belligerents begin to negotiate (Ruggeri, Gizelis, & Dorussen, 2013). This is to offer nonviolent alternatives to even such neutral armed forces, which still frighten some people and still fail in some cases (e.g., Rwanda, Somalia).

Is human nature violent? Of course; we see the evidence. We also see the evidence that human nature is nonviolent, and we can choose to access that creative repertoire of nonviolent paths. Gene Sharp (2005) points out that human babies will resist—they first cry and are then fed. And we see political theorists acknowledge that humans seek both consensus and the times to say no (Thomassen, 2013). Our imaginations—fed by the realities of past nonviolent victories—can be our incubation vessels for our ultimate strategic use of mass nonviolent resistance to invasion and occupation.

Ending wars that have already begun is much harder than preventing them, of course. Standard bargaining theory suggests that leadership changes its mind about continuing a war, while Stanley and Sawyer (2009) found in their research that actually changing the composition of the elite coalition is a path to peace in many cases. This is much more in line with strategic nonviolence, which holds two things central in this regard: one, that changing a belligerent ruler's mind is much harder than replacing him (this may be very different for philosophically or religiously based practitioners who, like Phil Berrigan (1996, p. 211), may believe in a vision or prophesy that includes such individual and societal peace conversions due to divine intervention); two, that replacing him is possible. Principled nonviolence posits that a ruler can be transformed, but the real transformation in the ideas of strategic nonviolence is the empowerment of civil society, which transforms from acceptance of an autocratic ruler to the realization that it has the latent and actionable power to replace that ruler—that civil society may choose to replace a noncompliant ruler rather than allowing a ruler to continue to forbid a noncompliant civil society. Replacement of the autocrat by violence—whether it is from an armed uprising or foreign armed invasion—virtually guarantees more of the same. Saddam Hussein was knocked out of power at a cost of hundreds of thousands of Iraq lives, thousands of U.S. and other nations' armed troops' lives, at least $1.5 trillion USD—and the "democratic" result is another autocrat, Nouri al-Malaki, who, like Saddam Hussein before him, has been "arresting and torturing political enemies and turning a blind eye to his allies' corruption and criminal acts" (Parker & Salman, 2013).

The beauty of nonviolent resistance is that it not only prevents violent conflict in many ways, but it is employed in order to address the structural violence. Nonviolence is therefore peace and justice. Per Christie (2011), using nonviolence to seek justice is also a violence prevention method. This is the game changer for which humankind has been waiting. Working to reduce grievances is done better and faster using nonviolence, as counterintuitive as that is to some people or some cultures. Overcoming the counterintuitive problem of nonviolence is a matter of education, thus making education a strategic concern for nonviolent strategists (Beyerle, 2008).

This method, civil society nonviolent power, holds hope in situations not often contemplated as hopeful and certainly not prepared for by those purporting to promote democracy by any means necessary. For example, the notion that capitalism won the Cold War, that capitalism and democracy are synonymous, and that of course democracy is the victor of the Cold War is greatly belied by the rise of new autocracies from the ashes of the Second World back when they were self-identified as communist and other-identified, therefore, presumably, as anti-democratic. Now capitalism, and its natural spread to globalization, is frequently overtly anti-democratic, as we see with the rise of China. The alternative is people power, nonviolent civil society force (Thornton & Thornton, 2012). True democracy, in which rights are equal and respected, is the essence of nonviolence, or at least makes war almost impossible (Stout, 2010).

Applying the counterfactual can help us think about the possibilities for war prevention. An example was the 1973 Yom Kippur War, driven into bloody practice by a terrible collusion of the Egyptian government under Anwar Sadat, the Syrian government under Hafiz al-Assad, the Israeli government led by Golda Meir, and the external meddling by the United States and the National Security Advisor (NSA), Henry Kissinger, in particular (Vanetik & Shalom, 2011). What if Sadat or al-Assad had refused to take it as far as war? What if Meir had determinedly pursued a land-for-peace agreement? What if Kissinger had not undermined every initiative toward peace? What if the U.S. citizenry had been informed of the U.S. government's role and had insisted it be an honest broker of peace instead of the weapons supplier to the devotees of a "Greater Israel" policy of land acquisition? The key on the nonviolence side is the role of civil society in each instance, the use of or—more often—the failure to use civil society power beginning with expressing opinions, moving to threats to remove officials from power, and, if necessary, noncooperation with a government working for war. This is the most important counterfactual to consider; and the most important one to learn to effect.

PART 3

Nonviolent Resistance: Invaded and Invading Nations

Saddam Hussein has brutalized and repressed the Iraqi people for more than 20 years and more recently has sought to acquire weapons of mass destruction that would never be useful to him inside Iraq. So President Bush is right to call him an international threat. Given these realities, anyone who opposes U.S. military action to dethrone him has a responsibility to suggest how he might otherwise be ushered out the backdoor of Baghdad. Fortunately there is an answer: Civilian-based, nonviolent resistance by the Iraqi people, developed and applied in accordance with a strategy to undermine Saddam's basis of power.
—Peter Ackerman and Jack DuVall, September 2002[1]

Nonviolent resistance from within the invading or potentially invading nation is important to the possibility of preventing such an act. Once there has been an invasion, nonviolent resistance from within the occupied nation is just as important as that from within the invading nation. Collaboration between the two is more powerful than either and can produce synergistic force to end an invasion and occupation (Alexander, 1984). The first hope is preventive and requires nonviolent resistance from within the potentially invading nation, something with the capacity to help transform destructive conflict into a creative nonviolent alternative (Dawoody, 2006).

Confounding factors that fall outside the simple classifications are more usual than not. For instance, though Pakistan has not been invaded by the United States or U.S.–led NATO alliance forces, and though they are an ally, officially, in the war on terror, their civil society holds a very different view, one that is strongly majority hostile to the United States, one that sees the United States as invading Pakistan, and one that regards U.S. aid to the Pakistan government as inimical to the Pakistani people. As the 92,000 documents of WikiLeaks revelations about the war on Afghanistan became known in the summer of 2010, and as Pakistanis learned more about the U.S.–backed Pakistan Inter-Service Intelligence (ISI) activities, a Pew poll showed the Obama administration remained as unpopular as that of Bush before him—some 60 percent of Pakistanis regarded the United States as the enemy (Ajami, 2011). Pakistanis know that the United States conducts assassinations on its soil, that armed drone aircraft are killing many more civilians than "militants," and that their own government is allowing this. With allies like the United States, Pakistanis feel, who needs enemies? What the American public learns is that Pakistanis are religious fundamentalists who support terrorism. This impasse is insoluble without nonviolence, and the nonviolence required will be far more complex than resistance, but will include a great deal of resistance in order to be effective. With a tiny fraction of the resources devoted to the ISI, Americans could actually transform the relationship, but will be unable to do so as long as the ISI is a U.S. partner. U.S. citizens are in a unique position to change that. Barack Obama received his Nobel Peace Prize in 2009, and perhaps he will earn it finally (Ben-Meir, 2013). The party that can guide him to do so is the American populace.

The objections to violent invasion are as many as there are people. No one likes another nation's armed forces on their sovereign soil. No one likes to feel a part of a collective imposing injustice or committing brutal suppression on others. The question is not whether to oppose an invasion, but rather how. The very first order of business is to convince the leadership of the coalition that nonviolence is key, and the more purely nonviolence can be practiced the more likely it is to succeed. This is quite counterintuitive to many, but students of how civil society exercises power point to that repeatedly, using terms for violent elements of resistance such as "contaminant" that justify a state crackdown and disincentivize recruitment (Helvey, 2004, p. 117).

Nonviolent Resistance from within the Invading Nation

I am ill. The name of my sickness is history.
—Daniel Berrigan (1968, p. 108)

When civil society stops a war there is never a smoking memo from the would-be invaders stating that, "Curses. Our plans to invade have been foiled by an aroused and committed civil society prepared to exact prohibitive costs in response to our invasion. We cannot proceed with our nefarious plans." It is impossible to prove a negative. If an invasion that seemed likely did not happen, it will be rationalized in other ways. "The timing isn't optimal." "They are now negotiating in good faith." "Other concerns are more pressing."

Nevertheless, strong evidence, including correlatives and previous outcomes in similar situations, can also instruct, if not produce dispositive mandates or replicable templates for civil society action. The Reagan administration threat to invade Nicaragua under the Sandinistas is a case in point. Civil society in the United States was significantly active, and the Reagan response to Nicaragua threatened invasion repeatedly yet never precipitated into U.S. "boots on the ground." The Vets Fast for Life started on September 1, 1986, on the Capitol steps in Washington, D.C., vowing to remain in situ and fast until they saw significant signs that the American people would not tolerate such an invasion. The veterans were George Mizo, U.S. Army, 1963–1970, Vietnam; S. Brian Willson, U.S. Air Force, 1966–1970, Vietnam; Duncan Murphy, U.S. Army, 1942–1945, ambulance driver, World War II; Charles Litekey, U.S. Army, 1966–1971, Vietnam, two tours.[2] Each of these veterans of war has his own story of peace conversion, something as important to examine as any other transformational story. Daniel Berrigan, brother to another peace conversion veteran, Phil, waxed poetic about the power of conversion, likening the effects to a commitment to suffer and sacrifice (1991, p. 254).

The signs that the Vets Fast for Life were seeking did emerge, and the veterans finally stopped their fast. Like Gandhi commenting on the damage to the soul of America after the atomic bombing of Hiroshima and Nagasaki (Berrigan, 1997, p. 75), the veterans knew they carried and could expose the damage to the national soul from Vietnam in particular and warn a traumatized nation that we were again flirting with the same tragic, criminal deadly error.

The Vets Fast for Life is an example of the synthesis of purely moral acts and strategy, a dialectical relationship either practiced by or noted by Gandhi, King, Havel and others. It is the sort of action that makes many claim that nonviolence takes longer than violence, since the moral action actually usually does take time to make a strategic impression, as noted by Vaclav Havel (Steger, 1999). If an inspirational witness act of great drama can ultimately inspire many more to act in accord with the basic goals of the higher risk action, that drama can lead to strategic advance. This can dissolve the debate between the realists and the moralists; actually, moral actions that may involve suffering by actors with moral credentials can be highly strategic, conceived as such or not. When a nun is arrested or beaten, that will arouse civil society to act more boldly itself. There is a reason the British did not want Gandhi fasting to death in their prisons and a reason the military dictatorship in Myanmar/Burma decided to keep Aung San Suu Kyi on house arrest instead of killing her for her dissidence. Of course, if there is a violent insurgency, killing moral leadership is not as harmful to the regime, as we saw with the assassination of Archbishop Oscar Romero in El Salvador. Violence is indeed a contaminant. Would Romero have been spared if he had beseeched rebel troops to lay down their arms in addition to his impassioned call to the El Salvadorian soldiers to lay down theirs? We cannot know, but his authentic, ringing denunciation of government violence was what set his assassination plot into motion. His sacrifice was more innocent blood shed and even with that, the military government was empowered by the violence it faced.

A Pledge of Resistance campaign emerged that promised high costs from individuals, both in civil resistance and legal protests. Specifically, this pledge promised nonviolent action from those who signed "If the United States invades, bombs, sends combat troops, or otherwise significantly escalates its intervention in Nicaragua ..."; the signers would either commit nonviolent civil disobedience or engage in support actions for that civil disobedience (Emergency Response Network, n.d.). Can it be said that the totality of these efforts prevented the invasion of Nicaragua? No. But it is noteworthy that high ranking U.S. officials with access to Reagan and his cabinet were speculating that invading Nicaragua was almost inevitable—and that it never occurred. The streets of U.S. towns were alive with demonstrations against the likely invasion. This author witnessed one in Minneapolis, Minnesota, in 1987 that began small, in response to a public comment from President Reagan that seemed to threaten invasion, and within 30 minutes had filled a major intersection in Minneapolis (Lake Street and Hennepin Avenue) during rush hour. This demonstration shut it down for the evening. I was leaning on the front of a stopped city bus, just talking with peace activists, and eventually the traffic backed up, including the buses, and a four-block area full of people was converted to a peace demonstration for the night. These sorts of nonviolent actions sent a strong signal to an administration still under the lingering political effects of the Vietnam War era; indeed, three of the four vets who fasted on the Capitol steps for nearly two months were combat veterans of that war.

Questions of moving from protest—that is, legal actions challenging a policy or presence—to resistance—that is, actions that might be deemed illegal and precipitate arrest or other violent sanctions—require understanding and framing by oppositional organizations. Most civil disobedience—that is, resistance—is framed as breaking a good law for a good reason, not breaking a bad law and attempting to overturn it (Goodin, 1987). Struggling for the high-value goals like sovereignty assumes mass (if latent) agreement that someone's sovereignty is being violated and that the risks of protest and resistance are not higher than the potential benefits and likely benefits of such actions.

In late 2002 and early 2003 the peace movement in the United States mobilized to stop the Bush regime plan to invade Iraq. We mounted many demonstrations, locally, regionally, and nationally. We talked to each other and to our surrounding communities. We vigiled, we held signs, we rallied, we walked, we talked, we sang, we wrote, and, in the end, we failed.

Why did we succeed in stopping the invasion of Nicaragua and fail to stop the invasion of Iraq? In both cases, after all, the citizens of those targeted countries had not attacked the United States or U.S. personnel. The Sandinistas in Nicaragua had even been servicing the debt to the United States that had been largely siphoned off to aggrandize the personal wealth of U.S.–backed dictator Somoza and his elite circle. In the case of Iraq, there were no Iraqis involved in the September 11 attacks,[3] nor in the previous attacks on U.S. personnel in New York city,[4] Somalia,[5] Yemen,[6] Saudi Arabia,[7] Kenya, or Tanzania.[8] There were no weapons of mass destruction and certainly no remotely legitimate claim of any likelihood of nuclear weapons in any foreseeable future.

If we are citizens of the United States, how could we have succeeded in stopping an aggressive neocon campaign based on lies and ignorant xenophobia? In the aftermath of the terror attacks of 11 September 2001, could we have succeeded or was there never any such chance? And how can we stop Russia, China, Israel and any other potential invader from aggressing across borders? What are our special advantages and challenges as citizens of these über nation-states? Why is stopping an invasion by our own nation-state the same or very different from stopping a civil war in, say, Nigeria? Is there an available template for success or will we need to experiment based on successes in different sorts of struggles? It is not enough to shrug off our loss and wait to help affix blame when the aggressive war fails, as the antiwar movement did finally in the 2004–2006 period of deterioration of the U.S. position in Iraq and the sadly ineffectual rallying around Cindy Sheehan, for example, as a symbol of unacceptable loss, as if all the peace movement cared about was the loss of American aggressor lives (Managhan, 2011). The only "success" that came of any of that entire process is the dubious ability to cite the Bush regime as criminal and similar lies as just that, lies. The efforts from within potentially invading countries need to become much more effective. Yes, there were powerful peace coalitions formed before the invasion and during the occupation, such as the Catholic peace movement—with its many affiliates such as Pax Christi, Catholic Workers, Atlantic Life Community, Pacific Life Community, Lakes and Prairies Life Community, Voices for Creative Nonviolence—and United for Peace and Justice, but those coalitions never attained enough timely influence to stop the invasion, halt the flow of tax dollars to support the invasion and occupation, nor even stop the surge.

Ironically, members of that coalition were even arrested at then–Senator

Barack Obama's office as they demanded that he agree to stop voting for supplemental funding for the occupation of Iraq (Huet-Vaughn, 2007). That national push certainly had some effect three long years into the occupation—in Oregon, for example, all the arrests at the various offices of Senator Gordon Smith and the negative publicity achieved by that media-savvy nonviolent campaign helped unseat Smith and affected many other races to some extent in both the 2006 and 2008 elections, including Obama's election on the promise that he would conclude U.S. military involvement with Iraq (though he did not tip off the public that he would almost immediately order a surge and far more warmaking in Afghanistan, to be supplemented by a radical increase in weaponized drone attacks). Observers might logically conclude that, indeed, to the extent the public did get involved, it affected the political will and the funding for the ongoing occupation of Iraq—but to the extent the U.S. public felt defeated and did not self-mobilize, it ceded the power of occupation to the various administrations.

Saul Alinsky, the famous community organizer from Chicago, taught that the fastest recruitment principle is "organize the organized." This might apply to forming a strong coalition quite rapidly to cut off and defeat proposals to go to war in the United States or any other nation contemplating the invasion of another nation. Religious organizations, professional associations, trade unions, and other large groups of citizens are potential partners in a unified strategic coalition that can stop war before it starts or end it after it has begun.

An example is the potential to muster the actions of the strand of social workers who are ideologically committed to working to protect and gain civil and human rights for all (Atkinson & Mattaini, 2013), which would certainly include a natural human right to live free of war and destruction. Sometimes these professionals are organized in sections of more massive associations and sometimes they have their own stand-alone organization. An example might be from the most logical peace affinity organization in the academy, the Peace and Justice Studies Association, a stand-alone association in the United States and Canada with several hundred members. The additional components of this sort of association would include the peace sections of much larger associations of sociologists or political scientists. No one attempted to organize these bodies of peace professionals to act in concert during that late 2002-early 2003 period, when organized opposition to invasion was so crucial. I suspect that we were not thinking strategically very well at all in that period, and that indeed, too many theorists failed to act on what they knew. That potential exists, however, in virtually every society, even unfree nation-states where people must organize using much more circumspection than in the free press democracies.

One almost invisible and small but hopeful component of the peace conversion process in the hegemonic nations is the increase in women conscientious objectors (Elster & Sørensen, 2010). Whether those female members of the military are Israeli women refusing to serve in Palestine or U.S. female soldiers deciding to nonviolently resist the invasion and occupation of Iraq, the trend is positive toward peace and, if publicized more, could begin a new strand of peace challenging from within the bellicose nations. Conscientious objectors are a moral force, even if there are relatively few of them, and when you have 20,000—as did the British in World War I (Hochschild, 2011), they can help shape post-war determination to avoid future wars.

One of the ongoing tasks in the United States in particular is to address the ongoing financial and global power projection nexus that keeps the U.S. Congress so intent on huge military budgets no matter the condition of war or peace for U.S. troops. The first mainstream mention of this concern came from President Eisenhower in his Farewell Address, 17 January 1961, when he coined the term *Military Industrial Complex*[9] to describe the unwarranted "total influence" of these various players in the very fabric of our democracy. While this speech stands as one of the most cogent and prescient warnings of our era, Eisenhower did not mention the other reasons for this "vast military establishment." U.S. corporations benefit from it in many ways, including but not limited to war profiteering, influence over foreign dictators who receive U.S. military aid to allow U.S. corporations to extract human and natural resources cheaply, long-term military contracts at the highest rates of profit, cost-plus and no-bid contracts that guarantee massive profits even for inefficiency and fraud, and high profits even in times of austerity for the rest of society (e.g., Ronald Reagan's comment to his OMB chief, David Stockman, "Defense is not a budget issue.") (Stockman, 1986). This "conflict industry" (Daniels & Walker, 2001) will fight with any means to retain its position of power and wealth. Understanding this is crucial in understanding the depth and breadth of the struggle necessary to prepare U.S. democracy for peace instead of permanent preparation for war. It is likely to remain a crippling problem to all peace efforts until it's addressed vigorously by civil society directly.

The times in between crises are fully as important as the times when the war drum beats. Every year there is another budget battle, and since it's a twice-annual process at a minimum in the United States (appropriations and authorizations), plus special budget wars such as the sequestration (fiscal cliff) struggle, it is always time for citizens to point out the deep problems generated by what the Global Peace Index terms "Violence Containment Spending."[10] The report determines that a 15 percent reduction in VCS in the United States could generate some 1.7 million new jobs, reprioritizing away from high-profit, capital-intensive sectors to labor-intensive, low-profit sectors that serve the daily needs of citizens rather than power projection, global hegemony, and violent intervention in other sovereign nations.

Coalition

Arguably, the strongest need for any movement within an invader nation to prevent an invasion or end any occupation is the size and robustness of its nonviolent coalition, that is, a coalition committed to nonviolence for the purposes and duration of the campaign in question (thus avoiding paralyzing and irrelevant philosophical debates). Even those (or especially those) groups who have a philosophical or religious commitment to nonviolence—or who prefer to portray themselves that way—are better served by being open to coalition partnering with groups not linked otherwise to pacifism. Potential coalition partners in the United States have been overlooked, often, by some admixture of white liberal guilt and easy accommodation to the war system. This is certainly the case for African Americans, who have used pacifism and who have on occasion claimed it as core to their beliefs—e.g., from 1955–65 when the U.S. Civil Rights movement was almost uniformly nonviolent and asserted that largely from a Christian standpoint. At this time in history, by contrast, says Juan Floyd-Thomas (2011, p. 158), "the African American community in general, and the Black Church more specifically, is allowing countless young women and men to become cannon fodder and collateral damage."

In Britain—where the nonviolent resistance to the invasion of Iraq was much more robust on a per capita basis than it was in the United States, many attempts to form viable coalitions between the natural antiwar constituencies of the Muslim population and the various brands of socialists were made, and none ultimately succeeded (Glynn, 2012). No coalition should be formed that does not, in fact, conditionally understand its ephemeral nature. Yes, it may lead to the formation of a third party—or fourth, or tenth—but its work is best understood as specific, time-limited, goal-oriented. It may lead to more permanent understanding and relationships organizationally or it may not. Certainly the increasingly religion-first approach taken by great numbers of British Muslims would, and did, and will, clash with secular socialists. A party such as George Galloway's Respect endeavor was bound to fail—a party is a permanent manifestation. A coalition can bring together the most disparate of parties for the time-limited purpose of achieving one goal with one campaign over a relatively short period. From the nonviolent perspective, if there is a time-limited agreement on methods—entirely nonviolent—and on the particularized, tightly bounded goal, the chances for success increase greatly.

In the film *A Force More Powerful* (York, 2000) in the episode "We Were Warriors," concerning the effort to desegregate public facilities in Nashville,

Tennessee, the Rev. James Lawson stands before a church full of black and white teams who will be sitting in the next day. He says that everyone should have a partner, but it should not be a partner of the opposite sex and the other race, because "We don't want to fight that battle." This is the sort of respect for the achievement of a particular tightly bounded goal rather than trying to show that he is the most radical leader who can demonstrate his positions on all issues. He not only allows for the inclusion in his coalition of those who want to see integration but not interracial romance, but also protects the image of the movement from that particular criticism. Coalitional formation is a strategic art requiring enormous finesse and humility. As a coalition forms, the inclusion of other organizations or constituencies may alter the tightly bounded goal. This is a delicate process that should serve as a caution to those whose impulse is to make the existence of the coalition and its precise goal public. If all potential large organizations or constituencies are in the coalition and the goal is clear and bright, it is set and should be made public. Media is the next consideration.

Media

> *He's a communist.*
> —U.S. President Richard M. Nixon, about CBS diplomatic
> correspondent Marvin Kalb, June 6, 1969, when
> displeased with reportage about the war in Vietnam
> (qtd. in Pach, 2010, p. 556).

> *The invasion of citizen-journalism videos into mainstream media during
> and because of Arab insurgencies in particular will certainly mark a new
> chapter in the history of the paradigms, practices, and regulations of
> broadcast news.*
> —Rasha Salti (2012, p. 167)

Nonviolence scholars Hardy Merriman and Jack DuVall (2007) note the role of media in creating a foundation for belief in or disbelief in the idea of nonviolence working to wage a successful fight for liberation or for relief from great injustice. Media can convince civil society that it has two choices: all-out violent revolution or fatalistic apathy. And, say Merriman and DuVall (p. 11), this is often exactly what the media give, and that is then reflected in the behavioral choices made by those who resist. They often eschew nonviolence as tantamount to treasonous collaboration with tyrants and are left with the extremely bad choices of taking up arms, begging others to take up arms for them, or, far more likely, doing nothing.

> Media coverage can be crucial in alerting people to the power of nonviolent
> struggle in overcoming oppression. Yet, much of the media's current reporting
> and analysis tends, subtly or obviously, to reinforce unintentionally the belief

that extreme violence is a logical default response to oppression, while also propagating misconceptions about nonviolent action.

The roles of state media and large corporate media are often indistinguishable, from a dictatorship by a military strongman or a theocratic ruler, to a freewheeling democracy or an old-line communist regime—they all seek to control the television, radio, newspaper, and now the various vectors and sites on the Internet. War proponents devote many more resources to controlling the narrative and limiting options; their basic message to the citizenry is two parts.

First, *Do you want to bomb and shoot somebody or do you want to just do nothing?*

Second, *Those who don't support our attack are traitorous cowards.*

Both pieces to the narrative were once more easily managed, but the Internet and proliferation of platforms within cyberspace have made that control harder and harder—not only can the online organizer reach her entire nation, but now the world, which can create external pressure on her behalf (Chander, 2011). It is the worldwide web. Still, it is a coevolving process; peace movements learn about new vectors of communication first and take advantage, or the war proponents jump into the lead and peace messaging must try to catch up. Technical competence becomes as crucial as wordsmithing or public speaking. From the Big Deal of candidate John F. Kennedy discovering make-up and keeping visibly cool during televised debates in 1960—while Nixon sweated and wiped his mouth with the back of his hand, looking like the crook he would eventually deny he was—to activists around the world jacking in and helping Iranians in their Green Revolution in 2009 in workarounds of the regime's sophisticated efforts to blunt all social media, the picture is now enormously fluid and complex. Probably the greatest value of social media is that it is not reliant upon mass media/tors but rather on individuals, unincorporated networks, and on actual relationships to relationships, that is, a social network that defies old methods of organizing simple strata, such as unions.

One misconception about traditional oppositional organizing is that it is driven, decided, and directed by nongovernmental organizations (NGOs) that somehow come in from the outside and take over civil society, instructing it to challenge power. Indeed, there are those who explicitly cite cases of spontaneous uprising (e.g., Biekart & Fowler, 2012), as though most challenger groups have been NGOs or NGO-driven in the past, something that no research nor general knowledge of social change would reasonably suggest. Most U.S.–based NGOs are in fact 501(c)3 nonprofit corporations that do not take political stances but operate educationally. Yes, their educational efforts may have political consequences—indeed, the progenitors of the modern NGO sector (or civil society organization—CSO, a more current label) were often women's transnational peace and disarmament educational associations (Boulding, 1995).

A more subtle but insidious aspect of mainstream media's manipulation of the responses of civil society to prospects of war is to treat media mistakes as one-off errors, unique and rare. Retractions and apologies should be respected, of course, but what is the effect? When mainstream media support an invasion, enable an invasion, by misreporting[11] the facts, by publishing lies that support arguments for war, and eventually acknowledge their mistakes, and offer their mea culpas, how does the electorate react? Do the journalists learn? Does the public learn? In short, does the apology do any good at all, or does it simply make it appear that the mistake was highly unusual, a blip in the normal smoothly factual reportage we can expect from highly qualified and trustworthy professionals? Does this make the reading public, the viewing citizenry, the electorate, more credulous or less? Does this make the next batch of disinformation more palatable or less? Does the appearance of good journalistic ethics belie a war journalism so deeply rooted that even apologia[12] for war enabling and war promoting only eliminates more potential friction in the slide toward the next war?

Some, perhaps many, have given up on corporate media in the United States and other ancillary belligerent partners in armed invasions. While it is perhaps adaptive to do so when one considers the cost-benefit analysis, the tough sell to editors predisposed to administration sources, and the unknown influence of the elite corporate culture on content (visible in some organizations, such as Rupert Murdoch's empire, but far less obvious in other corporate-influenced news organizations, even including the Corporation for Public Broadcasting, including National Public Radio), corporate media can still offer a platform on occasion for a critique of war, if not a promotion of peace directly.

Even when an invasion is done, the messaging is crucial and the struggle to control the narrative is key to preventing yet another invasion. The great myths of defeat are allowed to fester because it is almost invariable that social psychology dictates a defeated party will create any necessary scapegoat in order to justify the massive exercise in passive-aggressive behavior we see in those situations. In those cases, the struggle is to act like a mature, dignified and civilized culture, not like a sulking victim. Sadly, that struggle is often lost, if not on the surface, certainly amongst some constituencies.

Historian Jeffrey P. Kimball (2010, p. 577) describes this phenomenon in the United States:

From the post–Civil War period, these included the South's Myth of the Lost Cause; and from the Cold War era, they included the Yalta-conference-sellout myth, the appeasement-of-aggression theory, the Munich analogy, the loss-of-China accusation, and the domino theory. The stab-in-the-back legend and the Vietnam Syndrome critique, however, did not arise spontaneously. They were the fruit of human agency and intelligent design; they were the product of elites who purposefully concocted a narrative out of the amorphous conditions of defeat, bitterness, and recrimination accompanying a dirty war and its untidy denouement.

An empire is bound to have to balance apparently competing interests as it attempts to maintain itself and grow. The United States, for example, must balance the eight-decade relationship with the House of Saud in Saudi Arabia with the new leadership it made possible by invading Iraq—Shi'a leadership that hates and fears Saudi Arabia and is driven to deeper embrace of both Syria and Iran, two archenemies of Washington. The United States virtually installed the Nouri al-Malaki regime—fully as committed to Sunni and Kurd persecution as Saddam Hussein was to Shi'a and Kurd persecution—and finds itself with a virtually 100 percent negative image in all aspects of global Islam. Effectively, the U.S. violence has accomplished what no leadership or movement has achieved since the birth of Islam, the unification of all Muslims in the opinion that the United States is a rogue, anti–Muslim power that needs to be opposed. Unless American civil society understands this, it will likely remain open to being convinced yet again to accept U.S. military involvement in more invasion, more occupation, always done falsely in the name of security and democracy. A great deal of media work is necessary in order to correct this.

It will not help to adapt a Pollyannish view and narrative that Islam is the religion of peace—too many suicide attacks, too many Hamas rockets into civilian areas, too many beheadings and stonings, too many Muslims calling for the destruction of Israel, the UK, France, and the United States have gone very public worldwide for that silly line to convince anyone but the most credulous. Instead, by acknowledging that Muslims legitimately feel attacked and are going to react much the same as the "Christian" nations do when they legitimately feel under attack, that is, with a ferociously violent response, then our citizenry can understand that we are in perpetual war until, as John Lennon and Yoko Ono declared, "War is over, if you want it." The notion is expressed again and again in far more professional and academic terms in the conflict literature as unilateral gestures leading to bilateral dialog leading to multilateral negotiations. At this writing, indeed, the Taliban has made a unilateral gesture toward the United States by announcing that it does not support using Afghanistan's territory to harbor groups who intend to launch attacks on the United

States, and the United States has responded by opening talks with the Taliban in neutral Doha, Qatar.[13]

With a Little Help from Our Celebrity Friends

Jane Fonda. Joan Baez. John Lennon. Donald Sutherland. Dick Gregory. George Clooney. Yoko Ono. Matt Damon. Danny Glover. Odetta. Pete Seeger. Ronnie Gilbert. Susan Sarandon. Jackson Browne. Holly Near. Bonnie Raitt. Sean Penn. These celebrities and many more devoted themselves to peace at various times. Did their efforts help? Did they assist in recruiting, in getting a message of peace into our public discourse? If so, how? If not, why not?

Mary Hershberger (2012) exegetes the story of Jane Fonda and her complex and impressive commitment to antiwar work in the 1960s and '70s. Fonda started the Free the Army troupe that performed to large crowds of active-duty military near bases and the general peace-supporting public at universities and elsewhere. She traveled to Vietnam, visited the North, witnessed the devastation of U.S. bombing of civilian targets and infrastructure, brought mail to imprisoned American POWs, and carried home their messages of hope that such an unpopular and unwarranted war would quickly end. Fonda did outstandingly effective organizing during the war, including substantial contributions to most aspects of the Winter Soldier hearings. She was arrested or detained several times by Richard Nixon's agents from various agencies—NSA, Customs, various branches of the military, FBI, IRS, etc.—though none of those charges ever resulted in conviction. Then years later more vicious lies about her were spread, and she was portrayed as a tool who supported torturing U.S. pilots captured by the North Vietnamese. This served to redirect blame from American policymakers and the Pentagon; indeed, Hershberger asserts, the lies about Fonda were produced and disseminated by the Pentagon (p. 550).

Obviously, stopping a war in progress is vastly different from preventing an invasion and war of occupation. Once enough blood and treasure has produced overwhelming sunk costs, each of those who has paid—who has suffered—becomes invested in the war's succeeding. When it fails, as it so badly did in Vietnam, the celebrity who opposed the war with the most energy and effectiveness becomes the scapegoat. Fonda was bitterly stung and is not active in peace movements any longer, but she did—for the most part—outstandingly effective antiwar work during the Vietnam era. Perhaps she is an object lesson to other celebrities not to risk the traducement and bile inflicted on Fonda, and her own sacrifices may in fact have been a deterrent to some.

One of the key lessons from her involvement is that any celebrity must be exceedingly careful not to put herself into any situation that could be misunderstood or misused by war promoters. This is what Fonda stumbled into when she visited anti-aircraft gunners and was photographed there, wearing a North Vietnamese helmet. This was used to prove that she wanted Americans to die, to be shot down, and that her activism was anti–Americanism and reckless, not nonviolent and moral. Indeed, Fonda did assert that the anti-aircraft emplacements were legitimate self-defense against U.S. bombers attacking civilians, so she did willingly allow her words and her images to be used to reframe her entire antiwar campaign, producing the lingering hatred for her that is her legacy amongst unregenerate hawks from the Vietnam War era and the far right in the United States to this day. Would someone who believed in nonviolence be immune from that reframing? Only if she were very careful, nearly meticulous and highly informed. High-level peace work is a public relations gold mine *and* a minefield primed to explode with any misstep.

For all she did, for all the calumny inveighed against her, we should probably let Jane have the last word, spoken to an interviewer shortly after a series of politicians called for her trial on treason, one Talibanic pair of them calling for her execution and one demanding that her tongue be cut off. She said, at the conclusion of the Watergate trials and imprisonment of key Nixon regime officials, "I'm still here. The last government's in jail" (Hershberger, p. 569).

Transforming a War Culture to a Peace Culture

An invading and occupying nation builds a war culture, an imperial project with a domestic front. The public increasingly normalizes war in the collective mind and, after a time, nothing is more sacred than supporting veterans, nothing is abnormal about one or more parents at war (Bumiller, 2012), and the background rate of hate crimes against those who are tropes for "the enemy" increases.

This is the case in Israel, as peace groups are labeled treasonous if not terrorist, and the civil society pressure for peace talks evaporates with each new atrocity and each predictable frame of that atrocity. It is a legacy of imperialism in England, a vestige of times when both military and bureaucratic occupying forces were referred to popularly as "an old Indian hand" or other casual representative of the Union Jack, upon which "the sun never sets." This normalization of war, of armed occupation, of a background rate of expense and bloodshed, works itself deeply into the collective consciousness. Like the child who says out loud that the emperor has no clothes, it takes fearless public declaration and challenger messaging to counter this saturation. Fear of opprobrium is a powerful deterrent to that public stance and is either confronted and overcome or it becomes debilitating and self-fulfilling. *We are ineffective because we don't speak out because we are ineffective* is the mutually reinforcing dynamic toward this acceptance of permanent war. Peace promoters either develop the strategic combination of thick-skinned tolerance for public criticism and intolerance for public acceptance of war, or the war culture deepens.

Nonviolence from Within the Invaded and Occupied Nations

Over human history, invasions have occurred to build empires, seek new lands for burgeoning populations, regain lost lands, enrich foreign elites, fund other wars between hegemonic powers, and satisfy monomaniacal ambitions of greedy leaders. Some invaded countries are occupied by troops, some are fully colonized by settling, and some are co-opted by economic imperialism. Resisting the invaders has been natural forever. Gandhi succeeded in evicting the British invaders. Is it wise for those who are invaded now to look to Gandhi for some lessons?

In the modern decolonizing era from the colonial reach of Europe there were two key cases. First was the American Revolution and founding of the United States in 1776, accomplished largely by violence. This informed and guided most attempts from that point on, and continues to be the presumptive conflict management approach understood as viable by the American electorate, leading to a nest and network of problems today. Second was Gandhi's nonviolent liberation of India in 1947, touching off a Global South wave of liberation struggles (Trivedi, 2011). Why were most of those insurrections violent instead of nonviolent? I argue that there were two primary reasons.

One, it appeared that Gandhi's methods took too long, as he began his quest in India a bit after World War I and it thus took at least 27 years to liberate India using nonviolence. Few African or Asian colonies wanted to wait at all, let alone that long. Two, coincidentally, that image of a slow method was exacerbated by the sad coincidence that it was just as Gandhi finally achieved Indian independence that the Soviet Union began to export massive numbers of its new radical field weapon, the Automatic Kalashnikov–47, named for its function—automatic high-rate firing—its inventor—M. K. Kalashnikov—and the year of its invention, 1947. Along with the AK came the Leninist ideology dictating violence as the method of revolution. These liberation tools were intuitively seen as the fast way to force an occupying force to leave, and violence retains that intuitive attraction, even though the correlation of violence to speed of success does not exist.

Gandhi's great mistake in that regard—in hindsight—was his ongoing effort to pursue an end to structural violence and let the actual independence date be set for a distant future date. He was a holistic thinker, who slowly began to understand and reject all British influence on India, wearing simple cloth he spun and eroding British influence slowly as he convinced others to do so (Fischer, 1982; Gonsalvez, 2010). Had he achieved Indian independence sooner (arguably, even in the early 1920s, when he first practiced mass *hartal,* which virtually shut down the nation), perhaps nonviolence would have acquired a status as fast and effective.

From an intercultural forensics point of analysis, it is important as well to parse Gandhian nonviolence for components that are universally applicable and those which may have universal analogs but which are culturally specific.

Nonviolence is *ahimsa* in the Hindu culture, a concept derived from Jains and therefore less alluring for other sets of beliefs unless those beliefs also contain their own version of nonviolence. In his way, Gandhi did make that attempt, and arguably did so with some great sensitivity. He was approached repeatedly by Christians who so admired him that they inquired about converting to Hinduism in order to emulate him and his methods. Invariably, he would urge them to simply be better Christians.

Noncooperation in India is *asahayoga,* and again, Gandhi evoked a religious sympathy from Christians, who saw Christ offer complete nonviolence in response to arrest and crucifixion, even including the religious belief that Jesus healed the severed ear of the Roman soldier who was attacked by one of the apostles when the soldier came to arrest Jesus.

While the classic example of evicting the invaders and occupiers using nonviolence is Gandhi's movement that succeeded in getting the British out of India, other such nonviolent efforts before and since show a complex and strong set of possible paths to freedom for occupied peoples. Indeed, one of the contemporary, linked movements to the struggle to evict the British empire from South Asia and Central Asia began in Pashto tribal areas in 1929, continued until the British left in 1948, and is most often misconstrued as something Gandhi initiated in what was known as the Northwestern Frontier. In fact, it was the Pashtuns, or Pathans, under the leadership of Abdul Ghaffar Khan, who launched their own indigenous movement for liberation and only acted in coalition with Gandhi toward the end of getting the British out, not with the goal of giving up Pathan control over their own territory (Bala, 2013). This movement had no direct Western influence at all and is an example of a warrior culture practicing nonviolence with extreme discipline and a willingness to sacrifice but a commitment not to use violence. It is also an example of what research reveals as a typical concomitant to highly organized armed insurgency, which is the natural appropriation of preexisting social networks by the insurgency (Staniland, 2012). Unarmed insurgents use the same process to great advantage.

Certainly the strongest correlative to nonviolent victory is often the size and unity strength (bonding) of the coalition of civil society committed to nonviolent means of liberation—just as the strong correlative exists on the violent side of an insurgency or civil war, that is, the broader and deeper the coalition of coordinated anti-regime armed groups, the greater the chance for victory—and the weaker the chance for nonviolence or peace treaty (Akcinaroglu, 2012). Where the American empire is concerned, it has long favored the so-called hearts and minds approach—that is, the notion that of course citizens would welcome armed U.S. troops in their country if we could just show them the decided advantages and excellent intentions of our troops, our tanks, our attack helicopters, and our general counterinsurgency necessary to solidify the win generated by the initial aerial bombardment and massive kinetic overwhelming. The most recent codification of this philosophy is the U.S. Army-Marine Corps' Counterinsurgency Manual FM 3–24 of 2007, an example of what one peace reviewer calls "low-intensity colonialism" (Rossinow, 2009, p. 326). As the various surges, starting that year in Iraq, were scored as successes by official U.S. conflict counters, the violent opposition either simply moved the venue of combat or dropped into the woodwork temporarily like a virus hiding from an attempt at medicinal battle, prepared to roar back quickly when the vacuum reopened by a U.S. withdrawal—and prepared to take power anew. Not able to promote imperial occupation by nonviolent means, and most fearful of violent eviction by a coalition of armed opposition, the United States has now heavily invested in the counterinsurgency (COIN) model, even as it also scrambles to execute an "Asian pivot" and reinvest in huge armament arrays pointed at any nation-state who might also have imperial ambitions, the subjects of worry now being China and India (Felter, 2012).

But are the factors the same when dealing with civil society? Can nonviolent civil society more successfully resist occupation even while creating the conditions that will make the ascension to political power more possible for peaceful civil society leadership instead of an armed vanguard?

Perhaps, if we are to ever end war on Earth, we will begin by accepting that we are a warrior species, that war doesn't work, and that we can acknowledge that we still celebrate our willingness to fight for justice but we no longer ethically, morally, nor practically accept violence as the proper means by which we fight. Perhaps we can, as a species, emulate the warriors who have done exactly that, from Asoka the Buddhist king of ancient times to Phil Berrigan, S. Brian Willson, and Abu Ala Mansour of our day. Asoka fought his way to control a vast Indian empire and then renounced all violence, even in the defense of his empire, and performed great deeds of compassion, inclusivity and reconciliation for the remainder of his life. His methods were so revolutionary and won the hearts and minds of his people so completely that his administration lasted 47 years after his death. Phil Berrigan and S. Brian Willson, both members of the U.S. military, converted to peace and fought even harder and much longer for peace and nonviolence than they did in World War II and Vietnam, respectively. Abu Ala Mansour is a fighter from an occupied land, Palestine, who transformed himself from a violent liberation fighter into a nonviolent warrior. Berrigan and Willson and indeed the many erstwhile violent warriors from the armed forces of the empire, from the occupying nation, face opprobrium at home for advocating methods of conflict management that do not favor empire; indeed, their methods would guarantee the end of empire, since all imperial projects are predicated upon violent conquest. Obversely, the members of occupied lands who use nonviolence can expect withering blasts of criticism from those who accuse them of cowardly failure to battle for freedom. Having worked for and with Native American tribes seeking affirmation of treaty rights in their own homelands, I can attest that this happens on occasion to Native leaders who abjure violence; it happened to Gandhi quite regularly in India (though he never needed to convert from violence to nonviolence, of course); and this is typical for Palestinians in my direct experience with former Palestinian fighters who transform themselves into nonviolent practitioners.

Nizar Farsakh (2011), Kennedy School of Government, Harvard, and a former advisor to Palestinian leadership, documents the transformation of Abu Ala Mansour from his early career as a violent Palestinian fighter to his leadership of a nonviolent campaign in the Palestinian town of Bil'in, population 1,500. Like former fighter Ayad Morrar in Budrus, another small Palestinian town in the path of "the Wall" built by Israel to separate and sequester Palestinians into Bantustans in the West Bank, Mansour struggles against the occupying armed force using only nonviolent methods. Morrar succeeded, Mansour is still in that struggle. Gene Sharp observes that Mansour's Bil'in campaign is dealing with agents provocateurs, Israeli Defense Force (IDF) members masquerading as Palestinians and throwing stones at IDF members to provoke the violence that can kill both individuals and an otherwise nonviolent campaign (Najjab, 2006).

Certainly there are those who call upon the United States to be prepared to (thus threaten to) use military force in seeking peace in the Middle East, and in defense of Israel in particular (Ben-Meir, 2013), but that has proven inadequate literally every time it has been tried, for all parties.

A generation of Palestinian fighters emerged from the humiliating and imperialist Six Day War[14] launched in 1967 by Israel, won in six days, and generating hostilities ever since. Mansour fought using the methods adapted by Palestinian military organizations such as the Palestinian Liberation Organization and Fatah (the organization in which Mansour worked), including political organizing, recruiting, and insurgent and terrorist strikes (insurgents target military sites and personnel, terrorists include civilians). Mansour used a broad array of tactics over the years, including the political work on the ground in Israel, and eventually reached the conclusion that violence was simply ineffective. Many other Palestinians began to see this, and what emerged was the next iteration of Palestinian resistance, the first intifada, largely nonviolent.

> The intifada of 1987 and the first Gulf War in 1991 ushered in a new phase of the conflict. The intifada helped enable this change by putting the Palestinians in a stronger negotiating position and bringing world attention to the conflict. One result was the Oslo Accords in 1993, which committed the PLO and Israel to resolving their conflict through negotiations [Farsakh, 2011, p. 126].

The gains from that process seemed to evaporate easily, however, when spoilers from both Palestine and Israel committed acts of terrorism (ironically all against Israelis, which drew Israeli political leaders and its citizenry back into the use of violence, which in turn convinced most Palestinians to also return to what they also knew best, violence). Slowly, partially in response to the realization that return to violence in the Second Intifada[15] (September 2000–December 2005) was costly and ineffective, some of the Palestinian fighters began to convert to nonviolent methods, even during that Second Intifada (Norman, 2013). With the formation of Combatants for Peace[16] and with increasing numbers of Israeli refusniks, that is, Israeli Defense Force members who foreswore further deployments from the Israeli borders into occupied territories, some Israeli combatants joined the slow transformation to a nonviolent resistance to the methods of both sides, invader and invaded. The history of Jerusalemite Fatah members and Israelis working together for years against the occupation by Israel of Palestine may have been why the Jerusalemite Fatah members did not join the waves of terrorists from Hamas and Fatah in other Israeli cities (Cohen, H., 2013). Fatah members from Jerusalem may have respected their Israeli partners in peace and justice struggles and that translated, if true, into innocent lives saved.

Csapody and Weber (2007) examine the case of the Austrian occupation and rule of Hungary and the successful nonviolent resistance campaigns of the mid–19th century, inspirational to Gandhi a half-century later in South Africa and then India. It is a widely repeated story and yet the leader, Deak, did not claim to have discovered a method nor did he attempt to offer a strategic model as Gandhi did, so Gandhi remains the inventor of credit.

Radical Flank Reconsidered: Backfire Against Any Violence

Nonviolent resistance to occupation is usually one of the most stark examples of the problems of the so-called "radical flank" phenomenon, since an occupied land is openly the result of a military invasion and subsequent subjugation of people on their own land by a foreign power. Occupation, predicated upon the violent force advantage, can be resisted violently and successfully ended, though almost always with extremely high costs, almost never quickly, and usually with a residue of various sorts of debt to more powerful military external powers as well as an assumption of entire credit to the armed resistance, who usually then takes power and often wields it with violence over their subjects. Occupation resisted solely with nonviolence will also have costs (almost certainly much lower, however, than any violent resistance), will also take time, but will leave no legacy of political or financial obligation to either a foreign power or armed "vanguards." Indeed, the research shows that regime change in general results in stronger metrics of human rights, civil rights and democracy if done nonviolently (Karatnycky & Ackerman, 2005). Part of this success in a lasting legacy of trust in the leadership of nonviolent campaigns is the transparency and the interpersonal relationships that develop during nonviolent campaigns. In violent opposition or even coalition, the trust is usually low from leader to leader, although there have been important cases when an insincere but convincing leader has persuaded another credulous leader of authenticity (Hall & Yarhi-Milo, 2012). On the nonviolent side, we often discuss this aspect as gentle personalism, something nonexistent and logically unrecognizable on the violent side. While Neville Chamberlain may have been fooled by Hitler, and George W. Bush may have been a village idiot in claiming to have looked into Putin's eyes and found a trustable soul, nonviolent leadership can frequently and logically develop trust and even faith from both coalition partners and representatives from adversaries alike. Some of this will begin even just by the gesture of reaching out to the armed forces, to the police, to the representatives of other stakeholders, and establishing a contact, a first-name connection.

The sad case of Palestinian aspirations for statehood—and the Gazan example in particular—are ongoing testimony to the legion problems of violent response to occupation. Indeed, while Israel withdrew its settlers from Gaza in August 2005, it expanded the settlements in West Bank, which is also part of aspirational Palestine. The United States, under the direction of then–Secretary of State Condoleezza Rice, flooded Gaza with $80 million in anti–Hamas campaign materials, virtually guaranteeing a pro–Hamas reaction from an outraged Gazan citizenry, and Hamas was voted in, thus officially empowering the violent reactionaries in Gaza. We see the results again and again, with Operation Cast Lead killing Palestinian civilians at a ratio of 100:1 (more than 1,300 Palestinian mortalities to 13 Israeli mortalities). Maladaptively, Hamas continues to offer violence and, at a time of their choosing, Israel kills them. The IDF killed one of the Hamas military leaders in November 2012, and it starts all over, with enraged responses from Hamas such as, "It's an open war. We will use all our cards."[17] This then precipitates an Israeli response that adopts the von Clausewitzian notion that all Gazans are guilty and can be justly punished, since they chose Hamas (Abdul-Karim & Brulliard, 2012). The greatest mistake—and the most common one made by activists in many struggles, is personified by Palestinian nonviolence activist Zoughbi Zoughbi, who, at a Bethlehem conference on nonviolence in 2006, told hundreds in attendance that Palestinians did not need to worry about their actions, but rather that the focus should be on making Israeli society less violent (Najjab, 2006). The obvious problem with that is every act of Palestinian violence delays the desired change in Israeli society. Again, this is both unfair and reality.

Some analysts ignore or dismiss the violence of the armed wing or the radical flank as minor, as more or less irrelevant, and instead focus on the non-violent aspects, stressing the existence of those in portraying the violent crackdown of the state as unjust. In his analysis of the strengths and weaknesses of the international peace movement, the executive director of the Fellowship of Reconciliation, Mark C. Johnson (2010), describes the devotion to nonviolence by those who were preparing for the May 2010 flotilla to Gaza and stresses the impunity with which Israel boarded one of the vessels and killed nine of the activists on board, but Johnson failed to mention that the particular ship in question had many activists who were not trained in nonviolence and in fact at least some who had previously expressed a desire to be a jihadi martyr. Johnson prefaced some of his analysis with a cursory note that he was not going to make the "fine" distinctions between peace movements and antiwar movements, thereby dismissing the evaluative use of the presence of the radical flank, which is often the major difference between a true peace movement that only uses nonviolent tactics, and a movement with a "diversity" (i.e., inclusive of violence) of tactics in opposition to a *particular* war. Brushing aside these factors will make any analysis of the reasons for failure of a particular movement less than adequate (Ackerman & DuVall, 2000; Chenoweth & Stephan, 2011; Chernus, 2004; Lynd & Lynd, 1996; Martin, 2007; Sharp, G., 2005). Simply, the injection of violence into an otherwise nonviolent campaign furnishes the justification for the forces of the state to crack down mercilessly and removes the image of righteous purity from the movement, thus nullifying serious civil society support for the movement. The state gains equal moral footing in the eyes of much of the public, if not the moral high ground, and the majority of civil society often shifts from identification with the movement to alienation from it. At times the introduction of violence and the resultant state crackdown will simply reduce recruitment from civil society into the movement based on higher barriers to involvement and a reduction in the perceived ethical gap between the movement and the state, which is harmful enough; at times it will weaken support for the movement based on the perception of closer moral equivalency, which is more harmful; at times that movement violence will even result in civil society's gratitude for the "thin blue line" of police protecting civil society from the violence of the movement. These distinctions are not "fine." The presence of a violent wing of a movement can stall it and even finish it; obversely, guarantees of nonviolent principles can result in a quid pro quo in which perfectly prepared violent forces of the state will hold off employing violence as long as the insurgents remain committed to nonviolence (Sambatpoonsiri, 2013).

Simply, any violence has the possibility of backfire (Beyerle, 2008). Violence by the state, violence by paramilitaries, violence by insurgents, violence by victims—all carry the seeds of backfire. What is usually required is media attention and the generation of outrage. When racists beat nonviolent black protesters in the Deep South, the rest of the U.S. citizenry was outraged. The minute riots began in various U.S. cities, outrage shifted to fear and apathy about demands from black people. Racism was no longer the issue; black violence was, so the riots achieved two negatives. One, they took the grievance off the table and replaced it with fear of black violence. Two, they provided justification for the state to come in with arms and soldiers and occupy their neighborhoods, dominating and further humiliating black people where they lived.

This dynamic is always assisted by media. What nonviolent movements must do to counter this may be tough, but it's necessary. They need to use a media strategy that involves Dorothy Day's gentle personalism with every possible reporter and editor in mainstream media. In other words, they are most effective when they develop a personal relationship with the professionals in mainstream media. They obviously need to build and support alternative media as well, including social media. The campaigns that do this most effectively are generally the ones who win. This is part of how the radical flank actions can be blunted. Otherwise, they can do the work of provocateurs and destroy a movement. Social media can be exploited by anyone—those who work for positive peace, those who work for an autocratic regime, and those who unwittingly do the work of agents provocateurs; social media and the worldwide web are neutral tools that can assist in perpetuating a tyrant's regime or can help bring it down (Chander, 2011).

Syria, a nation ripe for a nonviolent Arab Spring that might have succeeded in ousting Bashar al-Assad, instead succumbed to violent insurgency, and rather than a few weeks to effect regime change with a handful of casualties, the much more potent violent insurgents have failed as of this writing to finish off the regime of Bashar al-Assad after two years of effort. Now, when anything goes wrong in Syria, it is easy and credible, even for the incredible al-Assad regime, to claim it's due to rebel actions. Power out in Damascus?

Rebel attack (Associated Press, 21 January 2013a).[18] Indeed, in regime language, all insurgents are terrorists, and sadly, some of the violent insurgents have been nearly as reckless in targeting civilians as has been the Syrian regime (Associated Press, 20 January 2013).[19] Syrians have long suffered under the rule of the al-Assad family—Hafiz and now Bashar—but when they see an Egyptian regime change, a Tunisian regime change, a Yemeni regime change, all done with nonviolence and all done quickly with few casualties, they are disaffected from violence, which has cost, as of this writing, more than 60,000 civilian lives and has transmogrified from an Arab Spring campaign beginning in February 2011 into civil war within a month, since March 2011 (Associated Press, 21 January 2013b). Syrian government troops do some battle with rebels but the indiscriminate bombing—which I argue would not happen to a nonviolent civil society campaign—takes a constant toll, killing children routinely (Associated Press, 20 January 2013). This leads American hawks, as usual, to summarily declare that any lack of military action by the United States is "failure," (Cohen, R., 2013) as though attacking a Russian ally is risk-free and decisive. The argument that an early declaration of a no-fly zone would have somehow helped is disingenuous—a no-fly zone is unnecessary where the only opposition is nonviolent civil society. Declaring a no-fly zone and then enforcing it with NATO flying and bombing such as what we did in Serbia in 1999 or Libya in 2011–12 is simply siding with an armed rebellion that will then overwhelm nonviolent civil society and drive up mortalities. The results from Libya, which include the subsequent attack on the U.S. embassy and murder of the U.S. ambassador can hardly be heralded as a brilliant victory, especially as Islamists seem to be now at least as much in control in Libya as ever.

Working to save Syrian lives would have included providing Syrian civil society with training and funding, not bombers. The U.S. State Department has indeed offered some of that help to civil society, but the rebel army is far too committed now to expect them to stop in this existential struggle. Indeed, the rebels say there is no negotiation that doesn't involve Assad's removal from power entirely. Assad logically understands they mean to end his life, and he will thus fight on unless he can somehow arrange a Ben Ali exit with a fortune to a safe place, an unlikely scenario now. Ending this civil war is ultimately a choice for Syrian civil society. They have suffered, and if they withheld all cooperation for either rebels or regime, they could fix this, but it would take massive commitment, courage, and acceptance of consequences.

Very Funny: Our Leaders Are Worth Laughing At, Not Dying For

Humor is used in both the invading and invaded nations to help in resistance. The similarities and differences are distinctive.

If we live in a country planning to invade another, and we succeed in convincing our fellow members of civil society that our leadership is risible, entertaining in their buffoonery and not worth following, we make it less likely that the invasion will happen. Who wants to send sons along with the village idiot to go die for a mistake? The challenge, of course, is to succeed in the use of humor, not insult an entire sector of the population who then ignores the humor and might actually be more inclined to support or even participate in the invasion. We saw this unfortunate phenomenon during 2002–2003, when George W. Bush was ridiculed as an ignorant redneck, stressing his simplistic Texas approach to everything. It is clear in retrospect that many who consider themselves proud Southerners, or Westerners, took umbrage at these characterizations and rallied around Bush and his invasion of Iraq. Humor backfire is unhelpful.

If we live in an occupied country, we can survive and create a camaraderie using humor, as is known from studies of Norwegians under Nazi occupation, Tibetans under Chinese rule, and other examples (Sørensen, 2008). And when ethnic division prompts secessionist goals, nonviolent but pointed humor can relieve the high stress of aspirational sovereignty struggle, as we have seen in a divided Burma (Myanmar), Serbs under Milosevic, and in apartheid South Africa.

One of the keys to successful use of humor is to be certain that it all tends to redirect all scorn, all laughter at anyone, upward, toward the ruling elite, and not toward an ethnic group, nor toward the police nor soldiers. Humor should be used to divide the elites from the people, not the people from each other.

Certainly humor has been used by activists in the occupying nation to oppose the occupation. The Yippies, and Abbie Hoffman in particular, used humor to poke fun at the elites who profited from the war in Vietnam, though neither Hoffman nor the Yippies in general seemed to have any strategic sense of the inadvisability of attacking entire swaths of working-class Americans in their random efforts to oppose that war and occupation. Their humor included letting live pigs loose in Lincoln Park during the 1968 Democratic Convention to taunt and provoke the Chicago police. Since the Yippies and the National Mobilization Committee to End the War in Vietnam (the MOBE) at once claimed to be nonviolent and concomitantly displayed violent tendencies and elements, most genuinely peaceful activists tended to stay away, and those who wanted to battle police were attracted to the convention (Shogan, 2002). Results were predictable; Chicago police proved that fantasies about seriously overmatching police power (backed by 5,000 mobilized Illinois National Guardsmen and 6,000 nearby available U.S. troops with units of the 101st Airborne armed with flamethrowers and bazookas) were fatuous at best. Of course, classic backfire occurred as well and the bone-crunching aggression of the Chicago police gave the demonstrators a "propaganda" victory, according to MOBE leader Tom Hayden, a tactical adherent to nonviolence at best. The mixed picture, complex in its welter of factors and forces, continued public pressure on the war makers but did not recruit many from a middle class and working class. Those people were ultimately mostly recruited to oppose the war by the draft, since young men were being slaughtered without the purpose that their fathers had in World War II.

PART 4

Nonviolent Resistance by the World

Two trends make it more likely that civil society can work alongside of or ahead of governments in interfering with, preventing, and ending invasions and occupations as they occur or might occur anywhere on Earth. One is that civil society is increasingly unwilling to cede all powers to the nation-states and has begun to seriously granularize power at multiple levels and layers of humanity rather than solely at the unit preferred by those who are in power in those nation-states (Benhabib, 2013). Two is that we are wired and increasingly possess a civil society infrastructure for action, worldwide (Sadri & Flammia, 2009; Stremmelaar & Wallert, 2012). While war makers are used to making all decisions, civil society is rapidly learning how to effect compensatory mass-action measures that can counter elite power. Divine right, presidential power, and corporate control are all in various stages of death throes and all still manifestly dangerous, but people power is becoming credible to more of humanity.

Assessment and inquiry into the best methods to support any nascent nonviolent indigenous movement is best when it features the same characteristics that constitute best practices in conflict assessment and research, including indigenous participation and empowerment, and assessor accountability and respect, as well as protective confidentiality and popularly understandable sharing of all assessment results (Schirch, 2013).

It is inappropriate to think in terms of one level, but instead to think in systemic terms about interactions and effects of power and force exercised throughout a sphere of sources. While Alexis-Charles-Henri Clérel de Tocqueville wrote extensively in the first half of the 19th century about the existence and effects of American civil society upon the young democracy, it is only relatively recently that many scholars outside the peace and conflict studies field have begun to write about the effects of transnational civil society.

Even those cases often focus nearly exclusively on the relatively apolitical non-governmental organizations that often even have the sort of nonprofit status that allows citizens to donate and deduct a portion of those donations from their taxable income, plus allows those organizations to themselves be exempt from paying taxes. These are the nonprofit humanitarian aid, human rights, and democracy capacity-building groups, most of which are dedicated to an increasingly cosmopolitan understanding that national boundaries do not define us categorically (Benhabib, 2013). Arguably, this status of approval by the nation-state means these organizations are regarded as no threat to the interests of those nation-states. As the power of civil society to overthrow corrupt dictators is increasingly recognized by security studies scholars and analysts, including those in the government, those calculations and those exemptions may change. Social capital may be ineffable to some, but it is a realistic source of great power to launch change (Ohmer, Warner, & Beck, 2010). It is easier for low-paid or unpaid volunteers to help create the bonds that unite within society and the bridges that connect and even unite different societies than it is for governments to force or formalize those natural processes.

When the United States invaded Iraq, most of the world recognized that as a manifestation of an imperial project using a couple of fig leaves: putative WMD and "cavorting with terrorists." Neither leaf convinced many outside the United States. Indeed, there was a global movement to bring law forward by holding a citizen tribunal named the World Tribunal on Iraq (WTI) between 2003 and 2005, a tribunal called by citizens and a process that generated much internal debate over basic issues of universality of some rights versus sovereignty in the face of militaristic empire (Çubukçu, 2011).

What value, if any, can citizens of one country bring to the struggle to help protect another country from being invaded and occupied? There are four ways to consider this. First, and primary, all internationals should take their cues from those on the ground in the affected countries (Anderson & Larmore, 1991; Beyerle, 2008).[1] Listening is a skill and a conflict art (Cunliffe, 2013). Second, how can citizens from a third country put pressure on the rulers of the invading and occupying nation-state? Third, can citizens convince their own governments to get involved *if* the civil society oppositional groups in the affected country wish for that support? (in the international governance system that does exist—the UN—or even just in an ad hoc international attempt to delegitimize another nation-state that is planning or actually invading and occupying a third nation). Fourth and finally, can civil society of one or more countries convince corporations to take financial action to deter or sanction the invading or occupying nation-state?

Into this mix comes the question of defections from police and military, usually prompted by persuasion from civil society, and those defections are so powerfully threatening to elites who profit in some way from war that those elites will at times attempt to manage against such defections by creating division between soldiers and peace activists, or, if possible, discourage information about such defections from becoming public (Mirra, 2011). Simply, defections from amongst the ranks represents a significant loss of legitimacy in the eyes of civil society, which drives further such losses. Indeed, writes Melissa Everett (1989), in her study of 13 members of the U.S. armed forces or intelligence agencies, some of the lead individuals who break ranks (all of them in her study) have come to the conclusion that "war is preventable" (p. 213). Such views, informed by an insider perspective, can begin to unravel the unquestioning assumptions upon which the validity of violence rests. Stopping that downward spiral can be one of the toughest challenges to an elite which has consolidated military power unto itself but which is losing the hearts and minds of those whose cooperation is key to holding power, the average citizens. Ironically, and strategically, the relatively small civil society group of peace activists who can help cause defections from within the armed forces can leverage that into a much larger peace movement with much more power to actually change events.

The intermediary vector is one form or another of media. As the antiwar movement grew in civil society in the United States during the war in Vietnam, that helped support a growing disaffection and defection movement inside the military, which in turn increased and in many ways enhanced the antiwar movement in the domestic United States, the invader and occupier. Both Lyndon Johnson and Richard Nixon stayed angry at the U.S. media for bringing open information to public view. Pach (2010, p. 555) describes Nixon's fixation on the role of media:

> Nixon repeatedly accused journalists of focusing on the problems instead of the achievements of Vietnamization, failing to give him credit for reversing the course of the war, and even hoping for U.S. failure and enemy success in Vietnam. When critics complained that Nixon was withdrawing U.S. troops too slowly or expanding the war with new military operations in Cambodia and Laos, the president and his aides tried to deflect that discontent by blaming the news media—and, in particular, the television networks—for distorted, even disloyal reporting.

Media, of course, shades into culture, and culture is critical in the consideration of building nonviolent movements from amongst civil society. Sørensen and Vinthagen (2012) identify three cultural aspects of strategic nonviolence: one, appropriating cultural artifacts to directly promote peace and justice (e.g., getting an endorsement for the complete abolition of nuclear weapons from Admiral Hyman Rickover or General Lee Butler); two, morphing a culturally important phenomenon toward peace (e.g., "Peace is patriotic; war profiteering is unpatriotic"); three, creating a new cultural norm (e.g., "Patriotism is maladaptive; matriotism is loyalty to all of life, all children from all countries, and to the very environment that makes our lives possible"). These culture battlegrounds require extraordinary cultural knowledge and sensitivity or risk movement diminution by failing to attract commitment and support from enough members of a given civil society. Woehrle, Coy, and Maney (2008) examined analogous attempts by various peace movement organizations to harness the values already proven culturally accepted. They called for further research into evaluation of the cases of success in achieving peace related to these messaging strategies.

One of the commonalities amongst many successful struggles is some version of visioning the future desired (Davies, 2011). It may be projected by a speech, as in Dr. King's 1963 "I have a dream" speech, or it may be hammered out by a coalition of civil society organizations with differing but overlapping goals; it can ultimately reveal the boundaries of a movement and even a cam-

Figure 1: Coalitional goal-setting

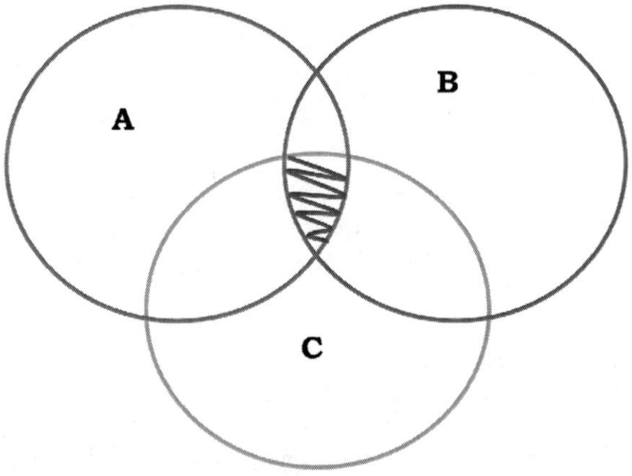

Figure 1: The entire set of goals for Party A includes many that do not overlap with Parties B or C. The same is true for all parties. The ultimate negotiated goal of a movement or a campaign that will stand most challenges and most attempts to divide the coalition is bounded by the bright lines that include a goal satisfactory to all coalitional parties. This goal may most strategically be negotiated by all potential coalitional parties before taking the campaign public. The parties may be influential individuals but are most likely larger sections of civil society in association (e.g., religious sect, labor union, student organization). The process of goal-setting includes goals for methods of waging the campaign (e.g., violence/nonviolence, legal/civil resistance). Unexamined goals can later fracture a coalition.

paign (see Figure 1). While each society is different, it is often the case that members of historically oppressed groups tend to be attracted to movements and campaigns that focus on justice and liberation, while members of privileged groups tend to be drawn into movements that stress the enlightened self-interest of peace as an intrinsic valued condition. Building coalitions between these groups means framing peace in a structural sense, highlighting correctly the enlightened self-interest of many groups, both historically oppressed and relatively privileged. Thus, for example, in a multi-campus study conducted on 159 undergraduate social work students, the more educated a student was made it more likely that student would support a peace position, and neither race nor gender were predictors for either pro-peace opinions or activism (Swank & Fahs, 2011). Elevating the analysis to include the peace journalism frames of structural violence (injustice) as a concomitant to most war can alter the appeal to a more diverse and thus larger and more effective coalition.

Visioning can thus be remarkably crucial to the strategic plan of any movement. It may be omitted from a process, and that movement may succeed, but the chances of that success are enhanced by this step. Elise Boulding first developed a formalized process.

Citizen-Based Direct Diplomacy

Citizen diplomacy, as used herein, refers to civil society acting independently, bringing a diplomatic presence, argument, or pressure to bear to effect or change foreign policy of a government—one's own or another. Some analysts focus on citizens acting on behalf of one's own government (Magbadelo, 2012), a practice essentially irrelevant to this problem of war except under rare, privileged circumstances at the pleasure of the governing elite.

Tapping into the power of civil diplomacy is more easily done if it is understood that acting upon the actual decision makers is sometimes a process of acting upon those who influence the decision makers, and that decisions that have narrow impacts can have broad and deep impacts when taken in aggregate and when done simultaneously or in a logical series. See Figure 2 for select examples of the sorts of decisions that fall to elites, to mid-level associations, and to grassroots civil society. The barriers between these are either permanent and impervious—in which case all real decisions with real power flow from the elites—or there is both communication and force operating between and among all levels, in which case the grassroots will need to be resilient, disciplined, and strategic, since the historical pathways all militate a top-down orientation of decision and implementation. Changing this cause-and-effect flow of influence is how most violence and most injustice ends.

Is it possible for civil society in one country to influence the government of another to postpone or cancel an invasion of a third country? Can civil society of one nation prevent, weaken, or otherwise hasten the end of the occupation of a third nation-state?

At times the apparently docile acceptance of—or even visible support for—one's own government engaging in aggression and brutality is perplexing to citizens of another nation-state (Abdullah, 2009). We might be from Venezuela shaking our heads at U.S. Americans who fail to stop their nation from invading Iraq. How could those supposedly educated Americans be so morally ignorant, so unwilling to take basic and easy action that would stop the invasion? After all, Congress voted on it in October of 2002, and how could Americans allow their elected officials to permit an illegal war based on lies? What does it take, a world citizen legitimately wonders, to arouse the complacent American public? How could the demonstrations against that patently outrageously criminal attack be so small in a nation priding itself on freedom of expression?

Anne Applebaum (2012) helps us think about this general principle, using the egregious examples of those who appeared to support Stalin and other brutal communist leaders in the height of the Cold War and Soviet state terrorism against their own people.[2] The psychology of collaboration with evil is powerfully linked to fear and can produce kneejerk—and even reasoned—support by otherwise good people for policies that are anathema to peace, freedom and justice. Patience and persistence with the cowed and vulnerable citizens of other nations—even nations where dissent is protected in many ways—is a key to cross-cultural and transnational civil society coalitions.

Cross-cultural workshops, trainings and dialog can facilitate transnational support for peace, for ending wars of invasion, occupation, or, for that matter, civil wars, but also offer perspectives on skilling up to continue effective action long after a particular conflict appears resolved (Shemesh, 2012; Williams & Miller, 2012). Transnational workshops for U.S. Americans can help American activists more strategically act on their own government to effect violence reduction internationally and domestically. The ability of U.S. activists to draw on these lessons can help reframe the issues to other Americans, resulting in an American civil society more oriented toward a universal understanding of how others view America and why. Similarly, any other belligerent nations, such as junior partner UK, can be assisted in becoming less compliant with the aggression of their nation.

While not a specific case of civil society stopping a likely invasion, the peace walks and other civil society initiatives in the 1980s helped reduce tensions between U.S.-S.U. Cold-Warring governments. The pugnacious and reckless rhetoric of Ronald Reagan forced fears to the surface amongst the citizens of both nations—as well as allies of both in Europe, who feared the growing likelihood of actual "limited" nuclear war in their countries, in the territory in which they lived but which was simply referred to by the superpowers as buffer states, as though a war in those nations comprising the Warsaw Pact and NATO nations would somehow be acceptable, contained losses to both global hegemons. Legal and illegal peace actions by citizens of both superpowers began to show the power of citizen-to-citizen peace initiatives, helping to bring about the *glasnost* and *perestroika* in Gorbachev's Soviet Union and Reagan's United States, alike. Soviet citizens began to hear of U.S. peace actions so robust—the Plowshares movement in particular, which featured public actions of direct disarmament of nuclear weapons using hand tools and no effort to escape legal consequences, resulting in harsh prison terms of up to 18 years in U.S. federal prisons—that they realized the American people were potential partners in actual peace efforts that could be promoted from civil society, not just the veneer of official Soviet "peace" statements or demonstrations engineered as crude public relations instruments to discredit the United States and frame the Soviet Union as the peace party.

In 1987, for example, 230 Americans and 200 Soviets joined in a premier act of citizen diplomacy, walking together for 450 miles from Leningrad to Moscow (Brigham, 2010). This helped lead to other collaborative acts of citizen diplomacy that pushed the rhetoric of peace to a new reality, and the culmination of these civil society efforts in the United States, the Soviet Union, and both NATO and Warsaw Pact nations resulted in the December 1987 Intermediate Nuclear Forces treaty mandating actual nuclear disarmament—the first such treaty in the nuclear age. While hawkish commentators claim the fall of the Soviet Union and all resultant peace benefits were a function of the U.S. willingness to spend itself into massive debt to acquire surreal levels of nuclear overkill, the effects of civil societies on all sides were prompted by and then dwarfed those spending commitments in their political effects.

The Louise Diamond and John MacDonald (1991) notion of multi-track diplomacy is more complex than Figure 2 but not unrelated. The wheel or pie of tracks—official, professional, citizen-to-citizen, business, education/ research, religion, funding, and communications—may portray a more egalitarian and accurate picture of realized rather than merely hypothetical power, and may reveal the nonhierarchical nature of reified power at all levels and from all sectors. The other distinct advantage to the multi-track orientation is that if all tracks are addressed, the outcome is a culture of peace (Shemesh, 2012), not merely a negative or imposed peace from official sources of power. Leaving the business community out of the peacemaking decisions is one example of courting the next round of violence, since war is often seen as economically stimulating. Leaving the religious track out of the peace negotiations

Figure 2: Categories of decisions and options
ascribed to levels of society

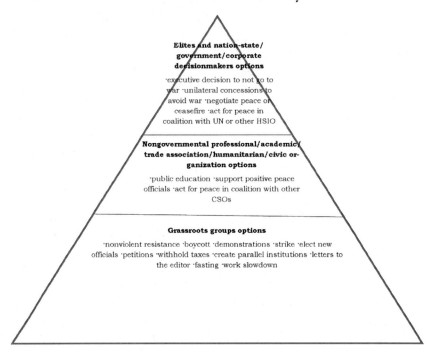

Elites and nation-state/government/corporate decisionmakers options

·executive decision to not go to war ·unilateral concessions to avoid war ·negotiate peace or ceasefire ·act for peace in coalition with UN or other HSIO

Nongovernmental professional/academic/trade association/humanitarian/civic organization options

·public education ·support positive peace officials ·act for peace in coalition with other CSOs

Grassroots groups options

·nonviolent resistance ·boycott ·demonstrations ·strike ·elect new officials ·petitions ·withhold taxes ·create parallel institutions ·letters to the editor ·fasting ·work slowdown

may open a pathway for a religious mandate to reignite war based on a retributive doctrine of violent justice. Leaving out the communications and public relations track is clearly maladaptive to peace, as it virtually guarantees a war journalism orientation—if it bleeds, it leads.

On the other hand, waiting for all tracks to be lined up and in consensus is not only unnecessary, it is prohibitively untenable and delays both peace and justice for no reason. The key is regarding the cease-fire or the signing of the peace accord not as the achievement of peace but rather as one small but crucial official step in a long journey toward the creation of a culture of peace. This also can strengthen resiliency.

When Israelis and Palestinians reached out to each other in bicommunal initiatives, they were creating a piece of the culture of peace, even when officials disagreed, even when Hamas was shooting rockets and the IDF was bombing Gaza. The citizen diplomacy never fails in the sense that it is building a consensus that it's possible and it's desirable. Giving up on people-to-people initiatives is never a wise option. Adjusting them toward more results and stronger peace outcomes is always the adaptive process.

Civil Society Prompting International Action

The historical view of the societal composition is that there are government, private enterprise, and nongovernmental sectors, but some analysts are finding it useful to consider society as a whole, as all are members of civil society, even those in government and presumably even those in the military (Biekart & Fowler, 2012). While this may be an extreme view, and while it may be unhelpful in direct contests between a coalition of corporations and government protected by the military, it has a helpful perspective from a nonviolent stance that everyone is a potential ally. In this view, then, civil society composed of disparate members of all groups can act to help nonviolently resist invasions and occupations. A member of a military who sets down his gun can become a member of a civic-driven action—and indeed, this has happened, just as it has happened that members of the ruling, governing elites have occasionally set aside their powers and stepped into the crowds offering nonviolent resistance.

Enabling Indigenous Conflict Management

Civil society on Earth comprises the global alert system for those who accompany indigenous conflict workers on the ground in countries either under occupation from external powers or whose own nation-state is oppressing them, especially if foreign powers are enabling the oppressors. So, for instance, Peace Brigades International was invited into Guatemala during the 1980s to accompany local community leaders who were trying to carve out more local sovereignty, more local power, defend local land, protect local children, bargain for local economic protection or gain, and generally nonviolently resist military occupation by the U.S.–backed Guatemalan military government. These international conflict workers would simply accompany local leadership and send back reports. When there was a strong enough threat, an emergency notice would go to the international network, citizens who would put immediate pressure on all parties to, in turn, put pressure on the Guatemalan military junta to order no harm to the particular threatened local leader. This proved so effective that the PBI teams saved many lives—every single local leader they accompanied survived that period. Later, one of the Guatemalan generals confirmed to two authors that the pressure on them was effective, since that pressure resulted in pressure from the U.S. politicians who voted on the military aid crucial to the power of the Guatemalan generals (Mahony and Eguren, 1997). Other indigenous populations under occupation have frequently appealed to the United Nations to move toward sovereignty and freedom for themselves on their own land (Natividad, 2013).

Kisiku Sa'qawei Paq'tism Randolph Bowers (2012) describes traditional indigenous conflict management for one North American tribe, the Mi'kmaq, as their "eco-psycho-social-spiritual methods for maintaining right relationships within human and natural systems" (p. 290). Simply accompanying people like this can create political space and conflict management space and introduce hope for sustainable resolution to direct mortal threat issues. Internationals require a good deal of training to be most effective in this, training in cultural sensitivity and de-escalation.

One of the greatest barriers to the recognition of indigenous nonviolent methods of conflict management is that the often robust and sustainable cultures of peace were so smashed and brutalized by the half-millennium of European colonization and the global militarized predatory capitalist imperialism that followed, that those indigenous lifeways—sometimes in successful and prosperous existence far longer than the war cultures that followed—were forgotten. Often, when those nonviolent methods of conflict management—so frequently so different from the zero-sum extractive models—were noted, they were labeled quaint and irrelevant, as unable to survive basic human evolutionary competition. In the short run, this is an interesting view. In the long run, it is a maladaptive view.

Elavie Ndura is a peace researcher and peace educator whose entire life, from childhood on, has been impacted by ethnic violence and war between and among the peoples of Burundi and Rwanda. She has impacted it back. She lost family members, including her husband, to the violence, and her father was crippled in one attack when she was a small child. Her response is to seek a global education and bring back the best methods of multicultural education to her homeland even as she enables the best of the indigenous methods of both education and communication in Burundi. She brings the best practices from global wisdom back to Burundi in frequent teacher-training trips home and, in turn, brings the indigenous wisdom from Burundi to the world through her publishing, her teaching at George Mason University, and her roles in many transnational associations. She protects her indigenous lifeways at the same time she seeks to be involved in their evolutionary development. Her peace education is a sort of inoculant against war. Supporting this sort of dialectical activity and creating more of it will sustain such violence prevention.

Nigerian nonviolent activist and scholar Judith Atiri (2009) points out that in countries that have a legacy of brutality and oppression, one act of "free speech" is often the sum of a person's nonviolent resistance, since the response of the state is frequently lethal. This knowledge gives a great deal of credibility and authenticity to indigenous nonviolent conflict management, a dedication and devotion worth valorizing and certainly supporting, even if it is not easy or even possible to emulate. Listening to and learning from nonviolent activists on the ground can teach the world to better support sustainable conflict transformation that worked well before invasion and occupation; bringing it back with new adaptive protections can show that the way forward is often to go back.

Civil Society–Initiated Corporation Action

Leon Howard Sullivan (1922–2001) was an African American child born October 16, 1922, into poverty in segregated Charleston, West Virginia. He experienced racism and segregation, recalling that he first vowed at age 12 that he would fight it. He grew to six feet, five inches tall and became an athlete, a basketball and football player in his segregated high school, winning an athletic scholarship in 1939 to West Virginia State College, where an injury ended his athletic career, and he worked to pay for the rest of his education. He became a Baptist minister at age 18.[3]

Leon Sullivan went on to change the world. He moved to New York City, earning degrees in religious studies from Union Theological Seminary and then Columbia University, finally earning a position as the minister of a large Baptist church in Philadelphia, where, perhaps inspired by the success of the Montgomery Bus Boycott in 1955–1956, he launched his own creatively different boycott of large corporations that refused to hire African Americans. His slogan was "Don't buy where you don't work," and this effort was so successful in Philadelphia that, Sullivan estimated, blacks garnered thousands of jobs as a result.

Sullivan went on to become the first African American to join the board of a major American corporation, General Motors, in 1971, and used his corporate connections to develop and implement his Sullivan's Principles beginning in 1977, a set of guidelines to help corporations join in an economic boycott of South Africa under apartheid. Sullivan approached corporations one by one, convincing them to join in this effort, and this became one of the powerful ancillary measures pressuring the business community of apartheid South Africa to defect from the ideological supporters of apartheid. By themselves, the Sullivan Principles could not have accomplished much, but joined with black South African boycotts of white businesses under apartheid, and with the transnational campaign to divest from South Africa, the full complement drove a wedge that flipped the usual model of "divide and conquer" from the top-down to bottom-up. The success of the Sullivan Principles then led to the development of the Global Sullivan Principles for Social Responsibility, introduced by the secretary-general of the United Nations to the UN in a ceremony on 2 November 1999 (Stewart, 2011). Other cases demonstrated that tactic, a logical product of a strategic nonviolent approach; for example, in 1960 in Nashville, Tennessee, the "Sit-in Kids" started desegregating lunch counters and, after the African American community began to feel support for those clean-cut college kids, the campaign began a boycott of white downtown businesses that accomplished the same goal—the ideologues—the fanatical racists—were separated from the business community, who were hurt by the boycott and just wanted to get back to business as usual (DuVall, 2007).

While this is a voluntary corporate code of conduct, and while only a very small number of multinationals signed on, and while some argue that the empirical value of the Global Principles is quite limited (e.g., Seidman, 2003), the case study offers hope to civil society wishing to develop and deploy more vectors of nonviolent force on potential invader and occupier nations. An expanded or parallel set of corporate conduct principles might explicitly sanction governments that invade or occupy—or they may even declare that profiteering from war or the threat of war is unethical and might prompt future sanctions. Other civil society instruments of convincing corporations to act in opposition to invasion or occupation are also possible.

Periodically boycott, divestment, and sanctions (BDS) actions garner global attention. From the Montgomery Bus Boycott to the boycott of South Africa to the various boycotts of corporations doing business in Burma (Myanmar) to the boycott of Israeli corporations or corporations tied to the Israeli occupation of Palestinian territories, the BDS instrument is a no-risk nonviolent tactic and can have great rewards for those seeking social change. There are various levels to all these BDS tactics and, to be clear, each must be well designed to have a nonviolent effect. From the killer sanctions in Iraq in the 1990s to a boycott of businesses owned by specific religious or ethnic groups, BDS may be contributing to structural violence that results in actual mortalities, or BDS can be a winning and completely nonviolent tactic.

Only a nation-state or group of nation-states can implement formal sanctions. Some subnational governments (states, provinces, tribes, counties or parishes, cities, towns and villages) can effect boycotts and divestment, and many civil society organizations and certainly individuals in or out of association with others can also use boycott and divestment. When BDS is done well it can be far more forceful than military threat under many circumstances and can clearly be employed when a military threat is impossible or flatly illogical. The United States is simply not going to attack Israel for their human rights abuses.

But the full range of potential BDS brought to bear upon Israel would radically alter that nation-state's behavior. Without U.S. backing, Israel simply could not act with impunity; they would have to become much better neighbors in the Middle East. This is why any form of BDS targeting Israel's conduct is met with fury by those who are convinced that only a U.S.–backed Israel can survive. Even a minor BDS gesture precipitates a major controversy, as evident when, in 2010, the student government at UC-Berkeley debated a boycott and divestment resolution. The frames of the debate from the opposing sides were cast in dire, existential terms, each claiming the moral, ethical, peace-loving high ground (Hallward & Shaver, 2012). Hundreds were in attendance, and media covered it nationally and internationally. The tempest almost cracked the teapot. Israelis harken back to the European Holocaust, which was not executed by Palestinians nor anyone else in the Middle East, weakening their arguments in the eyes of much of the world, and Palestinians and their allies talk and write in hyperbolic terms, comparing Israel to Nazi Germany or claiming that their occupation is so bad it should not even be called a military occupation (see Abed, 2007). This "oppression Olympics" may give a few sound bites to the convinced, but generally will alienate those who honestly seek solid information.

Possibly the most ruthless extractive industry operating today is the oil business. How, then, can it be convinced to assist in the slow transformation of an armed conflict into a nonviolent struggle? How can the oil business become a partner in the transformation from a costly "diversity of tactics" to a diversity of people that can counter a regime that has been able to use the armed opposition to garner international help, defuse domestic opposition, and stay one step ahead of all challengers? Some of the elements of this transformation and the regime's threatened adaptability are evident in Sudan's weakening Omar Hassan al-Bashar–led National Congress Party teetering government. Key activists in Khartoum say further slippage of the economy will make the regime—in power since its 1989 takeover—topple. Key to all remaining economic power is the oil revenue (Rosen, 2012).

Identifying the oil corporations profiting from Sudan and targeting those companies for conditional costs could put reform pressures on al-Bashar. Enlisting support from a broad coalition of governmental and nongovernmental sources to pressure the industry to, in turn, pressure the ruling NCP via a corporate sanctions effort would be a game changer. And it may be simpler and more possible to target one regime than to attempt to create a universal principle that the oil corporations are expected to follow, however ideal that would be. The al-Bashar regime has shape-shifted as necessary from its roots as a revolutionary Islamicist vanguard to a reactionary survivalist regime willing to aid its control of its vast security apparatus by massive deflection of its revenue—as high as 88 percent of its government spending—to its patronage-driven system of state terror. In the case of Sudan, the civil societies most able to have an effect on its oil revenues would be Chinese and Malaysians. This is because "the country's oil industry is a foreign project, largely owned and operated by China's national oil company and Petronas, the Malaysian energy giant."[4] If Chinese or Malaysian civil society could organize a strong campaign, they could achieve nonviolently what the Israeli government, with its bombing attack in October 2012, and the long civil war in Sudan failed to do—bring down an entrenched and highly adaptive dictator via actions taken by oil corporations. This would be historic and is only impossible until it happens.

At times the likelihood of flipping the "divide and conquer" paradigm is scant. Analyst Stephen Zunes notes, for example, that, "unlike Tunisia and Egypt, where the opposition was relatively united and was able to take advantage of divisions within the ruling circles, the elites in Syria have been united against a divided opposition" (2012, p. 21).[5] Understanding this, the civil society movement might have sought to focus on coalitional development and then noncoercive inducements, rather than simple street demonstrations against a regime with a legacy of brutality more pronounced than any other in the region.

The Ultimate Challenge: How About Those Nazis?

The notion that nonviolence is the best way to resist occupation is frequently countered by the Hitler shibboleth, What about the Nazis? In truth, nonviolent resistance was quite possible against the Nazi occupation forces, even in the "Fatherland," although it was radically counterintuitive and remains so. Still, examples show that when it was tried and when nonviolence was not besmirched by violent elements or violent identification, it generally succeeded against Nazis and their surrogates. From Ackerman and DuVall (2000, p. 3):

> Danish citizens during the German occupation in World War II refused to aid the Nazi war effort and brought their cities to a standstill in the summer of 1944, forcing the Germans to end curfews and blockades; other European peoples under Nazi domination resisted nonviolently as well.

Danes tried sabotage and work slowdowns and limited stoppages and strikes. They developed underground leadership that had great authority and eventually decided that the work stoppages achieved more benefit with fewer costs than any other tactic.

The Soviets offered nothing but violent resistance and lost more than 14 percent of their entire population, even though they never lost their government. Norwegians mostly offered nonviolent resistance, lost their government and lost 3.2 percent—that is, for every thousand Soviets alive in 1939, 140 were killed in the war. For every thousand Norwegians alive in 1939, 32 were killed. Raw numbers are ghastly: 23,954,000 Soviets and 9,500 Norwegians.

Norwegian religious leadership was supplanted by the Nazi puppet regime of Vidkun Quisling, eponymous with traitor ever since. The Norwegian religious leaders treated the Nazis and quislings with civility and civil disobedience, simply ignoring Nazi ecclesiastic leaders.

In his famous disastrous "advice" to European Jews, Gandhi reckoned they should commit suicide until Hitler stopping killing them. Never was there better reason to avoid mere hagiography; Gandhi was simply out of his depth in this matter, and every Jew in Europe knew it. But he was correct in thinking that nonviolence could have brought down Hitler with far fewer casualties (Gan & DuVall, n.d.). Jews, Gypsies, communists and others, joined in nonviolent resistance, could have won the hearts and minds of civil society everywhere. Instead, they allowed themselves to be slaughtered, waiting in vain for some sort of deus ex machina, some cavalry to ride over the hill, and it did not for years. These victims could have banded together and stood a far greater chance for survival using strategic nonviolence, but they did not yet understand it. Nonviolence insists in some cases that success depends on replacing many old paradigms, not just reliance on violence. Ideologies are rendered less and less important, superseded by choice of—and commitment to—a different method of conflict management that eschews violence. Failure to let the old divisions drop away can mean failure overall, as Glynn (2012) describes in her exegesis of a case study of leftists attempting to form an operating coalition with Muslims. If Marxists cannot abandon devotion to violence and secularism, and if Muslims cannot act in coalition with irreligious humanists, coalition is impossible—"stillborn"—and success is less likely.

Perduring Problems, Hypothetical Solutions: Ballots, Bullets, or Bodies

The world has known long and apparently endless occupations of someone's land by someone else. Some may never be solved. However, some have been. What are the lessons from those long conflicts and their eventual liberation? What can we learn about the restoration of sovereignty to previous inhabitants? When nonviolence has been the method of struggle, what can conflict forensics teach, even if the struggles have not succeeded? This book will end with a look at examples from the histories of occupations and nonviolent struggles against them and attempt to apply lessons to creating hypothetical solutions to select struggles that continue against ongoing occupations that have persisted despite efforts to evict the occupiers. In the end, it's all people power, whether that comes from ballots in democracy, bullets in an armed contest, or bodies in a nonviolent struggle. Unlike the other methods, nonviolence can be practiced by everyone, not just those who qualify to vote or who carry a gun. As theorist, trainer, and historically important James Lawson simply notes, "Everyone can do the work."[6]

Tibet

China won and lost Tibet over the millennia and has occupied that nation since 1959. During the ensuing years, Tibetans have used both violence and nonviolence to resist the occupation. Most notably, the Dalai Lama has gathered world support for Tibet's liberation. He has always advocated nonviolence, which has made it appear that the struggle is entirely nonviolent to the casual observer, including many journalists, but the relationship between Tibet and China is not based on that false image; indeed, China portrays Tibetan violence as terrorism from separatists who want to make a legitimate Chinese province a separate nation. China has used the settler model—import citizens from the mother country to settle in the occupied land—in order to create an image of a legitimate Chinese province and to give great numbers of Chinese people "skin in the game," so that many Chinese know or are related to someone who lives in Tibet under the rubric of living in a province of China, however remote. Time is not a friend to Tibetans as Chinese settlers now are in equal numbers in Lhasa, the capital, and increasing in other areas as well. Tibetans struggle to keep hopeful, and still mourn the 1 million or more lives lost to the invading Chinese "Peoples Liberation Army," lives lost by violence (Houston & Wright, 2003). No one has determined how many Tibetan lives were lost to disease and starvation when infrastructure was destroyed by the Chinese.

Could the transnational community offer sufficient help to Tibetans to regain sovereignty, or at least achieve what the Dalai Llama calls the Middle Way, in which Chinese are in charge of foreign policy and defense and Tibet is otherwise autonomous? It is certainly possible, but would require a massive, sustained, and strategic commitment. The backbone would likely be boycott. If enough people globally refused to buy anything made in China until Tibet was free, China would likely open negotiations. This is the mixed blessing of China's dramatic success in the global markets in recent times; China is now, finally, susceptible to external pressure to behave better or lose markets. That will not happen, in all likelihood, until civil society worldwide agrees and seriously undertakes a sustained boycott. If that doesn't happen, the other nonviolent options are limited. Unless there is a seriously organized campaign, one that has cracked the media code and has the resources to engage globally in many languages, a conditional and effective boycott against China is fantasy.

The Tibetans have retained a government-in-exile for decades, led for many years by the Dalai Lama, now with a more active administration of others. The head of the Tibetan administration in exile, the Kalon Tripa, Lobsang Sangay, carries on this work. On April 2, 2012, he met with former Japanese Prime Ministers Shinzo Abe and Taro Aso, as well as with two former government ministers and the Tokyo mayor Shintaro Ishihara. The results of the meeting included a statement from the Japanese expressing solidarity with the Tibetans in exile (News in brief, 2012). These sorts of statements are of value in and of themselves, with moral force delegitimizing the Chinese occupation, but that value only affects the liberation struggle if used to help generate additional sanctions that can add to the Chinese calculus of the occupation. Enough sanctions applied properly, along with enough inducements promised or unilaterally given in support of Tibetan sovereignty, will end that occupation.

The reason the world has such a profound and crucial role to play is that Tibet is small compared to China, settlers now regard Tibet as their land and there are many of them, and the citizens of China have been given information that bolsters the idea that Tibet is legitimately part of China. Efforts to sanction China need ongoing strategic outreach to Tibetans living in Tibet to encourage them to use nonviolent resistance exclusively, outreach to Chinese citizens to provide countervailing information on the illegitimacy of Chinese occupation, and outreach to the world to encourage compliance with an increasingly tough regime of sanctions on China until Tibet is once again sovereign.

Transnational Forces for Nonviolence

Much is made of the transnational terrorism based on Islamic fundamentalism; indeed, that was the genesis of al-Qa'ida, the transnational members of the mujahedeen who travelled to Afghanistan during the 1980s to battle the occupying Soviet forces, both military and civil functionaries (and helping to explain the al-Qa'ida adoption of the nearly von Clausewitzian notion of total war against all occupying forces, whether overtly military or civilian, still regarded as occupiers). Other transnational identity groups fall on the other side, the side of nonviolent conflict management; certainly humanitarian organizations have impacted the abilities of indigenous populations in some regions to build adaptive strategies for bolstering democracy-capacity building and strategies for navigating elite power structures. Other transnational identity groups promote nonviolence even more directly; Quakers, Mennonites and other peace churches operate at many levels in civil society and in supranational organizations such as the UN and UNESCO. Women, and in particular feminists of various sorts, are a transnational force for peace in an international elite phallocratic environment (Cockburn, 2010).

Gender and Feminism

> By understanding political opportunity structures as being bound by cultural norms that create distinct sets of opportunities and constraints for different groups of people, scholars can better understand the particular manifestation of social movement action and thereby more fully account for human agency in social and political structures.
> —Rachel V. Kutz-Flamenbaum (2012, p. 293)

In one study comparing U.S. college students' attitudes to Iranian college students' attitudes, Saba Torabian and Marina Abalakina (2012) found that, unsurprisingly, those who were male, authoritarian, religious, and had never experienced war (no matter which country they were from) tended to have a much more positive attitude toward war. While some of these characteristics are environmental and only one is biological, one might suggest that we need to find solutions that involve creativity and imagination rather than waiting for all humans to have experienced war in order to formulate a negative impression of it. One presumed challenge then is to get religious males who have never experienced war to think about changing their authoritarian attitudes and their positive impressions about war, using their own imaginations instead of waiting to actually experience the violence and chaos of war. Women in general, peace activists and feminists in particular, might explore their own creativity in searching for these routes to helping religious males.

While there are organized, transnational, feminist groups that work overtly to stop war, women also work invisibly to create the background conditions for a peace culture. Eleonora Barbieri Masini (2012) documents examples of that work, often done in individual families, in communities, and only with the most bare notion that women are doing this around the world. Rape and honor killings were commonplace and scarcely remarked upon in the mainstream media in India, though women were building a potential movement under the mainstream media radar—not because they were intentionally stealthy, but because women were not the story, women were quotidian victims, women had no power. However, women reached a point in India where they had enough of this power to say "Enough" to a nation where women had been oppressed and violated (Borpujari, 2013). Women—so often so involved in nonviolent civil society struggles since the earliest campaigns Gandhi organized in South Africa—have learned to access different power for themselves, nonhegemonic civil society power, and are challenging gender violence in India and in far tougher environments in places where the law doesn't merely ignore women, it actively, openly, structurally victimizes them, as in areas of Shari'a law that strips women of most human rights. From Afghanistan to Iran and other societies overtly biased against women and permissive of male violence against women, women are courageously contesting civic space (Beyerle, 2008). Violence and war are seen as strong power; nonviolence and peace are seen as weak, but women show instances of redefining power and strength (Dumont, 2013; Palmer-Mehta, 2009). And while support from outside is sometimes helpful, indigenous women will gain their own rights or those rights will be resented, painted as a foreign imposition, and therefore precarious. Moroccan women are exemplars of rights won using judicious nongovernmental outsider support but acting independently and speaking for themselves, earning their own rights in 2004, a precursor, possibly, to the frequent and high-priority women's rights goals almost invariably included by women in every Arab Spring struggle, noted human rights worker Nouzha Guessous (2012). In a globalized world, it is unlikely that wired-in women will forever suffer under the barbarism of seventh-century Islamic *Fiqh,* or Family Law, so disadvantageous to women in particular and more than tolerant of practices humankind is overcoming, discarding, and evolving past. In Morocco, as an example, even in comparison to 1960, when women married at 17, bore seven children, and were usually illiterate, now Moroccan women marry at 27, have two children, and are 52 percent of graduate students—of course they will rise up, however gently but firmly, and they have gained many more rights (Guessous, 2012).

In a study of several transnational feminist-identified peace groups and networks, including Women in Black, Code Pink, Women's International League for Peace and Freedom, and Women's Network Against Militarism, sociologist Cynthia Cockburn traveled to several countries on four continents to interview and observe these women as they worked to stop invasions and end occupations. Her conclusion was that peace and antiwar movements in general needed to consider stronger adoption of feminist values, rhetoric, processes and practices in order to present stronger visions of distinctly different futures and methods of conflict management at every level, that is, the braided pathways to a better, more democratic, and more peaceful day ahead. Cockburn also concludes that any narrow view of war and women, or any simplistic understanding of causal factors in precipitating war or producing peace, would be inadequate and that problematizing war means locating it as an outcome of an entire systemic myriad of forces, of subsystems and innumerable variables. This systemic approach to also feminizing potential solutions is an invitation to map militarism and consider the illimitable intersections and flows of force.

As Rachel V. Kutz-Flamenbaum (2012) argues in her study of an Israeli women's peace group, Machsom Watch, feminizing potential solutions is indeed idiosyncratic to each instance and means culturally mapping conflict in order to see the relative feminizing aspects. In her specific study, the Israeli women used the hegemonic gender norms of Israeli society to more boldly challenge threats to peace and justice at various checkpoints along the Israel-Palestine security borders. Like any effective political effort to effect policy change, that women's peace group must understand the political opportunity structures (POS), that is, the matrix of cultural and event factors that open or shut doors to change. Kutz-Flamenbaum found that the women in Machsom Watch indeed harnessed gendered attitudes, proscriptions and permissions, intentionally, using that detailed contextual information to negotiate risk and opportunity.

The women from Machsom Watch conducted observations at security checkpoints where frequent violations of civil and human rights occur. They gathered evidence and used it to "name and shame" such conduct, almost invariably done to Palestinians by Israeli Defense Force squads. The women explicitly formed as women-only in order to exploit their relative immunity from direct harm as a special group of all women, mostly Ashkenazi, mostly more than 50 years old. Each of those identity elements offered some cultural protection, enabling the women to push further than, for example, a young Palestinian man could push, or even a young Sephardic Israeli man. Machsom Watch acknowledges that their effectiveness as an all-women's group was anticipated not only because of the behaviors predicted of IDF members, but also the predictable behaviors of male activists, who might escalate conflict and provide an excuse to dismiss the group as just another fighter contingent in a fighter-rich environment.

The women reported misbehaviors as widely as possible, to the public and to policymakers. In the 950 cases Kutz-Flamenbaum analyzed, she found the norms were renegotiated situationally and over time, at times slipping and either blunting the effectiveness of the women or exposing them to greater risk, or both. The cultural antennae of each member of each group taking the field on each day are crucial to shaping actions to minimize costs and maximize benefits toward the policy change desired. Assumptions can create opportunities and can create danger. Course correction can connect culturally informed actors to sustainable success and ongoing adjustments in image to remain positive and effective. For instance, the Iranian women, who suffered violent repression following the 2005 election of Mahmoud Ahmadinijad, reassessed their movement and realized its image was that of a small group of disaffected privileged women from Teheran. They strategized how to correct that image and recruit from grassroots across the country much more effectively (Beyerle, 2008).

Can efforts to end invasions and occupations benefit from the lessons of the 1935 Swedish Win Without War campaign that prominently featured the 20,000-strong Women's Unarmed Uprising Against War? That campaign was the major flowering of a Swedish women's peace movement that had been one of the last to develop in Europe (only earlier in the entire list of European countries than Turkey) (Andersson, 2003). Indeed, while small numbers of men started European and then North American peace associations as early as 1815 (Shifferd, 2011), women's organizations often grew much larger much faster and more radically pacifist once they began. Amongst the many possible lessons we might draw from this campaign in Sweden and the history of development of women's peace associations elsewhere is that women are sometimes preparing for peace in ways that permit a quick and committed mobilization even though there is little or no visible sign of that in the period leading up to it. Looking for other correlatives might help peace movements expand much more effectively, and seeking coalition with organized groups of women might also contribute to a rapid mobilization of a forceful movement to stop war.

Clearly, the effectiveness of all-women's organizations can be quite powerful, even—or perhaps especially—in patriarchal, militaristic societies that tend to view women's motivations as apolitical and therefore inconsequential enough to permit to a degree. Those women's organizations may not pass muster as feminist groups to privileged self-identified feminist analysts, but when these women can effect political change by utilizing the worst patriarchal cultural assumptions to clear themselves a path forward, that is arguably one of the most salient feminist characteristics of those movements.

Food Justice and Sustainable Agriculture

The association between nonviolence and war prevention or war interruption is becoming more clear, and it is also becoming obvious that the way the world produces, trades, and consumes food is a contributory causal factor in war or peace. The wisdom on this is ancient and was formalized toward peace in our modern era by Mohandas Gandhi, who connected indigenous control over food and crop production to freedom, to the erosion of the foreign authority over his land, and to the sense of autonomy and egalitarian justice in his world of positive peace—peace and justice by peaceable means. His heirs have been practicing this in India ever since, and some places have continuously been producing food for local consumption under a philosophy of nonviolent liberation, making the connections that Gandhi made (Sanford, 2013).

In an era when climate chaos will cause massive numbers of internally displaced and even transnational refugees as the seas rise and storms worsen,

Gandhian nonviolence fits nicely into reduction of the carbon footprint of a people, preserving and sharing resources, and conflict reduction.

Mediation

As Dr. King wrote from a Birmingham jail, the purpose of direct action is to get to the negotiating table. Sometimes nonviolent direct action, a form of NCI, can impose costs at the same time that fears are lowered, an intersection of factors almost impossible if violence is used, and the dominant party—usually the state in some form, or a corporation—may actually seek direct negotiations, such as did in fact happen with Dr. King in Birmingham, Solidarity in Poland, the anti-apartheid coalition in South Africa, or many labor unions who strike against either a government or a corporation. At times, however, some factions of the resistance use violence and it is harder for the party in power to conceive of negotiations, fearing for their future, possibly even their lives. In these situations, certainly, a third-party neutral is the best option, and there are times, even, when the fear is so great that a single mediator cannot be found who is agreeable to all parties, usually because of fear of hidden—or even overtly projected—mediator agendas. Indeed, mediators have many personal choices as they enter the process and those choices will affect the content, process and outcomes of conflict management (Gould, 2013).

Hall & Yarhi-Milo (2012) suggest that understanding the various factors involved in the supply side (the mediators in a coalition of them working together on a particular case) and from the demand side (the various belligerent parties seeking some sort of outcome) is crucial to understanding probabilities of success of particular practices and configurations of coalitions of mediators. The results of their quantitative study of examples from 1950–2000 conclude that single-party mediation is significantly different from multiparty mediation (that is, a coalition of mediators acting as a team). They found the multiparty mediations often carried a stronger image of legitimacy, which is more likely to produce sustainable agreements. On the other hand, they also concluded that under some circumstances, multiparty mediation can make some parties appear to be negotiating from a position of weakness and may thus affect outcomes or the sustainability of any agreement reached.

Always in the consideration of mediation or negotiation is the best alternative to a negotiated agreement (BATNA) and the transparency factors. In other words, are credible costs projected into the talks? If a nonviolent campaign openly contemplates a boycott that would significantly redound upon the powerful party, is that a credible threat? Can it be framed as a more natural outcome rather than a pugnacious threat? Is it actually deliverable? Framing the BATNA can produce eagerness to settle or resolve to continue the destructive conflict, and is a nuanced, culturally challenging factor.

Filson and Werner (2002) address the opacity problem—the failure to reveal private information, and how that might affect the outbreak or outcome of war. Withholding information about one's strengths is a poker strategy, and it may be valuable in some of the imperial projects that have been dedicated to inflicting injustice, but it may be the worst strategy for a ruler who wishes to avoid blundering into a costly or even regime-threatening war. Knowing the worst that an opponent can do may promote the peace of deterrence. The ultimate fictitious exemplar of this comes in the film *Dr. Strangelove*, when the Americans launch some bombs against the Russians and the Russian diplomat tells them that their strikes will trigger the new Soviet bomb that will end life on Earth. The U.S. officials scream, "When were you going to tell us this?!" In other words, withholding this private information has just sealed our doom. This also applies to nonviolence in real life (possibly somewhat less dramatically, certainly less existentially), as when A. Phillip Randolph told then–President Franklin Roosevelt, upon determining that the United States would be entering war against Germany and would thus be spending enormous sums on armaments and creating enormous numbers of jobs, that Roosevelt had better produce jobs for African Americans or face a "thunderous march" on Washington. Roosevelt did, in fact, sign an order stipulating that federal contracts could only go to contractors who did not practice racial bias in hiring. Randolph's march was postponed until August of 1963. Nonviolent deterrence can also work. Indeed, "As an act conducted in the hope of stopping an anticipated act of aggression, accompaniment represents a form of deterrence" (Miller & King, 2005).

Research examining mediator characteristics as they relate to appeal and success show that perceived neutrality is attractive but bias tends to produce agreements—even though those agreements may or may not be sustainable. Thus bias in a mediator lends certain credibility (Crescenzi, Kadera, Mitchell & Thyne, 2011). The fundamental problem with "mediators" is that they are often not true mediators, and the ultimate misuse of that term is the so-called "mediation with muscle" approach of the mediator who is actually an armed party simply facilitating an outcome that is in part forced by his armed might. Sometimes this works to produce a long-standing agreement that undermines other parties in other conflicts, e.g., the 1978 Camp David Accords between Israel and Egypt that, in truth, produced more problems for the Palestinians, since on both sides of the equation the United States—the "mediator"—agreed to supply arms and training to both parties, effectively ghettoizing Palestinians. Mediators who supply arms can simply never be honest brokers of peace. This was seen again in the Balkans in the 1990s, when the Holbrooke-Talbot team from the United States ordered everyone to the table and then waged war when the talks didn't turn out correctly. This gives mediation a bad name.

The U.S. role in the Middle East is indeed frequently responsible for failure and rarely actually responsible for any success, despite the seemingly beneficent role of the Clinton administration in the 1993 Oslo Accords, which were actually negotiated successfully despite the Americans, not because of them, the famous South Lawn of the White House ceremony notwithstanding. And the U.S. role in the failure to gain a peace treaty between Syria and Israel despite a decade of negotiations was significant, if not key (Pressman, 2007). The Israel bias is so strong from U.S. officials that it is a hindrance for U.S. mediators to be involved, and the role of the U.S. government in approving the seemingly infinite arms transfers into the region militates strongly against the notion of the United States as an honest broker of peace there. The power that is pumping gasoline on the fire is not the power that is putting out the fire.

Hansen (2012) suggests that sequencing mediators or conducting parallel mediations to take advantage of the strengths and overcome the weaknesses of particular mediators can work well, and he brings the evidence of successful interstate and intrastate mediated peace accords to illustrate this notion. He also cites examples that are caveats for multiparty mediations that are not coordinated, referring to "forum shopping" (the parties going from mediator to mediator seeking the best dealmaker for them), "cherry picking" moments of advantage, willful misinterpretation of communications, and other problems of mediator competition, a truly sad and unnecessary problem.

While any particular mediator and mediation is a complex of factors that cannot be neatly categorized in their entirety, it is wise to understand the basic difference between the structuralist mediators—those who view mediation as little more than an exploration and negotiation of costs and benefits into tidy rational components of endgame agreements—and the social-psychological unpacking and development/repair of the superordinate values, meta-communication and the relationships. Both are vital.

Boycotts can be a broad tool where a focused instrument might be more appropriate. So, for instance, there has been a debate surrounding the question of whether to engage in an academic boycott of Israel as a protest of their occupation of West Bank and their oppression of Palestinians in Gaza. Arguments are made in favor that stress the potential effectiveness of such a boycott in affecting Israeli policy (Abed, 2007) and against such a boycott as potentially injurious to the Israeli peace academics (Nussbaum, 2007). It is difficult to imagine the ethical strength of such a boycott when the net is wide enough to include some of the foremost peace researchers alive (e.g., Daniel Bar-Tal) while there is no concomitant academic boycott on scholars from China (in protest of that country's far more brutal occupation of Tibet, at least from the perspective of killings), nor even an academic boycott of Sudan in the environment of genocidal practices in Darfur. And a boycott of Israeli scholars would almost certainly not be honored by the U.S. government nor by U.S. multinational corporations, thus immunizing the Israeli weapons researchers who would be the nominal target of such a boycott. The American Friends Service Committee, or the Peace and Justice Studies Association are going to boycott the Israeli peace intellectuals? That seems a pity, especially since the AFSC or PJSA boycott of the Israeli weaponeer academics with whom they normally engage is a null set.

Boycott, like any other tool in our nonviolent social change kit, is neutral; the context and motivation of its use is what defines it. For instance, when the Chinese staged the Olympic Torch run leading into the opening of the 2008 Beijing Olympics, they mobilized extraordinarily nationalistic Chinese in diaspora to show rampant enthusiasm as the torch made its way toward China. And when it was rumored that the French corporation Carrefour was underwriting the Dalai Lama, angry demonstrations erupted outside Carrefour stores with a corresponding boycott. Carrefour rolled over quickly to proclaim its support for the Beijing Olympics (Ayson & Taylor, 2008). The occupying nation can learn to use civil society to counter civil society pressures and effectively neutralize the striving for justice, for liberation, and for indigenous sovereignty; China's occupation of Tibet is one of the toughest challenges to any nonviolent movement. The only possible less effective methods than nonviolence in opposition to the undemocratic behemoth taking over a much smaller neighbor would be, a) violence, and b) apathy. China's massive global economic power, however, has the seeds of its vulnerability planted in its people's growing fondness for material possessions. With material success come new needs, higher expectations, and a new vulnerability to transnational economic pressures. China and its people would alter behavior in response to serious, committed, sustained transnational boycott. The history of civil society using economic boycott to reveal and exploit previously hidden cracks in the monolith of the ruling elite demonstrates a reversal of the divide and conquer strategy so effective for so long against civil society. In South Africa, the ideological racialists of apartheid rulers were separated from the realpolitik of the business class via the effective boycott of that ruling elite. The white businessmen finally removed the white supremacists from power and installed de Klerk, whose pragmatist approach saved the whites from slaughter and allowed the end of apartheid without the "inevitable" bloodbath. Similarly, in Montgomery, Alabama, in 1955–56, the boycott eventually helped the business community decide to end crippling segregation and, five years later, the same phenomenon helped the Nashville, Tennessee, freedom movement separate the white racists from practical businessmen who wanted an end to the boycott begun in support of the sit-in kids. So boycotts, designed well to account for circumstances, can bring justice and liberation where there was little—or they can reinforce inequality and subjugation when wielded cynically by oppressors.

One form of mediation is that generally negotiated by lawyers, Alternative Dispute Resolution (ADR). The reason this is normally the province of lawyers is that, unlike transactional bargaining—what mediation usually involves, bargaining without constant reference to what the law requires—dispute bargaining is a negotiation and fact-finding process that focuses on what the parties are required to do by the extant laws (Condlin, 2011). While it is helpful to make these distinctions, it is also crucial that any mediated agreement be legal. Getting all the stakeholders to the table, facilitating them along toward a beautiful agreement that breaks through all the grievances and brings in a win for all parties is an art—but is also utterly useless and dysfunctional if this agreement isn't legal. The law is both BATNA and boundary for successful mediation and ADR.

Conclusion: Nonviolence Is the Better Mousetrap

While ending war on Earth is not simple, nor easy, humankind has done a remarkable job of radically reducing international war and can potentially do just as remarkably at stopping civil war, invasion, and occupation. After all, we can note the obvious truth in Kenneth Boulding's so-called "First Law" ("Anything that exists is possible") (Evans Pim, 2010), and enjoy the perspective of most societies being at peace most of the time. While it is impossible to prove a negative, it is logical to assert that this has already happened in the Philippines, possibly in Zambia, probably in Serbia, potentially in Egypt, and remotely possibly in Tunisia, in Ghana, or in some of the Velvet Revolution or Colored Revolution countries—indeed, anywhere that there has been an overthrow or ouster of an autocratic regime is quite likely what happened instead of civil war. That used to be a small number; the number is arguably quite large and growing. The variables are nearly infinite, and the pressures toward war are sometimes apparently insurmountable, but with steady development of structural nonviolence—the fairness of institutions, the capacity of nonviolent forces to de-escalate, and the disarmament of both civil society and governments—we can produce moments, then months, and finally entire years or even decades without war on Earth. The erosion of the pillars of support for war is highly important work, and just as important are the design and construction of the pillars for a structural nonviolent world, one society at a time. Humans are hard-wired for war and peace, love and hate, violence and nonviolence, routine and creativity—no species ever on Earth has been given such a broad palette of choice. Saying we had no choice is never true; humankind is always at a crossroads and always on the move. Our creativity is as infinite as our capacity for self-destruction.

Human agency is a function of hope. Elites have always had hope; we are entering the era of hope for all of humanity. This is what will give us the edge and the resilience to achieve a stable peace on our lovely planet, reified for each of us, some argue, by the extent to which we seek and find an integrative approach, an integrative nature, and an integrative identity (Hiller & Vela, 2013; Van Hook, 2013). And this search for an end to civil wars, invasions, and occupations will not likely succeed based on a religion or even a philosophy; unless by that we mean an

> open-ended generative systems approach [that] appeals to infinite human creativity and variability, encouraging continuous explorations in the fields of education, research, social action and policy making, by developing a broad range of scientific, institutional, educational, political, economic and spiritual alternatives to human killing [Evans Pim, 2009, p. 15].

Peace and justice advocates who win often generate the sense of hope and possibility first in themselves by their own study of what has happened elsewhere. Gandhi did this (Hastings, 2002; Fischer, 1982 [1954]; Schock, 2013), looking at the struggles in Czarist Russia in 1905, in Bengal in 1905, and reading Tolstoy, Ruskin, Thoreau and others to cross-fertilize his own thinking first. Knowledge production is critical to increasing the learning that can save us from starting all over each time and can tell us what might work in some form wherever we are. The research is under way. Karatnycky and Ackerman (2005) noted that in 50 of the 67 regime changes they studied in the previous 35 years, nonviolent people power was the decisive factor and primary method. Merriman and DuVall (2007) describe this superior product and note that addressing this demand for most effective conflict management model can result in the demand for terrorism drying up—dissolving at the roots. The same will be true for rational choice insurgency, as clearly proven by Chenoweth and Stephan (2011). The better mousetrap is available and the world has noticed. Nonviolence, solar panels, electric cars, organic food, civil discourse—we have the brightness of the future proven and on the shelf. All the "new" products have old, old roots in fertile soil. Let's get some sun and water to those roots.

Notes

Preface

1. In a sort of throwback policy, Syrian males under 42 and in diaspora may purchase exemption from compulsory military service, if they've been living abroad for at least 11 years. The cost is $8,000 (approximately) unless they emigrated at younger than 12 years of age, in which case it is $3,000 (Beitin, 2012).

2. http://www.washingtonpost.com/world/national-security/for-mitt-romney-a-bigger-military-but-at-what-price/2012/10/29/877daa78-1ec1-11e2-9746-908f727990d8_story.html?wpisrc=nl_headlines.

Section I

1. http://www.aeinstein.org/selflib/Social_Power_excerpts_for_Self_Lib.pdf.

2. For example, see Jackson Diehl (Bacevich, et al., 2013, in the section authored by Diehl). Diehl uses the surge as a reason the United States should invade Syria, not accounting for the ongoing destruction in both places the United States has wasted lives and $billions on surges, Iraq and Afghanistan.

Part 1

1. Quoted in Bacevich et al. (2013) in the section authored by the editors.

2. There are two lists; the 10 wars are those with more than 1,000 battlefield deaths in 2012. Many more conflicts have produced fewer deaths but are unresolved. http://en.wikipedia.org/wiki/List_of_ongoing_military_conflicts.

3. http://www.nonviolent-conflict.org/images/stories/pdfs/defyingviolencewithdemocracy.pdf.

4. David Ignatius, *Washington Post* supporter of the U.S. invasion of Iraq in 2003, acknowledged his failures in one 2013 column and called President Obama's support for armed rebellion in Syria realism in another, subsequent column. http://www.washingtonpost.com/opinions/david-ignatius-obamas-pragmatic-approach-to-mideast/2013/03/27/80d1bbd2-96fe-11e2-814b-063623d80a60_story.html?wpisrc=nl_headlines.

5. Many stories of Syrian rebel atrocities are to be found, e.g., Barnard (8 November 2012) file:///C:/Writing2013/Background/In%20Syria,%20Missteps%20by%20Rebels%20Erode%20Their%20Support%20-%20NYTimes.com.htm.

6. A mixed but decidedly multilateral approach is advocated by the R2P Coalition, http://www.responsibilitytoprotect.org/.

7. From a report on National Public Radio, 4 March 2013, http://www.npr.org/2013/03/04/173442174/conscience-of-syrian-revolution-faces-challenge-from-islamists.

8. Indeed, say insiders in Syria, most of Bashar al–Assad's advisors are old line and hard line, remnants of his strongman father's regime, who warn him that he looks soft—his receding chin is weak-looking, his profession is ophthalmology, and so he is seen

as a gentle doctor and not a military defender of the state of Syria, and his personality was always shy and beta-male behind his "swaggering" older brother, who was the heir apparent to Hafiz al–Assad until he crashed his sports car and pushed Bashar into the inner circle. http://www.nytimes.com/2012/12/25/world/middleeast/no-easy-route-if-bashar-al-assad-opts-to-go-or-stay.html?pagewanted=all&_r=0.

9. Fawkes was discovered guarding 36 barrels of gunpowder, arrested, tried, hanged, drawn, and quartered along with several other "Jesuit Treason" plotters. http://en.wikipedia.org/wiki/Gunpowder_Plot.

10. Prospect theory was developed by Daniel Kahneman, who won a Nobel Prize in Economics for this decision-making science research. Most people have higher loss aversion than gain attraction, hence the decision to use nonviolence is easier than an "all-in" commitment to join a violent rebellion. http://en.wikipedia.org/wiki/Prospect_theory.

11. Take the quiz and think about reducing one or more of the variables in your life: http://www.footprintnetwork.org/en/index.php/GFN/page/calculators/.

12. More electrical efficiency can reduce coal and fracking pollution: http://www.nrdc.org/air/energy/genergy.asp.

13. http://en.wikipedia.org/wiki/Colombian_civil_war. The amount and stated reasons for the military aid to Colombia have shifted from leader to leader (U.S. leaders and Colombian leaders each affect it), and the alleged missions have related to civil war, a war on drugs, and a war on terror. Still, it's almost all military, benefitting U.S. military contracting corporations and particularly compliant individuals or factions in Colombia, much to the detriment of the people of both the United States (who pay in tax dollars) and the people of Colombia (who pay in blood).

14. http://www.newdimensions.org/program-archive/peaceful-warrior-with-robert-fuller/. Fuller has various podcasts and journalistic sources for his philosophy on peace by citizen diplomacy and sheer amount cross-border travel by many citizens. Fuller

called his initiative the Mo-Tzu project, after an ancient Chinese philosopher.

15. http://uscenterforcitizendiplomacy.org/. This is a newer coalition, dating to a founding conference in 2004 and associating more formally in 2006.

16. http://www.scotsman.com/news/scottish-independence-alex-salmond-given-to-end-of-2014-for-referendum-1-2576099.

17. In an effort to reconceptualize that set of disaster outcomes for Europe, many analysts are now calling for unilateral NATO nuclear disarmament without any treaty nor even expectation from Russia. Quite simply, the nuclear weapon only has strategic value if any society can justify incinerating millions of innocent people, and global social norms are increasingly declining that potential. See Yost, 2011. In a bid to get and maintain buy-in for a nuclear NATO, the United States arranged for other NATO national officers to control some nuclear weapons. This has been critiqued as similar to a crime boss insisting that multiple members of his crime syndicate participate in murder, in order to blunt the chances of defections.

18. Etzioni goes on to name particular leaders throughout the MENA who meet these criteria. http://stats.lib.pdx.edu/proxy.php?url=http://search.ebscohost.com/login.aspx?direct=true&db=a9h&AN=65165970&site=ehost-live.

19. http://www.nytimes.com/2012/10/15/world/middleeast/jihadists-receiving-most-arms-sent-to-syrian-rebels.html?nl=todaysheadlines&emc=edit_th_20121015.

20. http://www.foreignpolicy.com/articles/2012/10/10/holding_civil_society_workshops_while_syria_burns?page=0,0.

21. The HTML version available is unpaginated.

22. http://www.washingtonpost.com/world/national-security/on-benghazi-attack-angry-words-from-obama-and-republicans/2012/11/14/1483153e-2e94-11e2-beb2-4b4cf5087636_story.html?wpisrc=nl_headlines.

23. Syria is angry with all its neighbors, one permanently (Israel), the rest from time to time, and especially as all its neighbors

harbor refugees from the civil war there. U.S. military aid to a violent uprising is the most available conductor for the electricity of al–Assad anger. http://www.washingtonpost.com/world/world-digest-syrian-government-warns-jordan-over-aid-to-rebels/2013/04/04/8631e0de-9d34-11e2-a2db-efc5298a95e1_story.html?wpisrc=nl_headlines.

24. This treaty first requires ratification by 50 nations and then takes effect some three months later. http://www.washingtonpost.com/business/un-general-assembly-to-vote-tuesday-on-first-un-treaty-to-regulate-the-global-arms-trade/2013/04/02/eaa49ed0-9b5e-11e2-9219-51eb8387e8f1_story.html.

25. In the stew of refugees flowing out and foreign fighters pouring in, Assad is credible. http://www.nytimes.com/04/06/world/middleeast/un-says-aid-for-syria-refugees-is-running-out.html?nl=todaysheadlines&emc=edit_th_20130406&_r=0.

26. Israel will neither confirm nor deny, but it's almost a certain IDF signature strike. http://www.nytimes.com/2013/05/06/world/middleeast/after-strikes-in-syria-concerns-about-an-escalation-of-fighting.html?nl=todaysheadlines&emc=edit_th_20130506&_r=0.

27. http://www.fundforpeace.org/global/?q=fsi-grid2012.

28. Hezbollah loudly and persistently celebrated this as a great victory, never acknowledging how pyrrhic it was. http://en.wikipedia.org/wiki/Israel_Lebanon_conflict_of_2006.

29. Erick Torch, a member of the Balkan Peace Team in the 1990s, told this to a group of us standing in the snow around a bonfire behind my cabin by Lake Superior. Gallows humor, or black humor, is common in high stress and oppressed societies.

30. Janine di Giovanni is also a member of the Council on Foreign Relations. http://www.thedailybeast.com/newsweek/2013/03/11/syria-when-nonviolent-revolutions-spin-into-bloodshed.html.

31. Liel Leibowitz, media professor at New York University. http://www.theatlantic.com/magazine/archive/2012/03/the-revolutionist/308881/.

Part 2

1. http://www.nytimes.com/2012/10/20/world/middleeast/bomb-blast-in-beirut-lebanon.html?nl=todaysheadlines&emc=edit_th_20121020&_r=0.

2. The partisan sources are often quick to claim that any party with a different worldview is the party using violence. In the case of Syria, this is not difficult. http://www.globaltimes.cn/content/771732.shtml#.UVjUKaLm60c.

3. http://www.nytimes.com/2012/10/19/world/middleeast/horrific-bombing-in-northern-syria-kills-dozens.html?nl=todaysheadlines&emc=edit_th_20121019&_r=0.

4. Personal conversation with Soviet dissident, November 1984.

5. http://www.nimh.nih.gov/health/publications/the-numbers-count-mental-disorders-in-america/index.shtml. All mental health disorders together affect slightly more than one-quarter of all Americans; no comparable figures on all Lebanese, but depression alone is greater than all combined in the United States.

6. http://en.wikipedia.org/wiki/Truth_and_Reconciliation_Commission_%28Sierra_Leone%29.

7. http://en.wikiquote.org/wiki/Fran_Lebowitz.

8. China is vying to move Exxon out of some of the richest oil fields of Iraq and is claiming some 1.5 million barrels daily. Tim Arango & Clifford Krauss (2 June 2013), China is reaping biggest benefits of Iraq oil boom, http://www.nytimes.com/2013/06/03/world/middleeast/china-reaps-biggest-benefits-of-iraq-oil-boom.html?nl=todaysheadlines&emc=edit_th_20130603&_r=0. Wolfowitz was the first Bush high official to claim that the Iraqis would pay for the whole war with their oil. http://truth-out.org/opinion/item/16788-robert-scheer-china-benefits-from-bushs-folly.

9. http://www.nytimes.com/2012/10/18/world/americas/colombia-tries-again-to-end-drug-fed-war.html?_r=1&nl=todaysheadlines&emc=edit_th_20121018.

10. From an old television commercial. http://www.youtube.com/watch?v=u9o2I5Z0cpY.

11. http://www.ciponline.org/images/ uploads/publications/Hartung_IPR_0612_ NuclearLobbyReport_Final.pdf. William Hartung has produced decades of analysis of the Military Industrial Congressional Complex.

12. http://www.nytimes.com/2012/10/ 21/world/iran-said-ready-to-talk-to-us-about-nuclear-program.html?nl=todays headlines&emc=edit_th_20121021&_r= 0&pagewanted=all.

13. http://www.youtube.com/watch?v= ejvyDn1TPr8, Nixon on David Frost TV program, 20 May 1977.

14. http://en.wikipedia.org/wiki/ Police_use_of_firearms_in_the_United_ Kingdom.

Part 3

1. Ackerman and DuVall worked hard to make these methods known from their Washington, D.C.-based International Center on Nonviolent Conflict but that strategic plan was never tried in Arab lands until, arguably, Arab Spring. http://sojo.net/mag azine/2002/09/weapons-will.

2. http://www.williamgbecker.com/ veteransfast.html.

3. http://en.wikipedia.org/wiki/ Hijackers_in_the_September_11_attacks, 15 of the 19 terrorists were Saudi Arabian, others from Egypt and UAE.

4. http://en.wikipedia.org/wiki/ Ramzi_Ahmed_Yousef. The 1993 truck bombing of the World Trade Center was carried out by a Pakistani and a Jordanian.

5. Peter L. Bergen (2001), *Holy War, Inc., inside the secret world of Osama bin Laden*. New York: Free Press. Bin Laden claimed the Blackhawk attack in 1993 as a victory for al–Qa'ida, led by and committed by Somalis.

6. http://en.wikipedia.org/wiki/Abd_ al-Rahim_al-Nashiri. Likely USS *Cole* attackers were Saudi Arabian and Yemeni.

7. http://en.wikipedia.org/wiki/Ali_ Saed_Bin_Ali_El-Hoorie. The 1996 attack on the Khobar Towers was done by Saudi Arabians and one Lebanese participant.

8. http://en.wikipedia.org/wiki/1998_ United_States_embassy_bombings. The 1998 bombings of the U.S. embassies in Kenya and Tanzania were conducted by Egyptians and Saudi Arabians.

9. http://www.youtube.com/watch?v= 8y06NSBBRtY.

10. http://www.visionofhumanity.org/ info-center/violence-containment-images/; September 2012 special report.

11. The credulous reportage on so-called Iraqi intelligence sources was representative of this failure, as even the sources themselves have revealed ("Curveball," 2012).

12. This is not to impugn any particular journalist. David Ignatius was not the source of the lies that propped up the rationales or rhetorical falsehoods justifying the invasion of Iraq. He was one of many influential journalists who utterly failed to perform his job. http://www.washingtonpost.com/opin ions/david-ignatius-ten-years-later-recall ing-iraqs-hard-lessons/2013/03/20/5a05 890c-90d7-11e2-bdea-e32ad90da239_ story.html?hpid=z2.

13. Just as interesting and encouraging is the criticism of this dialog by some who call for the presence of more parties, more stakeholders, so the talks have a greater chance of sustainable success. http://www.theworld. org/2013/06/peace-talks-with-taliban/.

14. http://en.wikipedia.org/wiki/Six-Day_War. This war grew out of many sharply increasing border tensions on all land sides of Israel, and Israel launched June 5, 1967, against Egypt (capturing and occupying the Sinai Peninsula and Gaza Strip), Syria (capturing and occupying Golan Heights), and Jordan (capturing and occupying West Bank).

15. http://en.wikipedia.org/wiki/ Second_Intifada Beginning in September 2000, sparked by Ariel Sharon's provocative visit to the Temple Mount, or Al-Aqsa Temple to the Israelis and Muslims respectively.

16. http://en.wikipedia.org/wiki/Com batants_for_Peace. In 2005 this collaborative group of former Palestinian fighters and IDF members went public, after meeting for a year secretly to hammer out agreements and develop mutual trust.

17. http://www.washingtonpost.com/ world/middle_east/civilians-in-gaza-israel-

suffer-amid-conflict/2012/11/15/6cb99
006-2f6c-11e2-9f50-0308e1e75445_story.
html?wpisrc=nl_headlines.

18. http://www.washingtonpost.com/
world/middle_east/syrian-regime-says-
rebel-attack-on-main-power-line-causes-
overnight-blackout-in-damascus/2013/01/
21/1990329c-63a4–11e2–889b-f23c246aa
446_story.html. While power outages are
not infrequent in Damascus, this was the
first occasion of a citywide simultaneous
blackout.

19. http://www.washingtonpost.com/
world/middle_east/syrian-activists-say-gov
ernment-airstrike-near-damascus-kills-at-
least-7/2013/01/20/f1608450-6300-11e2-
889b-f23c246aa446_print.html. This AP
story sources a human rights group which
claims to have obtained more than 70 videos
showing Syrian rebels engaging in torture.

Part 4

1. This is a Prime Directive. If locals are
in violation of the ethics of any particular

internationals, the internationals should stay
out, should wait for a different group to ask
them for help who is not in such violation,
and it's also crucial to avoid being influenced
or recruited by those in diaspora, who have
little validity on the ground in the country
in conflict (*Economist,* 2006).

2. http://www.foreignpolicy.com/
articles/2012/10/31/the_collaborators_
song.

3. http://en.wikipedia.org/wiki/Leon_
Sullivan.

4. http://www.theatlantic.com/inter
national/archive/2012/11/its-basically-
over-the-sudanese-dictatorships-dwindling-
options/264406/.

5. Zunes frequently posts his observations about civil society struggle in the National Catholic Reporter. http://ncronline.
org/news/global/unarmed-resistance-still-
syrias-best-hope.

6. Lawson was a key interview subject for
the film series *A Force More Powerful.*

References

Abbasi, A.M. (2012). The Arab world: Democratization and Islamization? *International Journal on World Peace, 29,* no. 1, 7–19.

Abbyad, C. (2012). Life of a Syrian child. *Nursing Children & Young People, 24,* no. 10, 13.

Abdul-Karim, R., & Brulliard, K. (2012, November 15). Civilians in Gaza, Israel suffer amid conflict. WashingtonPost.com. Retrieved from http://www.washington post.com/world/middle_east/civilians-in-gaza-israel-suffer-amid-conflict/2012/ 11/15/6cb99006-2f6c-11e2-9f50-0308 e1e75445_story.html?wpisrc=nl_head lines.

Abdullah, S.M. (2009). *Creating a world that works for all.* Portland, OR: Commonway.

Abed, M. (2007, Fall). In defense of academic boycotts. *Dissent* (00123846), 83–87.

Ackerman, P., & DuVall, J. (2000). *A force more powerful: A century of nonviolent conflict.* New York: St. Martin's Press.

Ackerman, P., & DuVall, J. (2002, September-October). With weapons of the will: How to topple Saddam Hussein—nonviolently. *Sojourners.* Retrieved from http://sojo.net/magazine/2002/ 09/weapons-will.

Ackerman, P., & DuVall, J. (2005, Summer). People power primed: Civilian resistance and democratization. *Harvard International Review, 42–47.*

Ackerman, P., & Glennon, M. (2007). The right side of the law. *American Interest, 3,* no. 1, 41–47.

Ackerman, P., & Kruegler, C. (1994). *Strategic nonviolent conflict: The dynamics of people power in the twentieth century.* Westport, CT: Praeger.

Ajami, F. (2011). Pakistan and America. *Policy Review, 27–39.*

Akcinaroglu, S. (2012). Rebel interdependencies and civil war outcomes. *Journal of Conflict Resolution, 56,* no. 5, 879–903. doi:10.1177/0022002712445741.

Alexander, H. (1984, original 1969). *Gandhi through western eyes.* Philadelphia: New Society Publishers.

al-Gharbi, M. (2013). Syria contextualized: The numbers game. *Middle East Policy ,* no. 1, 56–67. doi:10.1111/mepo.12003.

Alpher, Y. (2012). Regional implications of the conflict in Syria: A view from Israel. Norwegian Peacebuilding Resource Centre. Retrieved from http://www.ciaonet. org/pbei/noref/0026064/f_0026064_ 21354.pdf.

Alvarez-Ossorio, I. (2012). Syria's struggling civil society. *Middle East Quarterly, 19,* no. 2, 23–32.

Anderson, J. (2012). The implosion. *New Yorker, 88,* no. 2, 58–67.

Anderson, J.H. (2011). After the fall. *World Affairs, 174,* no. 4, 16–22.

Anderson, S., & Larmore, J. (Eds.). (1991). *Nonviolent struggle and social defence.* London: War Resisters' International.

Andersson, I. (2003). 'Women's Unarmed Uprising Against War': A Swedish peace protest in 1935. *Journal of Peace Research, 40,* no. 4, 395.

Applebaum, A. (2012, October 31). The collaborator's song. *Foreign Policy*. Retrieved from http://www.foreignpolicy.com/articles/2012/10/31/the_collaborators_song.

Arango, T., & Krauss, C. (2013, June 2). China is reaping biggest benefits of Iraq oil boom. Retrieved from http://www.nytimes.com/2013/06/03/world/middleeast/china-reaps-biggest-benefits-of-iraq-oil-boom.html?nl=todaysheadlines&emc=edit_th_20130603&_r=0.

Aras, D. (2012). Turkish-Syrian relations go downhill. *Middle East Quarterly, 19*, no. 2, 41–50.

Arnove, Anthony, ed. (2000). *Iraq under siege: The deadly impact of sanctions and war*. Cambridge, MA: South End Press.

Associated Press. (2013, January 20). Syrian troops battle rebels around Damascus as air raid kills at least 7 outside the capital. *Washington Post*.

Associated Press. (2013a, January 21). Power outage leaves Damascus, south Syria in darkness; government blames rebel attack. *Washington Post*.

Associated Press. (2013b, January 21). Russian government to evacuate more than 100 Russians from Syria. *Washington Post*.

Associated Press. (2013, March 2). Syria, Iran accuse U.S. of double standard. *USA Today*. Retrieved from http://www.usatoday.com/story/news/world/2013/03/02/syria-double-standards/1958487/.

Associated Press. (2013, April 1). UN adopts landmark treaty to regulate multibillion-dollar global arms trade. Retrieved from http://www.washingtonpost.com/business/un-general-assembly-to-vote-tuesday-on-first-un-treaty-to-regulate-the-global-arms-trade/2013/04/02/eaa49ed0-9b5e-11e2-9219-51eb8387e8f1_story.html.

Associated Press. (2013, April 4). World Digest: Syrian government warns Jordan over aid to rebels. Retrieved from http://www.washingtonpost.com/world/world-digest-syrian-government-warns-jordan-over-aid-to-rebels/2013/04/04/8631e0de-9d34-11e2-a2db-efc5298a95e1_story.html?wpisrc=nl_headlines.

Associated Press. (2013, May 10). In Kenya's rough-edged democracy, lone protester, amplified by social media, gets a hearing. Retrieved from file:///C:/Writing2013/Background/In%20Kenya%E2%80%99s%20rough-edged%20democracy,%20lone%20protester,%20amplified%20by%20social%20media,%20gets%20a%20hearing%20-%20The%20Washington%20Post.htm.

Atiri, Judith (2009). Some thoughts on nonviolence. In Elavie Ndura-Ouédraogo & Matt Meyer (Eds.), *Seeds of new hope: Pan-African peace studies for the twenty-first century* (pp. 11–12). Trenton, NJ: Africa World Press.

Atkinson, K.N., & Mattaini, M.A. (2013). Constructive noncooperation as political resistance. *Journal of Progressive Human Services, 24*, no. 2, 99–116. doi:10.1080/10428232.2013.778180.

Atlas, P.M. (2012). U.S. foreign policy and the Arab Spring: Balancing values and interests. *DOMES: Digest of Middle East Studies, 21*, no. 2, 353–385. doi:10.1111/j.1949-3606.2012.00158.x.

Aydin, A., & Regan, P.M. (2012). Networks of third-party interveners and civil war duration. *European Journal of International Relations, 18*, no. 3, 573–597. doi:10.1177/1354066111403515.

Ayoob, M. (2012). The Arab Spring: Its geostrategic significance. *Middle East Policy, 19*, no. 3, 84–97. doi:10.1111/j.1475-4967.2012.00549.x.

Ayson, R., & Taylor, B. (2008). Carrying China's torch. *Survival* (00396338) 50, no. 4, 5–10. doi:10.1080/0039633080 2328776.

Bacevich, A.J., Diehl, J., Hayden, M.V., Laqueur, W., O'Sullivan, M.L., Perle, R., & Wolfowitz, P.D. (2013). Lessons learned. *World Affairs, 176*, no. 1, 8–34.

Bachrach, J. (2011). Wikihistory. *World Affairs, 174*, no. 2, 35–44.

Bah, A. (2012). State decay: A conceptual frame of failing and failed states in West Africa. *International Journal of Politics, Culture & Society, 25*, no. 1–3, 71–89. doi:10.1007/s10767–012–9120–9.

Bala, S. (2013). Waging nonviolence: Reflections on the history writing of the Pashtun nonviolent movement Khudai Khidmatgar. *Peace & Change, 38*, no. 2, 131–154. doi:10.1111/pech.12009.

Balmer, C. (2012, December 18). Insight: Rattled Israel holds key to Palestinian uprising. Reuters.

Bamidele, O. (2012). Disarmament, demobilization, and reintegration of children in armed conflict. *Peace Review, 24,* no. 3, 284–291. doi:10.1080/10402659.2012.704251.

Ban on democracy: A conversation with Ban Ki-moon. (2012). *World Policy Journal, 29,* no. 3, 49–55. doi:10.1177/0740277512461313.

Bannon, I., & Collier, P., (Eds.). (2003). *Natural resources and violent conflict: Options and actions.* Washington, D.C.: The World Bank.

Barnard, A. (2012, October 19). Blast in Beirut is seen as an extension of Syria's war. *New York Times.* Retrieved from http://www.nytimes.com/2012/10/20/world/middleeast/bomb-blast-in-beirut-lebanon.html?nl=todaysheadlines&emc=edit_th_20121020&_r=0&pagewanted=all.

Barnard, A. (2012, November 8). Missteps by rebels erode their support among Syrians. Retrieved from file:///C:/Writing 2013/Background/In%20Syria,%20Missteps%20by%20Rebels%20Erode%20Their%20Support%20-%20NY Times.com.htm.

Barnard, A. (2013, May 5). Syria blames Israel for fiery attack in Damascus. Retrieved from http://www.nytimes.com/2013/05/06/world/middleeast/after-strikes-in-syria-concerns-about-an-escalation-of-fighting.html?nl=todays headlines&emc=edit_th_20130506&_r=0.

Barnard, A., & Saad, H. (2012, October 19). Seized by rebels, town is crushed by Syrian forces. *New York Times.* Retrieved from http://www.nytimes.com/2012/10/19/world/middleeast/horrific-bombing-in-northern-syria-kills-dozens.html?nl=todaysheadlines&emc=edit_th_20121019&_r=0.

Barone, M. (2003). The next stage of war. *U.S. News & World Report, 134,* no. 8, 25.

Barter, S.J. (2012). Unarmed forces: Civilian strategy in violent conflicts. *Peace & Change, 37,* no. 4, 544–571.

Batton, J. (2004). Commentary: Considering conflict resolution education: Next steps for institutionalization. *Conflict Resolution Quarterly, 22,* no. 1/2, 269–278.

Bedrosian, T.A., & Nelson, R.J. (2012). Neurobiology of human killing. In Daniel J. Christie & Joám Evans Pim (Eds.), *Nonkilling psychology* (pp. 23–41). Honolulu, HI: Center for Global Nonkilling.

Beitin, B.K. (2012). Syrian self-initiated expatriates: Emotional connections from abroad. *International Migration, 50,* no. 6, 1–17. doi:10.1111/j.1468-2435.2012.00759.x.

Benhabib, S. (2013). Transnational legal sites and democracy-building: Reconfiguring political geographies. *Philosophy & Social Criticism, 39,* no. 4/5, 471–486. doi:10.1177/0191453713477351.

Ben-Meir, A. (2013). Earning the Nobel Peace Prize. *DOMES: Digest of Middle East Studies, 22,* no. 1, 1–7. doi:10.1111/dome.12009.

Bergen, P.L. (2001). *Holy War, Inc.: Inside the secret world of Osama bin Laden.* New York: Free Press.

Berrigan, Daniel. (1968). *Love, love at the end: Parables, prayers and meditations.* New York: Macmillan.

Berrigan, Daniel. (1991). *Whereon to stand: The Acts of the apostles and ourselves.* Baltimore, MD: Fortkamp.

Berrigan, Daniel. (1997). *Ezekiel: Vision in the dust.* Maryknoll, NY: Orbis.

Berrigan, Daniel. (1998). *Daniel: Under the siege of the Divine.* Farmington, PA: Plough Publishing.

Berrigan, Philip. (1996). *Fighting the Lamb's war: Skirmishes with the American empire.* Monroe, ME: Common Courage.

Beyerle, S. (2008). Courage, creativity, and capacity in Iran: Mobilizing for women's rights and gender equality. *Georgetown Journal of International Affairs, 9,* no. 2, 41–49.

Beyerle, S. (2010). People count: How citizen engagement and action challenge corruption and abuse. Paper, International Peace Research Association, University of Sydney.

Beyerle, S. (2013). "We want freedom!" Nonviolent conflict to curb corruption.

In Rhea DuMont, Tom H. Hastings, & Emiko Noma (Eds.), *Conflict transformation: Essays on methods of nonviolence* (pp. 66–85). Jefferson, NC: McFarland.

Bhatt, C. (2012). Human rights and the transformations of war. *Sociology, 46,* no. 5, 813–828. doi:10.1177/003803851245 0102.

Biazoto, J. (2011). Peace journalism where there is no war. *Conflict & communication online, 10,* no. 2, 1–19.

Biekart, K., & Fowler, A. (2012). A civic agency perspective on change. *Development, 55,* no. 2, 181–189. doi:10.1057/dev.2012.9.

Binnendijk, A.L., & Marovic, I. (2006). Power and persuasion: Nonviolent strategies to influence state security forces in Serbia (2000) and Ukraine (2004). *Communist and Post-Communist Studies, 39,* 411.

Boaz, Cynthia. (2013). Foreword. In Rhea DuMont, Tom H. Hastings, & Emiko Noma (Eds.), *Conflict transformation: Essays on methods of nonviolence* (pp. 1–3). Jefferson, NC: McFarland.

Boaz, Cynthia, & DuVall, Jack. (2006, September/October). Defying violence with democracy: Why grassroots civil society—and not "nation building" from on high—is key to the future of Iraq. *Sojourners.*

Boesak, A.A. (2011). "For the tyrant shall be no more": Reflections on and lessons from "The Arab Spring" in North Africa, the Middle East and the Civil Rights and anti-apartheid struggles. *Hervormde Teologiese Studies, 67,* no. 3, 1–9. doi:10. 4102/hts.v67i3.1159.

Böhmelt, T. (2012). Why many cooks if they can spoil the broth? The determinants of multiparty mediation. *Journal of Peace Research, 49,* no. 5, 701–715. doi:10.1177/0022343312437774.

Borpujari, P. (2013, January 6). Outrage over the culture of rape in India. *Boston Globe.* Retrieved from http://bostonglobe.com/opinion/2013/01/06/borpujari/HoXh EZNRU6kUuL2qqmOGqJ/story.html.

Borshchevskaya, A. (2010). Sponsored corruption and neglected reform in Syria. *Middle East Quarterly, 17,* no. 3, 41–50.

Boulding, Elise (2002). Foreword. In Krishna Mallick & Doris Hunter (Eds.), *An anthology of nonviolence: Historical and contemporary voices* (pp. xiii-xvi). Westport, CT: Greenwood.

Bowers, K. (2012). From little things big things grow, from big things little things manifest. *Alternative: An International Journal of Indigenous Scholarship, 8,* no. 3, 290–304.

Brading, R. (2012). The Anti-Bolivarian student movement: New social actors challenge the advancement of Venezuela's Bolivarian socialism. *Asian Journal of Latin American Studies, 25,* no. 3, 23–46.

Brady, C. (2010, November 8). Climate change and peacebuilding. Retrieved from http://transition.usaid.gov/our_work/cross-cutting_programs/conflict/publications/docs/CMMBRADYAfP-ClimateandPeacebuildingNov10.pdf.

Brigham, S. (2010). The American-Soviet walks: Large-scale citizen diplomacy at glasnost's outset. *Peace & Change, 35,* no. 4, 594–625. doi:10.1111/j.1468-0130. 2010.00657.x.

Buchan, R. (2011). The international law of naval blockade and Israel's interception of the Mavi Marmara. *Netherlands International Law Review, 58,* no. 2, 209–241. doi:10.1017/S0165070X11200032.

Buchanan, A., & Keohane, R.O. (2005). Justifying preventive force. *Ethics & International Affairs* (Wiley-Blackwell) 19, no. 2, 109–111.

Buller, J. (2011). A Review of Reporting Conflict: New Directions in Peace Journalism. *Peace Review, 23,* no. 2, 252–254. doi:10.1080/10402659.2011.571623.

Bumiller, E. (2012, December 24). With a parent off again at war, a holiday of pride and isolation. *New York Times.*

Burston, J. (2003). War and the entertainment industries: New research priorities in an era of cyber-patriotism. In Daya Kishan Thussu & Des Freedman (Eds.), *War and the media* (pp. 163–175). Thousand Oaks, CA: Sage.

Call, Charles T. (2012). *Why peace fails: The causes and prevention of civil war recurrence.* Washington, D.C.: Georgetown University Press.

Cannistraro, V. (2011). Arab Spring: A partial awakening. *Mediterranean Quarterly,* 22, no. 4, 36–45. doi:10.1215/10474552–1471494.

Carpenter, T. (2013). Tangled web: The Syrian civil war and its implications. *Mediterranean Quarterly, 24,* no. 1, 1–11. doi:10.1215/10474552-2018988.

Carrington, Christopher. (2013). *Civil resistance or rebellion: The impact of country-level factors on revolutionary strategy* (Master's thesis). Duke University, ProQuest, UMI Dissertations Publishing, 2013. 1535836.

Carroll, Berenice A. (1969). How wars end: An analysis of some current hypotheses. *Journal of Peace Research, 4,* 295–322.

Cerván, D. (2010). Armed violence reduction and prevention: A promising contribution to the solution for the Nigerian ethno-religious conflict. *International Journal of Interdisciplinary Social Sciences, 5,* no. 3, 225–236.

Chander, A. (2011). Googling freedom. *California Law Review, 99,* no. 1, 1–45.

Chenoweth, E., & Cunningham, K.G. (2013). Understanding nonviolent resistance: An introduction. *Journal of Peace Research, 50,* no. 3, 271–276. doi: 10.1177/0022343313480381.

Chenoweth, E., & Stephan, M.J. (2011). *Why civil resistance works: The strategic logic of nonviolent conflict.* New York: Columbia University Press.

Cherbo, J. (2009). An initiative to facilitate international cultural exchanges: The RCCE project. *Journal of Arts Management, Law & Society, 39,* no. 4, 285–289.

Chernus, I. (2004). *American nonviolence: The history of an idea.* Maryknoll, NY: Orbis.

Christie, D.J. (2006). What is peace psychology the psychology of? *Journal of Social Issues, 62,* no. 1, 1–17. doi:10.1111/j.1540-4560.2006.00436.x.

Christie, D.J., & Evans Pim, J. (Eds.). (2011). *Nonkilling psychology.* Honolulu, HI: Center for Global Nonkilling.

Clouser, R. (2012). (Im)possibilities of truth and reconciliation. *Cultural Studies, 26,* no. 6, 987–990. doi:10.1080/09502386.2012.698290.

Cockburn, C. (2010). Gender relations as causal in militarization and war. *International Feminist Journal of Politics, 12,* no. 2, 139–157. doi:10.1080/14616741003665169.

Cohen, H. (2013). Palestinian armed struggle, Israel's peace camp, and the unique case of Fatah Jerusalem. *Israel Studies, 18,* no. 1, 101–123.

Cohen, J. (2009). Effective participation of national minorities as a tool for conflict prevention. *International Journal on Minority & Group Rights, 16,* no. 4, 539–548. doi:10.1163/156918509X12537882648381.

Cohen, R. (2013, January 21). Obama's failure in Syria. *Washington Post.* Retrieved from http://www.washingtonpost.com/opinions/richard-cohen-obamas-failure-in-syria/2013/01/21/613d9afa-63ed-11e2-9e1b-07db1d2ccd5b_story.html.

Condlin, R.J. (2011). Bargaining without law. *New York Law School Law Review, 56,* no. 2, 281–328.

Cortright, D. (2009). *Gandhi and beyond: Nonviolence for a new political age,* 2nd ed. Boulder, CO: Paradigm Publishers.

Cortright, D., & Lopez, G. (2000). *The sanctions decade: Assessing UN strategies in the 1990s.* Boulder, CO: Lynne Rienner.

Cortright, D., & Lopez, G. (2002). *Sanctions and the search for security: Challenges to UN action.* Boulder, CO: Lynne Rienner.

Crescenzi, M.C., Kadera, K.M., Mitchell, S., & Thyne, C.L. (2011). A supply side theory of mediation. *International Studies Quarterly, 55,* no. 4, 1,069–1,094. doi:10.1111/j.1468-2478.2011.00681.x.

Csapody, T., & Weber, T. (2007). Hungarian nonviolent resistance against Austria and its place in the history of nonviolence. *Peace & Change, 32,* no. 4, 499–519. doi:10.1111/j.1468-0130.2007.00464.x.

Çubukçu, A. (2011). On cosmopolitan occupations. *Interventions: The International Journal of Postcolonial Studies, 13,* no. 3, 422–442. doi:10.1080/1369801X.2011.597599.

Cumming-Bruce, N., & Arsu, S. (2013, April

5). U.N. says it is running out of money to assist wave of refugees from Syria. Retrieved from http://www.nytimes.com/2013/04/06/world/middleeast/un-says-aid-for-syria-refugees-is-running-out.html?nl=todaysheadlines&emc=edit_th_20130406&_r=0.

Cunliffe, R.H. (2013). Listening as a practice of conflict transformation: Learnings from a death penalty compassionate listening project. In Rhea DuMont, Tom H. Hastings, & Emiko Noma (Eds.), *Conflict transformation: Essays on methods of nonviolence* (pp. 167–179). Jefferson, NC: McFarland.

Cunningham, K. (2013). Understanding strategic choice: The determinants of civil war and nonviolent campaign in self-determination disputes. *Journal of Peace Research, 50,* no. 3, 291–304. doi:10.1177/0022343313475467.

Curtis-Wendlandt, L. (2012). No right to resist? Elise Reimarus's freedom as a Kantian response to the problem of violent revolt. *Hypatia, 27,* no. 4, 755–773. doi:10.1111/j.1527-2001.2011.01213.x.

"Curveball" reiterates confession about Iraq War lies. (2012). *New American* (08856540) 28, no. 8, 7.

Dahi, O., & Munif, Y. (2012). Revolts in Syria: Tracking the convergence between authoritarianism and neoliberalism. *Journal of Asian & African Studies* (Sage Publications, Ltd.) 47, no. 4, 323–332. doi:10.1177/0021909611431682.

Dalacoura, K. (2012). The 2011 uprisings in the Arab Middle East: Political change and geopolitical implications. *International Affairs, 88,* no. 1, 63–79. doi:10.1111/j.1468-2346.2012.01057.x.

Daniels, S.E., & Walker, G.B. (2001). *Working through environmental conflict: The collaborative learning approach.* Westport, CT: Praeger.

Davenport, J.J. (2011). Just war theory, humanitarian intervention, and the need for a democratic federation. *Journal of Religious Ethics, 39,* no. 3, 493–555. doi:10.1111/j.1467-9795.2011.00491.x.

Davies, K. (2011). The power list. *Alternatives Journal, 37,* no. 5, 30–34.

Dawoody, A.R. (2006). Examining the pre-emptive war on Iraq. *Public Integrity, 9,* no. 1, 63–77. doi:10.2753/PIN1099-9922090104.

Demirtaş, B. (2013). Turkish-Syrian relations: From friend "Esad" to enemy "Esed." *Middle East Policy, 20,* no. 1, 111–120. doi:10.1111/mepo.12008.

Denton, J.S. (2012). Letter from the editor. *World Affairs, 175,* no. 1, 4–6.

Dorent, N. (2011). Transitory cities: Emergency architecture and the challenge of climate change. *Development, 54,* no. 3, 345–351. doi:10.1057/dev.2011.60.

Douzinas, C. (2013). The paradoxes of human rights. *Constellations: An International Journal of Critical & Democratic Theory, 20,* no. 1, 51–67. doi:10.1111/cons.12021.

Dudouet, V. (2013). Conflict transformation through nonviolent resistance. In Rhea DuMont, Tom H. Hastings, & Emiko Noma (Eds.), *Conflict transformation: Essays on methods of nonviolence* (pp. 9–33). Jefferson, NC: McFarland.

DuMont, R., & Noma, E. (2013). Introduction. In Rhea DuMont, Tom H. Hastings, & Emiko Noma (Eds.), *Conflict transformation: Essays on methods of nonviolence* (pp. 7–8). Jefferson, NC: McFarland.

DuMont, R., Hastings, T.H. & Noma, E. (Eds.). (2013). *Conflict transformation: Essays on methods of nonviolence.* Jefferson, NC: McFarland.

DuMont, R.A. (2013). Mainstreaming feminism in Conflict Resolution. In Rhea DuMont, Tom H. Hastings, & Emiko Noma (Eds.), *Conflict transformation: Essays on methods of nonviolence* (pp. 126–133). Jefferson, NC: McFarland.

DuVall, Jack (2007, Spring/Summer). Fierce urgency for the rights of all: Democratic power and the choice of conflict. *Bridges.*

Dyrstad, K. (2012). After ethnic civil war: Ethno-nationalism in the Western Balkans. *Journal of Peace Research, 49,* no. 6, 817–831. doi:10.1177/0022343312439202.

Eastwood, B.M. (2007). A note on the new face of citizen diplomacy: Education city and American Universities in the Middle East. *American Foreign Policy Interests, 29,* no. 6, 443–449.

Eckert, A.E. (2012). The responsibility to protect in the anarchical society: Power, interest, and the protection of civilians in Libya and Syria. *Denver Journal of International Law & Policy, 41,* no. 1, 87–99.

Economist. (2006, January 19). A rainbow of revolutions.

Editorial, B. (2012, February 29). Syria protests must stick to nonviolence. *Christian Science Monitor.*

Egin, O. (2013). The game changer. *World Affairs, 176,* no. 1, 64–72.

Ehrenreich, B. (1997). *Blood rites: Origins and history of the passions of war.* New York: Metropolitan.

Elster, E., & Sørensen, M.J. (Eds.). (2010). *Women conscientious objectors: An anthology.* London: War Resisters' International.

Emergency Response Network. (n.d.). *No mandate for war: Basta! A pledge of resistance handbook.* San Francisco, CA: Emergency Response Network.

Etzioni, A. (2011). Toward a nonviolent, pluralistic Middle East. *Middle East Quarterly, 18,* no. 4, 27–38.

Evans Pim, J. (Ed.). (2009). *Toward a nonkilling paradigm.* Honolulu, HI: Global Center for Nonkilling.

Evans Pim, J. (Ed.). (2010). *Nonkilling societies.* Honolulu, HI: Global Center for Nonkilling.

Everett, M. (1989). *Breaking ranks.* Philadelphia: New Society Publishers.

Farsakh, N. (2011). From militant to peace activist in Palestine: The transformation of Abu Ala Mansour. *Kennedy School Review, 11,* 124–131.

Fawcett, L. (2013). The Iraq War ten years on: Assessing the fallout. *International Affairs, 89,* no. 2, 325–343. doi:10.1111/1468-2346.12020.

Felter, J.H. (2012). Why do insurgencies fail? Causes and effects, governance and military force in counterinsurgency strategies. *Historical Methods, 45,* no. 4, 183–186. doi:10.1080/01615440.2012.721337.

Filiatreau, S. (2009). Christian faith, nonviolence and Ukraine's Orange Revolution: A case study of the Embassy of God Church. *Religion in Eastern Europe, 29,* no. 3, 10–22.

Filson, D., & Werner, S. (2002). A bargaining model of war and peace: Anticipating the onset, duration, and outcome of war. *American Journal of Political Science, 46,* no. 4, 819.

Fischer, L. (1982). *Gandhi: His life and message for the world.* New York: Mentor (original 1954).

Fish, M., Jensenius, F.R., & Michel, K.E. (2010). Islam and large-scale political violence: Is there a connection? *Comparative Political Studies, 43,* no. 11, 1,327–1,362. doi:10.1177/0010414010376912.

Flintoff, John-Paul. (2013, January 3). Gene Sharp: The Machiavelli of non-violence. *New Statesman.* file:///C:/Writing/ Writing2013/Background/Flintoff Gene%20Sharp%20%20The%20Machi avelli%20of%20non-violence.htm.

Flores, A. (2012). A competing risks model of war termination and leader change. *International Studies Quarterly, 56,* no. 4, 809–819. doi:10.1111/j.1468–2478.2012.00735.x.

Floyd-Thomas, J.M. (2011). More than conquerors: Just war theory and the need for a black Christian antiwar movement. *Black Theology: An International Journal, 9,* no. 2, 136–160. doi:10.1558/blth.v9iv.136.

Förster, T. (2012). Imagining the nation. *African Arts, 45,* no. 3, 42–55.

Fouda, T. (2011, January 4). In Syria, a kernel of democracy. *Christian Science Monitor.*

Fuller, G.E.(2011). The Arab Revolution is beyond America's control. *NPQ: New Perspectives Quarterly, 28,* no. 2, 35–39. doi:10.1111/j.1540–5842.2011.01239.x.

Galperin, E. (2012, May 21). Don't get your sources in Syria killed. Committee to Protect Journalists. Retrieved from http:// www.cpj.org/security/2012/05/dont-get-your-sources-in-syria-killed.php.

Galtung, J. (1992). Reporting on a war: The Gulf War. *Social Alternatives, 11,* no. 1, 8–11.

Galtung, J., & Ruge, M.H. (1965). The structure of foreign news: The presentation of the Congo, Cuba and Cyprus crises in four Norwegian newspapers. *Journal of Peace Research* 2, 64–90. doi:10.1177/002234336500200104.

Gan, B., & DuVall, J. (n.d.). Gandhi a fighter, not a quitter.

George-Williams, D. (2006). *"Bite not one another": Selected accounts of nonviolent struggle in Africa*. Addis Ababa, Ethiopia: University of Peace: Africa Programme.

Ghaemi, N. (2011). *A first-rate madness: Uncovering the links between leadership and mental illness*. New York: Penguin.

Ghazi, Y., & Hauser, C. (2012, December 31). Violence in Iraq swells at year's end, leaving at least 3 dozen dead. *New York Times*.

Giovanni, J. (2013). Syria's cycle of retribution. *Newsweek, 161*, no. 10, 1.

Glynn, S. (2012). Muslims and the Left: An English case study. *Ethnicities, 12*, no. 5, 581–602. doi:10.1177/1468796811435315.

Gonsalvez, P. (2010). *Clothing for liberation: A communication analysis of Gandhi's swadeshi revolution*. Thousand Oaks, CA: Sage.

Goodin, R.E. (1987). Civil disobedience and nuclear protest. *Political Studies, 35*, no. 3, 461–466.

Gould, R.J. (2013). A paradoxical identity: From conflicted to hybrid. In Rhea DuMont, Tom H. Hastings, & Emiko Noma (Eds.), *Conflict transformation: Essays on methods of nonviolence* (pp. 141–151). Jefferson, NC: McFarland.

Greenberg, J., & Dehghanpisheh, B. (2013, January 31). Hezbollah, Russia condemn Israeli airstrike inside Syria. *Washington Post*. Retrieved from http://www.washingtonpost.com/world/middle_east/reports-israeli-aircraft-fired-missile-along-lebanon-syria-border/2013/01/30/60fab2be-6adf-11e2-ada3-d86a4806d5ee_story.html?wpisrc=nl_headlines.

Greenstein, R. (2012). Making sense of Israeli politics today. *International Sociology, 27*, no. 5, 599–608. doi:10.1177/0268580912452359.

Guessous, N. (2012). Women's rights in Muslim societies: Lessons from the Moroccan experience. *Philosophy & Social Criticism, 38*, no. 4/5, 525–533. doi:10.1177/0191453712448000.

Hall, T., & Yarhi-Milo, K. (2012). The personal touch: Leaders' impressions, costly signaling, and assessments of sincerity in international affairs. *International Studies Quarterly, 56*, no. 3, 560–573.

Hallward, M., & Shaver, P. (2012). "War by other means" or nonviolent resistance? Examining the discourses surrounding Berkeley's divestment bill. *Peace & Change, 37*, no. 3, 389–412. doi:10.1111/j.1468-0130.2012.00756.x.

Hamburg, D.A. (2010). Recent advances in preventing mass violence. *Annals of the New York Academy of Sciences, 1208*, no. 1, 10–14. doi:10.1111/j.1749-6632.2010.05792.x.

Hansen, M. (2012). Parallel mediation: Ordering the chaos of multiparty mediation. *International Negotiation, 17*, no. 2, 237–263. doi:10.1163/157180612X651430.

Hartung, W.D., & Anderson, C. (2012). *Bombs versus budgets: Inside the nuclear weapons lobby*. Washington, D.C.: Center for International Policy.

Hasan, M. (2012). Exploding the four myths about intervention in Syria. *New Statesman, 141*, no. 5110, 21.

Hastings, T.H. (2000). *Ecology of war & peace: Counting costs of conflict*. Lanham, MD: University Press of America.

Hastings, T.H. (2002). *Meek ain't weak: Nonviolent power and people of color*. Lanham, MD: University Press of America.

Hastings, T.H. (2004). *Nonviolent response to terrorism*. Jefferson, NC: McFarland.

Hastings, T.H. (2013). Preface. In Rhea DuMont, Tom H. Hastings, & Emiko Noma (Eds.), *Conflict transformation: Essays on methods of nonviolence* (p, 5). Jefferson, NC: McFarland.

Hazbun, W. (2012). Itineraries of peace through tourism: Excavating territorial attachments across the Arab/Israeli frontier. *Peace & Change, 37*, no. 1, 3–36. doi:10.1111/j.1468-0130.2011.00730.x.

Helvey, Robert L. (2004). *On strategic nonviolent conflict: Thinking about the fundamentals*. Boston, MA: The Albert Einstein Institution. Retrieved from http://www.aeinstein.org/organizations/org/OSNC.pdf.

Henne, P. (2012). The two swords: Religion-state connections and interstate disputes. *Journal of Peace Research, 49*, no. 6, 753–768. doi:10.1177/0022343312456225.

Hershberger, M. (2004). Peace work, war myths: Jane Fonda and the antiwar movement. *Peace & Change, 29*, no. 3/4, 549–579. doi:10.1111/j.0149–0508.2004.00302.x.

Hiller, P.T., & Ayala Vela, P. (2013). The journey to conflict resolver: Peace-scapes. In Rhea DuMont, Tom H. Hastings, & Emiko Noma (Eds.), *Conflict transformation: Essays on methods of nonviolence* (pp. 152–166). Jefferson, NC: McFarland.

Hinnebusch, R. (2012). Europe and the Middle East: from imperialism to liberal peace? *Review of European Studies, 4*, no. 3, 18–31. doi:10.5539/res.v4n3pl8.

Hochschild, A. (2011). "I tried to stop the bloody thing": In World War I, nearly as many British men refused the draft—20,000—as were killed on the Somme's first day. Why were those who fought for peace forgotten? *American Scholar, 80*, no. 2, 51–63.

Houston, S., & Wright, R. (2003). Making and remaking Tibetan diasporic identities. *Social & Cultural Geography, 4*, no. 2, 217.

Howard, B.H., Shegog, R., Grussendorf, J., Benjamins, L.J., Stelzig, D., & McAlister, A.L. (2007). www.PeaceTest.org: Development, implementation, and evaluation of a web-based war-prevention program in a time of war. *Journal of Peace Research, 44*, no. 5, 559–571.

Hrynkow, C. (2012). The Israeli peace movement: A shattered dream. *Peace & Change, 37*, no, 4, 609–611. doi:10.1111/j.1468–0130.2012.00774.x.

Huet-Vaughn, E. (2007). Hands off Iraq. *National Catholic Reporter, 43*, no. 17, 5–6.

Jameson, A.K. & Sharp, G. (1963). Nonviolent resistance and the Nazis: The case of Norway. In Mulford Q. Sibley (Ed.), *The quiet battle: Writings on the theory and practice of non-violent resistance.* Boston: Beacon Press.

Jan, M., Paracha, S., Sultana, I., Sherazi, A., & Ali, S. (2011). News paradigms: Reporting of conflict-oriented events. *European Journal of Scientific Research, 55*, no. 2, 188–195.

Jasper, J.M., & Young, M.P. (2007). The rhetoric of sociological facts. *Sociological Forum, 22*, no. 3, 270–299. doi: 10.1111/j.1573–7861.2007.00020.x.

Jeffrey, A., & Jakala, M. (2012). Beyond trial justice in the former Yugoslavia. *Geographical Journal, 178*, no. 4, 290–295. doi:10.1111/j.1475–4959.2012.00461.x.

Jeffrey, C. (2013). Geographies of children and youth III: Alchemists of the revolution? *Progress in Human Geography, 37*, no. 1, 145–152. doi:10.1177/030913251 1434902.

Jenkins, S. (2012). Ethnicity, violence, and the immigrant-guest metaphor in Kenya. *African Affairs, 111*, no. 445, 576–596.

Johnson, K., Asher, J., Kisielewski, M., & Lawry, L. (2012). Former combatants in Liberia: The burden of possible traumatic brain injury among demobilized combatants. *Military Medicine, 177*, no. 5, 531–540.

Johnson, M.C. (2010, November). International peacemaking and the anti-war movement. *Political Theology*, 641–645. doi:10.1558/poth.v11i5.641.

Johnstad, P.G. (2012). When the time is right: Regime legitimacy as a predictor of nonviolent protest outcome. *Peace & Change, 37*, no. 4, 516–543.

Jones, T.S. (2004). Conflict Resolution Education: The field, the findings, and the future. *Conflict Resolution Quarterly, 22*, no. 1–2, 233–267.

Kahf, M. (2013). *Then and now: The Syrian revolution to date.* St. Paul, MN: Friends for a Nonviolent World.

Karatnycky, A., & Ackerman, P. (2005). *How freedom is won: From civic resistance to durable democracy.* New York: Freedom House.

Kárníková, A. (2012). Do they actually matter? The impact of NGOs on the European Instrument for Democracy and Human Rights (EIDHR). *Perspectives: Central European Review of International Affairs, 20*, no. 1, 83–109.

Karreth, J., & Tir, J. (2013). International institutions and civil war prevention. *Journal of Politics, 75*, no. 1, 96–109. doi:10.1017/S0022381612000898.

Kegley, C.W., Jr., & Raymond, G.A. (1999).

How nations make peace. New York: St. Martin's/Worth.

Kent, L. (2012). Interrogating the "gap" between law and justice: East Timor's Serious Crimes Process. *Human Rights Quarterly, 34,* no. 4, 1,021–1,044.

Khashan, H. (2013). Will Syria's strife rip Lebanon apart? *Middle East Quarterly, 20,* no. 1, 75–80.

Kimball, J.P. (2010). Out of primordial cultural ooze: Inventing political and policy legacies about the U.S. exit from Vietnam. *Diplomatic History, 34,* no. 3, 577–587. doi:10.1111/j.1467–7709.2010.00871.x.

Kingsbury, D. (2007). Timor-Leste: The harsh reality after independence. *Southeast Asian Affairs,* 363–377.

Kingsbury, D. (2009). East Timor in 2008. *Southeast Asian Affairs,* 357–369.

Kingston, J. (2006). Regaining dignity: Justice and reconciliation in East Timor. *Brown Journal of World Affairs, 13,* no. 1, 227–240.

Kisala, R. (1999). *Prophets of peace: Pacifism and cultural identity in Japan's new religions.* Honolulu: University of Hawai'i Press.

Klare, M.T. (2012). *The race for what's left.* New York: Metropolitan.

Klein, A.G. (2012). Measuring media compliance and divergence in the nondemocratic press system. *Communication Monographs, 79,* no. 1, 115–136. doi:10.1080/03637751.2011.646488.

Klug, T. (2012). Have the Arab uprisings lost their spring? *Palestine-Israel Journal of Politics, Economics & Culture, 18,* no. 1, 34–40.

Kouskouvelis, I.I. (2013). The problem with Turkey's "Zero Problems." *Middle East Quarterly, 20,* no. 1, 47–56.

Krajeski, J. (2012). Taking refuge: The Syrian revolution in Turkey. *World Policy Journal, 29,* no. 2, 59–67. doi:10.1177/0740277512451489.

Kriesberg, L. (2012). Reverberations of the Arab Spring. *Palestine-Israel Journal of Politics, Economics & Culture, 18*(1), 88–92.

Kriesberg, L., & Dayton, B.W. (2012). *Constructive conflicts: From escalation to resolution,* 4th ed. Lanham, MD: Rowman & Littlefield.

Kubo, K. (2010). Why Kosovar Albanians took up arms against the Serbian Regime: The genesis and expansion of the UCK in Kosovo. *Europe-Asia Studies, 62,* no. 7, 1,135–1,152. doi:10.1080/09668136.2010.497022.

Kutz-Flamenbaum, R. (2012). Mobilizing gender to promote peace: The case of Machsom Watch. *Qualitative Sociology, 35,* no. 3, 293–310. doi:10.1007/s11133–012–9231–7.

Kyi, Aung San Suu, & Clements, Alan. (1997). *The voice of hope.* New York: Seven Stories.

Le Billon, P. (2008). Diamond wars? Conflict diamonds and geographies of resource wars. *Annals of the Association of American Geographers, 98,* no. 2, 345–372. doi:10.1080/00045600801922422.

Lederach, J.P. (1997). *Building peace: Sustainable reconciliation in divided societies.* Washington, D.C.: United States Institute of Peace Press.

Lederach, J.P. (2003). *The little book of conflict transformation.* Intercourse, PA: Good Books.

Lee, S. (2010). Peace journalism: Principles and structural limitations in the news coverage of three conflicts. *Mass Communication & Society, 13,* no. 4, 361–384. doi:10.1080/15205430903348829.

Lee, S.T., Maslog, C.C., & Kim, H.S. (2006). Asian conflicts and the Iraq war: A comparative framing analysis. *International Communication Gazette, 68,* no. 5/6, 499–518.

Lesch, D.W. (2012). Prudence suggests staying out of Syria. *Current History, 111,* no. 748, 299–304.

Letendre, K., Fincher, C.L., & Thornhill, R. (2010). Does infectious disease cause global variation in the frequency of intrastate armed conflict and civil war? *Biological Reviews, 85,* no. 3, 669–683. doi:10.1111/j.1469–185X.2010.00133.x.

Liska, A.J., & Perrin, R.K. (2010). Securing foreign oil: A case for including military operations in the climate change impact of fuels. *Environment, 52,* no. 4, 9–22.

Lynch, J., & McGoldrick, A. (2005a). *Peace journalism.* Gloucestershire, UK: Hawthorn House.

Magbadelo, J. (2012). Nigeria's citizen diplomacy: Theoretical genesis and empirical exegesis. *Journal of Third World Studies, 29*, no. 1, 326–328.

Mahony, L., & Eguren, L.E. (1997). *Unarmed bodyguards: International accompaniment for the protection of human rights.* West Hartford, CT: Kumarian Press.

Mallat, C. (2011). The philosophy of the Middle East Revolution, take one: nonviolence. *Middle Eastern Law & Governance, 3*, no. 1/2, 136–147. doi:10.1163/187633711X591495.

Managhan, T. (2011). Grieving dead soldiers, disavowing loss: Cindy Sheehan and the im/possibility of the American antiwar movement. *Geopolitics, 16*, no. 2, 438–466. doi:10.1080/14650045.2010.539081.

Martin, B. (2007). *Justice ignited: The dynamics of backfire.* Plymouth, United Kingdom: Rowman and Littlefield.

Masini, E.B. (2012). Women's invisible role in building nonkilling societies. In James A. Dator & Joám Evans Pim (Eds.), *Nonkilling futures: Visions* (pp. 189–196). Honolulu, HI: Global Center for Nonkilling.

McDonald, P.J. (2011). Complicating commitment: Free resources, power shifts, and the fiscal politics of preventive war. *International Studies Quarterly, 55*, no. 4, 1,095–1,120. doi:10.1111/j.1468–2478.2011.00682.x.

McDoom, O. (2012). The psychology of threat in intergroup conflict. *International Security, 37*, no. 2, 119–155.

McIntire, M. (2012, April 21). Conservative nonprofit acts as a stealth business lobbyist. *New York Times.*

Mellor, N. (2009). Strategies for autonomy. *Journalism Studies, 10*, no. 3, 307–321. doi:10.1080/14616700802636243.

Menon, R. (2012). Beijing and Moscow balk at "interference." *Current History, 111*, no. 748, 310–316.

Merriman, H., & DuVall, J. (2007). Dissolving terrorism at its roots. In Senthil Ram & Ralph Summy (Eds.), *Nonviolence: An alternative for defeating global terror(ism)* (pp. 1–14). New York: Nova Science.

Retrieved from http://www.nonviolent-conflict.org/images/stories/pdfs/dissolving_terrorism_at_its_roots.pdf.

Michaud, M. (2013). Violent worldviews and self-projected use of violence. In Rhea DuMont, Tom H. Hastings, & Emiko Noma (Eds.), *Conflict transformation: Essays on methods of nonviolence* (pp. 180–198). Jefferson, NC: McFarland.

Millar, G. (2012). "Our brothers who went to the bush": Post-identity conflict and the experience of reconciliation in Sierra Leone. *Journal of Peace Research, 49*, no. 5, 717–729. doi:10.1177/0022343312440114.

Miller, C., & King, M.E. (2005). *A glossary of terms and concepts used in peace and conflict studies,* 2nd ed. Addis Ababa, Ethiopia: University of Peace.

Mirra, C. (2011). The mutation of the Vietnam Syndrome: Underreported resistance during the 1991 Persian Gulf War. *Peace & Change, 36*, no. 2, 262–284. doi:10.1111/j.1468–0130.2010.00691.x.

Najjab, J. (2006). Nonviolent resistance conference held in Bethlehem. *Washington Report on Middle East Affairs, 25*, no. 3, 67–68.

Natividad, LisaLinda (2013). Chamoru values guiding nonviolence. In Rhea DuMont, Tom H. Hastings, & Emiko Noma (Eds.), *Conflict transformation: Essays on methods of nonviolence* (pp. 134–139). Jefferson, NC: McFarland.

Ndlovu-Gatsheni, S.J. (2012). The death of the Subject with a capital "S" and the perils of belonging: A study of the construction of ethnocracy in Zimbabwe. *Critical Arts: A South-North Journal of Cultural & Media Studies, 26*, no. 4, 525–546. doi:10.1080/02560046.2012.723844.

Neuman, W. (2012, October 17). Colombia tries again to end drug-fed war. *New York Times*: Retrieved from http://www.nytimes.com/2012/10/18/world/americas/colombia-tries-again-to-end-drug-fed-war.html?_r=1&nl=todaysheadlines&emc=edit_th_20121018.

News in brief. (2012). *Tibetan Review: The Monthly Magazine on all Aspects of Tibet, 47*, no. 5/6, 14–17.

Newton-Small, J. (2013). Blood for oil. *Time, 181*, no. 6, 38–41.

Norman, J.M. (2013). The activist and the olive tree: Nonviolent resistance in the Second Intifada. In Rhea DuMont, Tom H. Hastings, & Emiko Noma (Eds.), *Conflict transformation: Essays on methods of nonviolence* (pp. 34–51). Jefferson, NC: McFarland.

O'Hanlon, M. (2006, March 27). How to stop a civil war. *Washington Post*. Retrieved from http://www.washingtonpost.com/wp-dyn/content/article/2006/03/26/AR2006032600875_pf.html.

Ohmer, M.L., Warner, B.D., & Beck, E. (2010). Preventing violence in low-income communities: Facilitating residents' ability to intervene in neighborhood problems. *Journal of Sociology & Social Welfare, 37*, no. 2, 161–181.

O'Leary, B. (2012). The federalization of Iraq and the break-up of Sudan. *Government & Opposition, 47*, no. 4, 481–516. doi:10.1111/j.1477-7053.2012.01372.x.

Olmert, J. (2011). Israel-Syria: The elusive peace. *DOMES: Digest of Middle East Studies, 20*, no. 2, 202–211. doi:10.1111/j.1949-3606.2011.00094.x.

Onazi, O., Valenti, M., Swomen, H., & John, I. (2010). Bringing peace education to youth via independent radio in Nigeria. *Injury Prevention* 16: A50-A51.

Orr, D. (2008). At the end of our tether: The rationality of nonviolence. *Conservation Biology, 22*, no. 2, 235–238 DOI: 10.1111/j.1523-1739.2008.00902.x.

Owen, P. (2013, April 2). "6,000 killed" in bloodiest month for Syria crisis. *Guardian*. Retrieved from http://www.guardian.co.uk/world/middle-east-live/2013/apr/02/6-000-killed-in-bloodiest-month-for-syria-crisis-live-updates.

Pach, C. (2010). "Our worst enemy seems to be the press": TV news, the Nixon administration, and U.S. troop withdrawal from Vietnam, 1969–1973. *Diplomatic History, 34*, no. 3, 555–565. doi:10.1111/j.1467-7709.2010.00869.x.

Paige, G.D. (2000). Political Science: To kill or not to kill? *Social Alternatives, 19*, no. 2, 11–18.

Paige, G.D. (2009). *Nonkilling global political science*. Honolulu, HI: Global Center for Nonkilling.

Pal, A. (2011). Gene Sharp. *Progressive* 75/76, no. 12/1, 52–53.

Palmer-Mehta, V. (2009). Aung San Suu Kyi and the rhetoric of social protest in Burma. *Women's Studies in Communication, 32*, no. 2, 151–179.

Panayiotides, N. (2012). Is the "Arab Spring" Israel's winter? Strategic instability in the Middle East. *International Journal on World Peace, 29*, no. 1, 21–40.

Parker, N., & Salman, R. (2013). Notes from the underground: The rise of Nouri al-Maliki and the new Islamists. *World Policy Journal, 30*, no. 1, 63–76. doi:10.1177/0740277513482618.

Pauling, L. (1998). *Linus Pauling on peace: A scientist speaks out on humanism and world survival*. Los Altos, CA: Rising Star Press.

Pearse-Smith, S.D. (2012). "Water war" in the Mekong Basin? *Asia Pacific Viewpoint, 53*, no. 2, 147–162. doi:10.1111/j.1467-8373.2012.01484.x.

Phillips, C. (2012). Turkey's Syria problem. *Public Policy Research, 19*, no. 2, 137–140. doi:10.1111/j.1744-540X.2012.00698.x.

Pincus, W. (2012, October 29). For Mitt Romney, a bigger military, but at what price? *Washington Post*. Retrieved from http://www.washingtonpost.com/world/national-security/for-mitt-romney-a-bigger-military-but-at-what-price/2012/10/29/877daa78-1ec1-11e2-9746-908f727990d8_story.html?wpisrc=nl_headlines.

Pinto, A., Crespin, E., John, I., Mtonga, R., Valenti, M., & Zavala, D. (2010). North-south collaboration on research and advocacy to reduce armed violence. *Injury Prevention* 16: A217.

Pressman, J. (2007). Mediation, domestic politics, and the Israeli-Syrian negotiations, 1991–2000. *Security Studies, 16*, no. 3, 350–381. doi:10.1080/09636410701547733.

Prince, S. (2011). Narrative and the start of the Northern Irish Troubles: Ireland's revolutionary tradition in comparative perspective. *Journal of British Studies, 50*, no. 4, 941–964.

Ramos-Horta, J. (2001). The rich should not forget the ROW (Rest of the World).

NPQ: New Perspectives Quarterly, 18, no. 4, 16.

Rand Corporation. (2009). Policy options to address U.S. national security concerns linked to imported oil. Retrieved from http://www.rand.org/pubs/mono graphs/2009/RAND_MG838.pdf.

Raz, A. (2013). The generous peace offer that was never offered: The Israeli Cabinet Resolution of June 19, 1967. *Diplomatic History, 37,* no. 1, 85–108.

Riga, L., & Kennedy, J. (2012). "Putting cruelty first": Interpreting war crimes as human rights atrocities in U.S. policy in Bosnia and Herzegovina. *Sociology, 46,* no. 5, 861–875. doi:10.1177/00380385 12451529.

Robins, P. (2013). Turkey's "double gravity" predicament: The foreign policy of a newly activist power. *International Affairs, 89,* no. 2, 381–397. doi:10.1111/ 1468-2346.12023.

Rosa, A. (2012). "To make a better world tomorrow": St. Clair Drake and the Quakers of Pendle Hill. *Race & Class, 54,* no. 1, 67–90. doi:10.1177/0306396812444822.

Rosen, A. (2012, November 1). "It's Basically Over": The Sudanese dictatorship's dwindling options. *Atlantic.* Retrieved from http://www.theatlantic.com/inter national/archive/2012/11/its-basically-over-the-sudanese-dictatorships-dwindling-options/264406/.

Ross, M. (2003). The natural resource curse: How wealth can make you poor. In Ian Bannon & Paul Collier (Eds.), *Natural resources and violent conflict: Options and actions* (pp. 17–42). Washington, D.C.: The World Bank.

Rossinow, D. (2009). The U.S. Army–Marine Corps Counterinsurgency Field Manual (U.S. Army Field Manual No. 3–24/Marine Corps Warfighting Publication No. 3–33.5). *Peace & Change, 34,* no. 3, 325–329. doi:10.1111/j.1468-0130. 2009.00569.x.

Ruggeri, A., Gizelis, T., & Dorussen, H. (2013). Managing mistrust: An analysis of cooperation with UN peacekeeping in Africa. *Journal of Conflict Resolution, 57,* no. 3, 387–409. doi:10.1177/00220027 12448906.

Rustad, S., & Binningsbø, H. (2012). A price worth fighting for? Natural resources and conflict recurrence. *Journal of Peace Research, 49,* no. 4, 531–546. doi:10. 1177/0022343312444942.

Ryan, C.R. (2006). The odd couple: Ending the Jordanian-Syrian "Cold War." *Middle East Journal, 60,* no. 1, 33–56.

Sadri, H., & Flammia, M. (2009). Using technology to prepare students for the challenges of global citizenship. *Journal of Systemics, Cybernetics & Informatics, 7,* no. 5, 66–71.

Salti, R. (2012). Shall we dance? *Cinema Journal, 52,* no. 1, 166–171.

Samarasinghe, V. (2012). "A theme revisited?" The impact of the ethnic conflict on women and politics in Sri Lanka. *Journal of Women, Politics & Policy, 33,* no. 4, 345–364. doi:10.1080/1554477X.2012. 722431.

Sanford, A. (2013). Gandhi's agrarian legacy: Practicing food, justice, and sustainability in India. *Journal for the Study of Religion, Nature & Culture, 7,* no. 1, 65–87. doi:10.1558/jsrnc.v7i1.65.

Sanger, D.E. (2012, October 14). Rebel arms flow is said to benefit jihadists in Syria. *New York Times.*

Sarquís, D.J. (2012). Democratization after the Arab Spring: The case of Egypt's political transition. *Politics & Policy, 40,* no. 5, 871–903. doi:10.1111/j.1747–1346. 2012.00381.x.

Satha-Anand, C. (2002). Forgiveness as a nonviolent security policy: An analysis of Thai Prime Ministerial Order 66/23. *Social Alternatives, 21,* no. 2, 29–36.

Scheer, Robert (2013, June 05). China benefits from Bush's folly. Retrieved from http://truth-out.org/opinion/item/ 16788-robert-scheer-china-benefits-from-bushs-folly.

Schirch, Lisa (2013). *Conflict assessment & peacebuilding planning: Toward a participatory approach to human security.* Boulder, CO: Lynne Rienner.

Schock, K. (2013). The practice and study of civil resistance. *Journal of Peace Research, 50,* no. 3, 277–290. doi:10.1177/ 0022343313476530.

Seidman, G.W. (2003). Monitoring multinationals: Lessons from the anti-apartheid era. *Politics & Society, 31,* no. 3, 381.

Seigneurie, K. (2012). Discourses of the 2011 Arab revolutions. *Journal of Arabic Literature, 43,* no. 2/3, 484–509. doi:10.1163/1570064x-12341243.

Selimian, H. (2011). A message from Rev. Haroutune Selimian. *International Congregational Journal, 10,* no. 2, 9.

Shabaev, I.P. (2009). Ethnic conflicts in the European North of Russia. *Anthropology & Archeology of Eurasia, 48,* no. 3, 31–75. doi:10.2753/AAE1061-1959480302.

Sharp, G. (1973). *The politics of nonviolent action: Part one: Power and struggle.* Boston: Porter Sargent.

Sharp, G. (1980). *Social power and political freedom* [excerpts]. Retrieved from http://www.aeinstein.org/selflib/Social_Power_excerpts_for_Self_Lib.pdf.

Sharp, G. (2005). *Waging nonviolent struggle: 20th century practice and 21st century potential.* Boston: Extending Horizon Books.

Shemesh, A. (2012). Citizen diplomacy— creating a culture of peace: The Israeli-Palestinian case. *Palestine-Israel Journal of Politics, Economics & Culture, 18,* no. 2/3, 58–65.

Shifferd, K.D. (2011). *From war to peace: A guide to the next hundred years.* Jefferson, NC: McFarland.

Shogan, R. (2002). *War without end: Cultural conflict and the struggle for America's political future.* Cambridge, MA: Westview Press.

Sly, L. (2013, April 9). In Syria, some brace for the next war. Retrieved from http://www.washingtonpost.com/world/middle_east/in-syria-some-brace-for-the-next-war/2013/04/09/284fa018-a11d-11e2-82bc-511538ae90a4_story.html?wpisrc=nl_headlines.

Sly, L. (2013, May 10). Assad forces gaining ground in Syria. Retrieved from http://www.washingtonpost.com/world/assad-forces-gaining-ground-in-syria/2013/05/11/79147c34-b99c-11e2-b568-6917f6ac6d9d_story.html?wpisrc=nl_headlines.

Smith, S.W. (2011). Sudan: In a Procrustean Bed with crisis. *International Negotiation,* 16, no. 1, 169–189. doi:10.1163/157180611X553917.

Smith-Christopher, D.L. (Ed.). (2007). *Subverting hatred: The challenge of nonviolence in religious traditions,* 2nd ed. Maryknoll, NY: Orbis Books.

Sørensen, M. (2008). Humor as a serious strategy of nonviolent resistance to oppression. *Peace & Change, 33,* no. 2, 167–190. doi:10.1111/j.1468-0130.2008.00488.x.

Sørensen, M., & Vinthagen, S. (2012). Nonviolent resistance and culture. *Peace & Change, 37,* no. 3, 444–470. doi:10.1111/j.1468-0130.2012.00758.x.

Sougato Baroi, H. (2012). Peoples' uprising in North Africa and Middle East: Lessons learnt and challenges of policy implication—Egypt as an illustrative case. *Canadian Social Science, 8,* no. 2, 108–116. doi:10.3968/j.css.1923669720120802.1377.

Soyinka, W., Pamuk, O., D'Estaing, V., Gandhi, S., Wahid, A., & Ramos-Horta, J. (2003). Islam, soft and hard. *NPQ: New Perspectives Quarterly, 20,* no. 1, 22.

Spyer, J. (2012). Defying a dictator. *World Affairs, 175,* no. 1, 45–52.

Staniland, P. (2012). Organizing insurgency. *International Security, 37,* no. 1, 142–177.

Stanley, E.A., & Sawyer, J.P. (2009). The equifinality of war termination: Multiple paths to ending war. *Journal of Conflict Resolution, 53,* no. 5, 651–676.

Steger, M.B. (1999). Of means and ends: 1989 as ethico-political imperative. *New Political Science, 21,* no. 4, 501.

Stephan, M.J., & Chenoweth, E. (2008). Why civil resistance works. *International Security, 33,* no. 1, 7–44.

Stewart, J.B. (2011). Amandla! The Sullivan Principles and the battle to end apartheid in South Africa, 1975–1987. *Journal of African American History, 96,* no. 1, 62–89.

Stockman, D.A. (1986). *The triumph of politics: The inside story of the Reagan Revolution.* New York: Avon.

Stokes, D. (2009). The war gamble: Understanding US interests in Iraq. *Globalizations, 6,* no. 1, 107–112. doi:10.1080/14747730802692658.

Stoll, R.J. (2011). Civil engineering: Does a realist world influence the onset of civil wars? *Simulation & Gaming, 42,* no. 6, 748–771. doi:10.1177/1046878109341765.

Stout, J. (2010). *Blessed are the organized: Grassroots democracy in America.* Princeton, NJ: Princeton University Press.

Stremmelaar, J., & Wallert, E. (2012). Illustrating the changing face of citizen action. *Development, 55,* no. 2, 239–242. doi:10.1057/dev.2012.20.

Swank, E., & Fahs, B. (2011). Students for peace: Contextual and framing motivations of antiwar activism. *Journal of Sociology & Social Welfare, 38,* no. 2, 111–136.

Szanto, E. (2013). Beyond the Karbala Paradigm: rethinking revolution and redemption in Twelver Shi'a mourning rituals. *Journal of Shi'a Islamic Studies, 6,* no. 1, 75–91.

Taydas, Z., & Peksen, D. (2012). Can states buy peace? Social welfare spending and civil conflicts. *Journal of Peace Research, 49,* no. 2, 273–287. doi:10.1177/0022343311431286.

Taylor, L.K. (2013). The roots of resistance: Victims' responses to genocide. In Rhea DuMont, Tom H. Hastings, & Emiko Noma (Eds.), *Conflict transformation: Essays on methods of nonviolence* (pp. 86–107). Jefferson, NC: McFarland.

Taylor, R.K. (1994, 2011). *Training manual for nonviolent defense against the coup d'état,* 2nd ed. Nonviolence International. Retrieved from http://nonviolenceinternational.net/.

Thomassen, L. (2013). Communicative reason, deconstruction, and foundationalism: Reply to White and Farr. *Political Theory, 41,* no. 3, 482–488. doi:10.1177/0090591713476871.

Thompson, L.G., & Kuo, G. (2012). Climate change: The evidence and our options. *World Future Review, 4,* no. 2, 114–122.

Thornton, W.H., & Thornton, S. (2012). The contest of rival capitalisms: Mandate for a global third way. *Journal of Developing Societies* (Sage Publications Inc.) 28, no. 1, 115–128. doi:10.1177/0169796X1102800105.

Tint, B., Koehler, J., Chrimwami, V., Abi-

Juru, M., Haji, S.M., Dogo, D., Lass, C.R., & Johnson, M. (2013). Voices from the diaspora: Reconciliation and capacity building in refugee communities from the Great Lakes region of Africa. In Rhea DuMont, Tom H. Hastings, & Emiko Noma (Eds.), *Conflict transformation: Essays on methods of nonviolence* (pp. 109–125). Jefferson, NC: McFarland.

Torabian, S., & Abalakina, M. (2012). Attitudes toward war in the United States and Iran. *Iranian Studies, 45,* no. 4, 463–478. doi:10.1080/00210862.2012.673825.

Totten, M.J. (2012). Assad Delenda Est. *World Affairs, 175,* no. 2, 15–21.

Trivedi, H. (2011). Revolutionary nonviolence. *Interventions: The International Journal of Postcolonial Studies, 13,* no. 4, 521–549. doi:10.1080/1369801X.2011.628114.

Tsagourias, N. (2012). Nicolas Politis' initiatives to outlaw war and define aggression, and the narrative of progress in international law. *European Journal of International Law, 23,* no. 1, 255–266.

Vanetik, B., & Shalom, Z. (2011). The White House Middle East policy in 1973 as a catalyst for the outbreak of the Yom Kippur War. *Israel Studies, 16,* no. 1, 53–78.

Van Hook, S. (2013). Power in the people: Urgent transformation toward integration. In Rhea DuMont, Tom H. Hastings, & Emiko Noma (Eds.), *Conflict transformation: Essays on methods of nonviolence* (pp. 208–212). Jefferson, NC: McFarland.

van Wilgenburg, W. (2012). Breaking from Baghdad. *World Affairs, 175,* no. 4, 47–54.

Villacampa, J. (2008). The mine ban treaty, new diplomacy and human security ten years later. *European Political Science, 7,* no. 4, 519–529. doi:10.1057/eps.2008.30.

Vines, A. (2012). The effectiveness of UN and EU sanctions: Lessons for the twenty-first century. *International Affairs, 88,* no. 4, 867–877. doi:10.1111/j.1468-2346.2012.01106.x.

Whelan, J. (2012). How not to have a revolution. *Eureka Street, 22,* no. 16, 6–8.

Wight, D.M. (2013). Kissinger's Levantine

dilemma: The Ford administration and the Syrian occupation of Lebanon. *Diplomatic History, 37,* no. 1, 144–177.

Williams, K., & Miller, R. (2012, October 26). Why we need to support civil society in Syria. *Inclusive Security blog.* Retrieved from http://blog.inclusive security.org/why-we-need-to-support-civil-society-in-syria/.

Wilmot, W.W., & Hocker, J.L. (2007, original 1978). *Interpersonal conflict,* 7th ed. New York: McGraw-Hill.

Woehrle, L.M., Coy, P.G., & Maney, G.M. (2008). *Contesting patriotism: Culture, power, and strategy in the peace movement.* Lanham, MD: Rowman & Littlefield.

Woolsey, J. (2003). This is World War IV. *NPQ: New Perspectives Quarterly, 20,* no. 3, 10–11.

Wort, O. (2012). Reception without the theory: On the study of religion in early modern England. *Annual Bulletin of Historical Literature, 96,* no. 1, 8–15. doi:10.1111/j.1467–8314.2012.01294.x.

Wulf, H., & Debiel, T. (2010). Systemic disconnects: Why regional organizations fail to use early warning and response mechanisms. *Global Governance, 16,* no. 4, 525–547.

Yost, D.S. (2011). The US debate on NATO nuclear deterrence. *International Affairs, 87,* no. 6, 1,401–1,438. doi:10.1111/j.1468–2346.2011.01043.x.

Youmans, W., & York, J.C. (2012). Social media and the activist toolkit: User agreements, corporate interests, and the information infrastructure of modern social movements. *Journal of Communication, 62,* no. 2, 315–329. doi:10.1111/j.1460–2466.2012.01636.x.

Zifcak, S. (2012). The responsibility to protect after Libya and Syria. *Melbourne Journal of International Law, 13,* no. 1, 59–93.

Zisser, E. (2013). Can Assad's Syria survive revolution? *Middle East Quarterly, 20,* no. 2, 65–41.

Zunes, S. (2009). The US invasion of Iraq: The military side of globalization. *Globalizations, 6,* no. 1, 99–105. doi:10.1080/14747730802692625.

Zunes, S. (2011). Nonviolent revolution in the Middle East. *Peace Review, 23,* no. 3, 396–403. doi:10.1080/10402659.2011.596088.

Zunes, S. (2012, January 26). Unarmed resistance still Syria's best hope. *National Catholic Reporter, 48,* no. 7, 21.

Index